Measuring Globalization

Volume 2

Measuring Globalization

Better Trade Statistics for Better Policy

Volume 2

Factoryless Manufacturing, Global Supply Chains, and Trade in Intangibles and Data

Susan N. Houseman
and
Michael Mandel
Editors

2015

W.E. Upjohn Institute for Employment Research
Kalamazoo, Michigan

Library of Congress Cataloging-in-Publication Data

Measuring globalization : better trade statistics for better policy / Susan N. Houseman and Michael Mandel, editors.
volumes cm
Includes bibliographical references and indexes.
ISBN 978-0-88099-488-0 (v. 1 : pbk. : alk. paper) — ISBN 0-88099-488-6 (v. 1 : pbk. : alk. paper) —ISBN 978-0-88099-489-7 (v. 1 : hardcover : alk. paper) — ISBN 0-88099-489-4 (v. 1 : hardcover : alk. paper)
1. Commercial statistics. I. Houseman, Susan N., 1956- II. Mandel, Michael J.
HF1016.M44 2015
382.01'5195—dc23
2014047579

W.E. Upjohn Institute for Employment Research
300 S. Westnedge Avenue
Kalamazoo, Michigan 49007-4686

Cover design by Alcorn Publication Design.
Index prepared by Diane Worden.
Printed in the United States of America.
Printed on recycled paper.

Contents

Acknowledgments

This book and its companion volume are the culmination of a research and conference project to document data gaps and biases in national statistics arising from the growth of globalization and to propose solutions for statistical agencies. We are indebted to the members of our advisory committee—Bill Alterman, Carol Corrado, Richard Freeman, David Friedman, Mike Horrigan, Ron Jarmin, Brad Jensen, Marshall Reinsdorf, and Marcel Timmer—who provided guidance on research topics and authors for commissioned papers as well as on directions for future research. We thank Mike Horrigan and the U.S. Bureau of Labor Statistics for hosting a preconference meeting, Diana Carew for organizing the final conference, and Lillian Vesic-Petrovic for providing outstanding research assistance.

The work for this project was supported by a generous grant from the Alfred P. Sloan Foundation.

1
Introduction

Michael Mandel
Progressive Policy Institute

Why should economists care about correctly measuring globalization? Obviously having a better picture of the global economy is a desirable end in itself. But more important is the relationship between good data and good policy: An accurate description of the global links among nations, businesses, and individuals is essential to optimal decision making by policymakers. Without such knowledge, policymakers are essentially flying blind.

Consider policy toward manufacturing enterprises. The federal, state, and local tax codes contain quite a few explicit beneficial provisions for manufacturing, in addition to direct and indirect subsidies. Moreover, there's an intense debate about whether manufacturing in countries such as the United States has been hollowed out or remains robust.

From this perspective, policymakers at every level of government would find it helpful to have direct information about the sorts of jobs that are created when manufacturers outsource production but keep the highly paid research and development (R&D), product development, and marketing jobs at home. Yet very little such data has existed heretofore.

This volume covers three topics where current statistical methodologies for tracking trade don't provide enough information for policymakers. These areas are "factoryless manufacturing," value-added trade in supply chains, and trade in services, intangibles, and data.

These areas are connected by a common thread: Rapid changes in the global economy have outstripped the traditional statistical presentation of export and import data by commodity and industry, as published by national and international statistical agencies. This has meant that such agencies no longer provide enough information for policymakers and researchers. The traditional presentation of trade statistics does not allow economists to trace out the implications of global supply chains, which disaggregate production among countries in new and unexpected ways. Moreover, economists have very little data on cross-border flows of intangibles and data, which are poorly reported in the conventional trade statistics and yet increasingly important.

Chapters 2, 3, and 4 describe a way of augmenting the conventional industrial classifications by creating a new category called "factoryless goods producers" (FGP). Such a change—and the data collection changes that would accompany it—would have the effect of providing policymakers with a new source of information about the impacts of global supply chains in manufacturing.

Chapters 5, 6, and 7 examine the measurement of value-added trade. In a world of global supply chains, policymakers need to know more than straightforward gross exports and imports for each commodity. An export may contain large amounts of imported components, while a particular imported commodity may be an essential part of high-value exports. As a result, trade negotiators would greatly benefit from having access to value-added trade statistics so they can determine which categories of exports are most beneficial to the domestic economy.

Similarly, value-added trade statistics would be invaluable for state and local economic development policy. Governments often offer tax and training incentives to companies without being able to correctly measure the true spillover benefits to the local economy.

Even domestic macroeconomic policy relies heavily on a good understanding of globalization. As we saw during the financial crisis, the credit contraction leapt across national borders in unanticipated ways. Today, U.S. consumption, investment, and production are heavily dependent on global supply chains. A credit or political shock in China, for example, could plausibly have large effects on inflation or consumption in the United States and other countries.

Finally, Chapters 8 and 9 address the difficult issues of measuring cross-border flows of intangibles and data. Like value-added trade, getting better measurements of these increasingly important components of the global economy could significantly affect trade policy, tax policy, economic development policy, and even macro policy.

FACTORYLESS GOODS PRODUCTION

Chapters 2, 3, and 4 deal with correctly measuring the increasingly important phenomenon of factoryless goods production and contract manufacturing services (CMS). Companies such as Apple and Nike—which do research in new technology, design new products, market the products, and receive the profits from the sale of the products—are subcontracting out most or all of their actual production to other companies, either in the United States or globally. The issue is whether the first type of company—which may own no factories but may perform all the high-end functions of manufacturers—should be classified in the manufacturing industry.

On one level, this is a straightforward classification question. Under the North American Industry Classification System (NAICS) currently used in the United States, a company that outsources production could be classified in either manufacturing, wholesaling, or some other industry altogether. What's needed is a consistent way of identifying such firms that the main statistical agencies—the U.S. Census Bureau, the Bureau of Labor Statistics (BLS), and the Bureau of Economic Analysis (BEA)—can agree on. Then the FGPs would buy manufacturing services from other companies (providers of CMS), which would do the actual factory production.

But the topic of FGPs turns out to raise some profound theoretical, practical, and policy issues as well, going beyond the narrow sphere of economic statistics. Manufacturing is important as a source of high-paying jobs and innovation for the economy. By separating out the production aspect of manufacturing from the product development and marketing aspect, FGPs make it possible to understand where the value-added and high-paying jobs are created in the research/product development/production/marketing chain.

In turn, if FGPs are buying manufacturing services from overseas contract manufacturers, the statistical agencies have to explicitly measure the quantity and price of purchased manufacturing services as part of imports.

At the time of the conference that these volumes grew out of, "Measuring the Effects of Globalization," held February 28–March 1, 2013, in Washington, D.C., U.S. statistical agencies were operating under a

2011 mandate from the Office of Management and Budget (OMB) to integrate the concept of FGPs into the sprawling U.S. system of economic statistics. As a result, agencies began planning and researching how to best track FGPs, and the three chapters in this volume reflect that effort.

However, since then, the OMB has relaxed its mandate. An August 8, 2014, OMB directive in the *Federal Register* notes the following:

> The Economic Classification Policy Committee (ECPC), which advises OMB on periodic revisions to NAICS, recently reported to OMB that results of preliminary research on the effectiveness of survey questions designed to identify Factoryless Goods Producers (FGPs) [show] inconsistent results. These results indicate that questions tested in the 2012 Economic Census fail to yield responses that provide accurate and reliable identification and classification of FGPs. The ECPC has advised that additional research, testing, and evaluation are required to find a method for accurate identification and classification of FGPs, and that this process could take several years. Given these initial research results and the large number of public comments submitted on the topic of FGPs, OMB here announces that the FGP recommendation will not be implemented in 2017. (*Federal Register* 2014, p. 46558)

The *Federal Register* note goes on to say this:

> Without the deadline imposed by the 2017 NAICS revisions, the relevant statistical agencies will now have the opportunity to complete the additional research, testing, and evaluation needed to determine the feasibility of developing methods for the consistent identification and classification of FGPs that are accurate and reliable. (Ibid.)

From this perspective, the chapters in this volume stand as a road map for future research. In Chapter 2, "Reflecting Factoryless Goods Production in the U.S. Statistical System," Maureen Doherty gives a brief history and overview of the rationale behind creating the category of factoryless goods production. She shows how the United States chose a somewhat different approach from international statistical organizations.

In Chapter 3, "Measuring 'Factoryless' Manufacturing: Evidence from U.S. Surveys," Fariha Kamal, Brent R. Moulton, and Jennifer Ribarsky identify data that the BEA and the Census Bureau are already collecting on both producers and users of CMS. Using this data, the chapter provides a snapshot of companies that are engaged in these activities.

Chapter 4, "The Scope of U.S. 'Factoryless Manufacturing,'" by Kimberly Bayard, David Byrne, and Dominic Smith, estimates the extent of U.S. factoryless manufacturing using corporate financial reports and Economic Census microdata. The authors calculate that manufacturing value-added would have been 5 to 20 percent greater for 2007 if all FGPs were reclassified to manufacturing, and that value-added would have been 20 to 30 percent greater for 2007 for semiconductor manufacturing if FGPs were included.

VALUE-ADDED TRADE

Factoryless goods producers make up only one aspect of global supply chains, however. The next three chapters take a more general look at value-added measures of trade. Value-added measures of trade acknowledge that exports of many goods and services are actually heavily dependent on imported intermediates. For example, a smartphone exported from China may contain chips originally made in Japan or South Korea (Kraemer, Linden, and Dedrick 2011). Similarly, exports of financial services from New York investment banks may in theory rely on intermediate services generated in the London offices of these banks.

Value-added measures of trade, rather than reporting gross exports, account for these imported intermediates by subtracting them out. Thus, value-added trade in theory represents the actual domestic value generated by exports.

Value-added trade measures are a very useful conceptual step forward. They are not a full solution, however. First, most countries do not have the right surveys in place to directly track usage of imported intermediates by industry. Second, value-added trade measures do not solve the import price bias issues raised in the first volume. For example, consider a piece of electronics assembled in China from imported components, and then exported to the United States. China's share of the final sales price might be quite low in this calculation. However, that assumes Chinese wages for the cost of assembly. If assembly was shifted to the United States, then the cost of assembly at U.S. wages would be a much bigger share of the final sales price.

Nevertheless, major steps have been made in assessing value-added trade, as described in the chapters in this volume. In Chapter 5, "Incomes and Jobs in Global Production of Manufactures: New Measures of Competitiveness Based on the World Input-Output Database," Marcel P. Timmer, Bart Los, and Gaaitzen J. de Vries analyze global value chain income ("GVC income") for 20 countries, including the United States, Japan, Brazil, China, India, Russia, and the major economies of Europe. The authors define GVC income as the income generated in a country by participating in global manufacturing production, including the large contribution of nonmanufacturing industries.

The authors show that in advanced countries, GVC income generated by capital and high-skilled labor is rising. This fits the common story that global shifts in manufacturing have benefited workers with more education. Some of these gains are coming in service jobs, since the authors demonstrate that the manufacturing sector is the direct source of only half of the GVC income. On the downside, the same analysis shows that high-skilled-job opportunities have declined in the United States since 1995, while rising in Europe and Japan.

The methodology described in the chapter relies on tracing out cross-border flows of intermediates, as described in the World Input-Output Database (WIOD), an effort funded in part by the European Commission (Timmer 2012). A similar effort, funded by the Organisation for Economic Co-operation and Development (OECD) and the World Trade Organization (WTO), is described in Chapter 6, "Measuring Trade in Value-Added and Beyond," by Nadim Ahmad. This chapter describes the methodology behind the Trade in Value-Added (TiVA) database, the assumptions behind the methodology, and the initiatives launched to improve the quality of those assumptions and the underlying data.

An August 2013 report that draws on the TiVA database, published subsequent to the 2013 globalization conference, estimates that between 30 and 60 percent of the value of the exports of G20 countries are either composed of imported inputs or are intermediate inputs for other countries (OECD, WTO, and UNCTAD 2013). In addition, 42 percent of the value-added of exports for G20 economies are made up of services, which closely matches the estimate in the previous chapter.

Finally, there's a broader policy point that often escapes policymakers—succeeding in international markets requires an ability to import high-quality intermediate inputs, as countries such as China have done.

From both a political and economic framework, China represents one particularly important application of the value-added framework. In Chapter 7, "Import Uses and Domestic Value-Added in Chinese Exports: What Can We Learn from Chinese Microdata?," Shunli Yao, Hong Ma, and Jiansuo Pei estimate China's domestic value-added share in exports by combining two enterprise-level sources of microdata. The chapter provides an excellent background for the types of data that the Chinese statistical authorities are collecting, as well as upper and lower bounds for domestic value-added shares.

INTANGIBLES AND DATA

The next two chapters address the difficult questions of measuring cross-border flows of intangibles and data. Chapter 8, "A Formulary Approach for Attributing Measured Production to Foreign Affiliates of U.S. Parents," by Dylan G. Rassier and Jennifer Koncz-Bruner, focuses on the proper geographical attribution of the income generated by intangible capital such as patents, software, and other intellectual property. The problem is that the knowledge embodied in intangible capital is a "shared input" across an entire enterprise. The return on intangible capital could in theory be attributed to the country where the capital was created, the country where the intangible capital was used for production, the country where the product that incorporates the intangible capital is sold, or the country where the intangible capital is nominally located for legal or tax purposes.

The BEA publishes data on income and assets by country for foreign affiliates of U.S. multinationals. The current methodology is to attribute the income generated by intangible capital owned by a multinational to the country where the capital resides for legal or tax purposes. That results in apparent anomalies where certain countries such as Bermuda and Ireland show relatively high levels of assets and income for the foreign affiliates of U.S multinationals, apparently out of proportion with the actual economic significance of those countries.

Rassier and Koncz-Bruner propose using proxy measures such as compensation, net physical assets, and sales in order to provide a better estimate of the location of income and economic activity of foreign affiliates of U.S multinationals. The proposed methodology results in only a small shift of income, in the aggregate, between foreign affiliates and U.S. parents. But the global location of income outside the United States shifts significantly. In particular, the proposed methodology shifts income across global regions including Africa, Asia, Europe, Latin America, and the Middle East by more than 10 percent of value-added.

The proposed methodology, however, does not actually deal with some of the conceptual problems raised by shared inputs. It would be better, in some sense, to be able to measure the creation and use of intangible capital separately, and provide some theoretical guidance for how the data can be used

In the final chapter, "Data, Trade, and Growth," Michael Mandel examines a topic that is rarely considered—how to measure cross-border flows of data. These days no international commerce can be conducted without an associated flow of data. That includes financial data, entertainment, the data that accompanies back-office functions such as human resources, sales data, and production data. Estimates from TeleGeography suggest that cross-border data flows rose at an average annual rate of 49 percent between 2008 and 2012.

The problem is that these cross-border flows of data, while clearly economically valuable, are often not picked up by the trade statistics. In the current methodology used by the BEA and most other statistical agencies globally, data is classed as a service—and a service export by definition occurs when a foreign person pays a domestic person for a service. Similarly, an import of services by definition occurs when a domestic person pays a foreign person for services.

However, the global architecture of the Internet allows and even encourages data to cross national borders without leaving a significant monetary footprint. In particular, major Internet providers exchange data without exchanging money, opening up the possibility of a packet of data traveling around the world without leaving a single monetary trace.

As a result, Chapter 9 offers evidence that economically important cross-border data flows are simply not being counted by current international economic statistics. It is likely that both the level and the rate of growth of data trade are being significantly understated.

This mismeasurement issue has several important policy implications. First, it seems likely that the data sector, and the companies making up the data sector, are bigger contributors to domestic and global growth than policymakers realize. That in turn leads to the second implication: To the degree that trade negotiators for the United States (and for other countries) prioritize their negotiation objectives according to the relative economic importance of different sectors of the economy, the undermeasurement of the data sector will adversely affect policy. To put it a different way, if wheat exports are easier to measure than trade in data, then U.S. trade policy will place too much emphasis on reducing barriers to agriculture exports and not enough on maintaining the free flow of data.

The second policy implication is that international tax policy may be distorted by undermeasurement of cross-border data flows. Tax policy is, at base, a balancing act between revenue raised and distortions to market outcomes. But it requires good information about the economy in order to make good choices.

And third, attempts by various countries to implement barriers to the free flow of data may do considerably more economic damage than the current trade statistics show.

Taken together, these two volumes show that progress is being made in the difficult problems of measuring globalization. However, there's a long way to go before global trade statistics truly provide policymakers with the information that they need.

References

Federal Register. 2014. "2017 North American Industry Classification System (NAICS) Revision." *Federal Register* 79(153): 46558. https://www.federalregister.gov/articles/2014/08/08/2014-18766/2017-north-american-industry-classification-system-naics-revision (accessed October 6, 2014).

Kraemer, Kenneth L., Greg Linden, and Jason Dedrick. 2011. "Capturing Value in Global Networks: Apple's iPad and iPhone." Working paper. Irvine, CA: Personal Computing Industry Center. http://pcic.merage.uci.edu/papers/2011/value_ipad_iphone.pdf (accessed October 6, 2014).

Organisation for Economic Co-operation and Development (OECD), World

Trade Organization (WTO), and United Nations Conference on Trade and Development (UNCTAD). 2013. *Implications Of Global Value Chains For Trade, Investment, Development, and Jobs*. Paris: Organisation for Economic Co-operation and Development; and Geneva: World Trade Organization; United Nations Conference on Trade and Development.

Timmer, Marcel P., ed. 2012. "The World Input-Output Database (WIOD): Contents, Sources, and Methods." WIOD Working Paper No. 10. Brussels: European Commission, Directorate-General for Research.

Part 1

Factoryless Manufacturing

2
Reflecting Factoryless Goods Production in the U.S. Statistical System

Maureen Doherty
Bureau of Labor Statistics

BACKGROUND

The goal of a country's national statistical agencies is to provide relevant, timely, and accurate information on that country's economy.[1] Over time, as technology changes and organizations mature and change the way they operate, there can be changes in both the mix of outputs produced in an economy and in the way firms operate to achieve their goals. One of the biggest challenges faced by producers of national economic statistics is to adapt to these structural changes in the economy in order to continue to provide relevant data. Usually, structural economic alterations occur gradually over time; however, with the continual rapid technological advances of the past 20 years, there have been significant shifts in the way firms operate. Two of the biggest changes are the growth of global value chains and the fragmentation of production.

Global value chains and production fragmentation are interrelated phenomena. A value chain is the set of interrelated economic activities that contribute to the provision of a good or service, starting with product development and ending with customer service. When some of the economic activities occur in different countries, the chain is considered a global value chain (Center on Globalization, Governance, and Competitiveness 2006). A production chain is the set of economic activities within or among firms in a global value chain that are required to produce specific products. A production chain is typically controlled by a lead firm and is considered to be global when the production activities are dispersed across countries (Chang, Bayhaqi, and Yuhua 2012). The relationship between production chains and global value chains is illustrated in Figure 2.1.

Traditionally, product development and at least some transformation activities of the production chain for manufactured products were performed by establishments classified as manufacturers. Over the past two decades, vast improvements in technology, communications, and transportation have allowed firms to share intellectual property and closely control all steps of the transformation process without directly performing any of the transformation steps. This allowed firms to improve profitability by focusing on innovation and product and marketing decisions instead of on the generic services and volume production portions of the value chain, which were then outsourced (Gereffi, Humphrey, and Sturgeon 2005). As a result, some establishments revolutionized their business processes even further and began to perform all of the functions typically associated with manufacturing except for the transformation steps.

These changes have introduced complexities into the production of economic statistics, forcing a reexamination of traditional economic measurement concepts related to industry classification for establishments and to the value of a country's outputs, exports, and imports by both the U.S. and international statistical communities. Economic activity classification systems did not address how to handle the output of establishments that outsourced certain production tasks. In addition, to the extent that production tasks were outsourced internationally, questions were raised concerning how the outsourced activities were handled in national accounts and balance of trade statistics.

This chapter will first look at the response of international statistical organizations to these phenomena and then turn its attention to the U.S. response, highlighting how the latter differed in some aspects from the international response. The chapter will then review implementation planning and issues within the U.S. statistical system.

Figure 2.1 Global Value/Supply/Production Chains

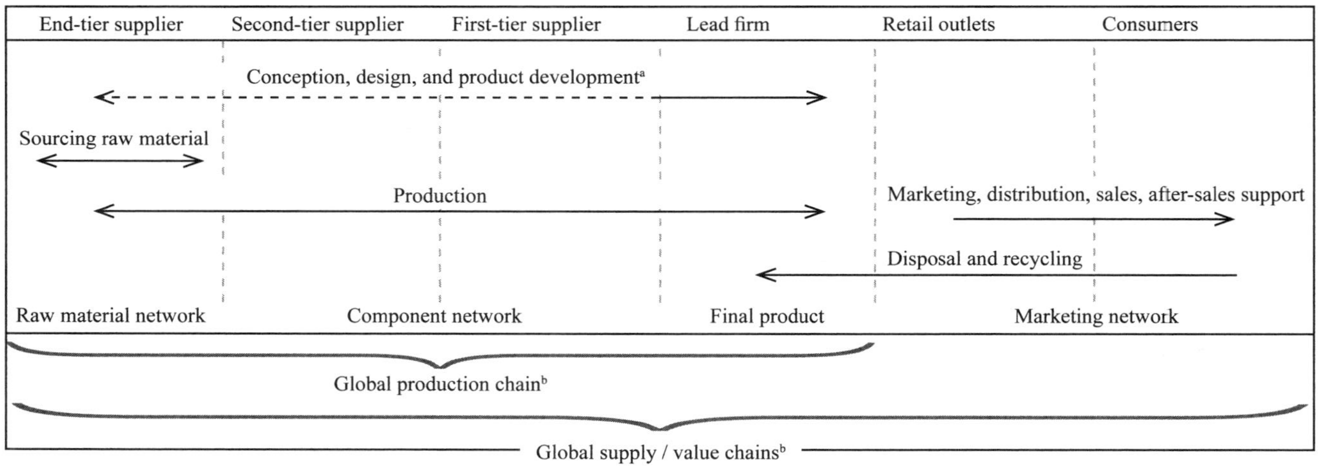

[a] Traditionally, conception, design, and product development are controlled by the lead firm; nowadays, however, some of these activities are outsourced to other firms, as is indicated by the dashed line. Arrows on both ends of a line indicate that a process can go in either direction.

[b] The players in the global production/supply/value chain include domestic and foreign firms.

SOURCE: Chang, Bayhaqi, and Yuhua (2012) of the Asia-Pacific Economic Cooperation (APEC) Policy Support Unit.

INTERNATIONAL RESPONSE

The United Nations Statistics Division and the International Monetary Fund (IMF) Statistics Department set standards and produce manuals and guidelines for a number of different international economic statistics. These groups routinely evaluate their standards and make periodic updates in order to stay current as businesses change the way they operate over time. In the past decade, each undertook an extensive multiyear evaluation and update of their processes, at least in part to reflect the impact of globalization. There were some differences in the timing of these efforts, but there was a great deal of collaboration across projects, and each project included widespread outreach to both gather input and obtain comments on drafts.

One of the standards that the United Nations Statistics Division is responsible for is the International Standard Industrial Classification of All Economic Activities (ISIC). As the name implies, this classification is the international standard for the classification of productive economic activities. The main purpose is to provide a standard set of economic activities so that entities can be classified according to the activity they carry out. The United Nations Statistics Division, along with the Technical Subgroup of the Expert Group on International Economic and Social Classifications, began planning a regularly scheduled update of ISIC in 2001. A draft of ISIC Revision 4 was approved in 2006 by the United Nations Statistics Division and released in 2008 (United Nations Statistical Commission 2006).

Clarification of the classification of an establishment that outsources its principle economic activity was one of the many issues addressed in this revision of the ISIC. With respect to outsourcing, it was determined that if any establishment outsources part but not all of its production activities, it should be classified as if it were carrying out the complete process. If an establishment outsources its complete production process, it is also classified as if it were carrying out the complete production process, as long as the output of the production process is not goods. Goods producers that outsource their entire production process are classified as if they were carrying out the complete process only if they are the economic owner of the output. Under these rules, an establishment is the economic owner of an output only if they are the legal owner of the physical input materials (Becker and Havinga 2007). If an establishment engaged in a goods-producing activity has all the production done by others and does not legally own the material inputs, it is considered to be buying the completed goods from the contractor with the intent to sell them and would usually be classified in the appropriate trade activity (European Commission et al. 2009).[2]

The System of National Accounts (SNA) is the internationally agreed-upon standard set of recommendations on how to compile measures of economic activity and is produced by the National Accounts section of the United Nations Statistics Division. It describes a coherent, consistent, and integrated set of macroeconomic accounts in the context of a set of internationally agreed-upon concepts, definitions, classifications, and accounting rules. In 2003, the United Nations Statistical Commission identified the need for a comprehensive update of the 1993 System of National Accounts manual based, at least in part, on the impact of globalization.

The main issue related to globalization was the treatment of goods that are sent from one country to another without a change in economic ownership. Under the 1993 SNA, when goods are sent abroad for processing and the processed goods are later returned, a change in ownership is imputed in each case, even when there is none, and the values of imports and exports reflect this imputed ownership change. The 2008 SNA recommended that imports and exports should be recorded on a strict change-of-ownership basis, with imputed changes no longer assumed. Economic ownership is the criterion that is used to determine whether a change in ownership takes place. For establishments involved in goods production activities, the SNA uses the ISIC criteria that an establishment must be the legal owner of input materials for the material used in the production process in order to be considered the economic owner of the output of that process.

According to the 2008 SNA, when goods are transferred from the economic owner in one country to an establishment in another country for further processing and the processed goods are then returned to the economic owner, the goods sent for processing should not be recorded as an export from the economic owner or an import to the processor in national accounts treatment. In addition, the returned processed goods should not be recorded as an export of the processor or as an import to the economic owner. Instead, the fee paid to the processing unit should be recorded as the import of processing services by the country owning the goods and an export of processing services by the country providing it (European Commission et al. 2009).

The IMF Statistics Department produces standards for concepts, definitions, classifications, and conventions for the compilation of balance of payments and international investment position statistics. As the international standard, its *Balance of Payments Manual* serves as a guide for IMF member countries that regularly report balance of payments data to the IMF. In 2003, the IMF Statistics Department also began working on an update to its *Balance of Payments Manual* in response to changes in the economic and financial environment. The final *Balance of Payments and International Investment Position Manual, Sixth Revision* (BPM6), was adopted in November 2008 (IMF 2009, p. 4).

Because BPM6 (IMF 2009) and SNA2008 (European Commission et al. 2009) were updated simultaneously, BPM6 reflects the same changes in the treatment of goods sent for processing and completed processed goods as described in the national accounts discussion above. BPM6, however, is not entirely consistent with SNA2008 in that it explicitly includes some additional guidelines related to the ownership of materials to be processed and to the location of the buyer of the goods after processing—these are not mentioned in SNA2008. As long as the economic owner of the processed goods is also the economic owner of the material inputs to be processed, that owner may obtain the materials from the owner's economy, the economy of the processor, or a third economy. Additionally, the fee charged by a processor to the owner of a processed good may cover the cost of materials purchased by the processor. When the goods for processing are obtained from a different economy than that of the economic owner, the value of those goods should be recorded as an import to the economic owner. Furthermore, the economic owner of the processed goods does not need to physically take possession of them before ownership is transferred to a buyer. If ownership of the goods is transferred to a buyer in a different economy than that of the economic owner, the sale should be recorded as an export from the economic owner's country (IMF 2009, pp. 161–163).

The International Merchandise Trade Statistics (IMTS), produced by the United Nations Statistics Division, is a set of official statistics that provides data on the movement of goods between countries and serves many different users with a wide variety of needs. In 2007, the need for a revision of these statistics was recognized because of many factors, including the impacts of globalization and the changes in related statistical frameworks like the *System of National Accounts Manual* and the *Balance of Payments and International Investment Position Manual.* As a result of these efforts, IMTS2010 was adopted in February 2010.

The need for compatibility with SNA2008 and BPM6 was one of the goals of the IMTS revision; however, when the needs of all data users were considered, priority was given to the need for statistics that reflect the physical cross-border movement of goods. As a result, IMTS differs conceptually from BPM6 and SNA2008 with respect to goods for processing and the return of processed goods. Specifically, IMTS recommends that goods for processing be recorded when they enter or leave the economic territory, irrespective of whether a change in ownership takes place. Because of these differences, it was recognized that adjustments to IMTS data would be necessary prior to use in the compilation of other statistics. In order to support the need to make such adjustments, IMTS2010 encourages the identification (preferably by special coding) of goods for processing and goods resulting from such processing in trade statistics. IMTS2010 also encourages the identification and special coding of goods that cross borders as a result of transactions between related parties (United Nations Department of Economic and Social Affairs 2011).

U.S. RESPONSE

The North American Industry Classification System (NAICS) is the standard used by U.S. statistical agencies in classifying business establishments for the purpose of collecting, analyzing, and publishing statistical data related to the U.S. business economy. It was developed jointly by the U.S. Economic Classification Policy Committee (ECPC 2010),[3] Statistics Canada, and Mexico's Instituto Nacional de Estadistica y Geografia to allow for a high level of comparability in business statistics among the North American countries, and it was adopted in 1997. NAICS did not explicitly include guidance for the classification of establishments that owned the design and controlled the production and sale of goods but outsourced all the production. From 1997 through 2007, the NAICS manual indicated that establishments that were engaged in the mechanical, physical, or chemical transformation of materials, substances, or components into new products should be classified in the manufacturing sector. Furthermore, it suggested that manufacturing establishments may process materials or may contract with other establishments to process their materials for them (OMB 2007, p. 197).[4] NAICS has historically classified as belonging to the manufacturing sector apparel jobbers who perform entrepreneurial functions involved in other apparel and accessory manufacture; however, the manual did not define exactly what was meant by entrepreneurial functions, nor did it differentiate between establishments that contract out some versus all of the transformation activities (p. 246).

By the late 1990s, individual U.S. statistical programs were beginning to adapt in response to the changes in the economy, but there was no consistent approach—particularly with respect to establishments that perform entrepreneurial functions related to production but don't perform transformation activities. Some programs interpreted the NAICS manual's statement related to contracting with other establishments as applying only to the specifically mentioned apparel jobbers and classified other such establishments in wholesale trade or management of corporations. Others interpreted this statement more broadly but provided their own interpretation of what was meant by "performing entrepreneurial functions." This led to inconsistent NAICS classification decisions across statistical programs for some establishments, making it difficult to draw conclusions when analyzing NAICS data across programs.

In response to these inconsistencies, the ECPC formed the Manufacturing Transformation Outsourcing Subcommittee in July 2008 and charged its members with defining manufacturing transformation outsourcing and identifying characteristics of establishments that outsource manufacturing transformation activities. The team was also responsible for researching international classification efforts and developing classification options for both establishments that outsource transformation activities and those that perform transformation activities for others. The group identified three different types of establishments that could be involved in the production of goods: 1) the traditional integrated manufacturer (IM), 2) the manufacturing service provider (MSP), and

3) the factoryless goods producer (FGP). The characteristics of each type of goods-producing establishment are depicted in Table 2.1.

The team's report also described a wide variety of classification options along with the strengths and weaknesses of each, based on the appropriateness of product valuations and whether the option would support analysis. The team focused on five basic classification options, with variations for some of them. The classification options are described in detail below.

1) Classification in manufacturing

Under the assumption that outsourcing the transformation steps of the manufacturing process is no different than outsourcing other steps, all FGPs could be classified in the manufacturing sector, along with IMs and MSPs. This allows the full value of all goods, including returns to intellectual property, to be included in the manufacturing sector, whether produced by an IM or an FGP.

Within the manufacturing sector, several potential options for classifying establishments were described. All three types of establishments could be included in the appropriate manufacturing industry, with or without breakouts by type of establishment. Breakouts by establishment by type, where possible, would facilitate data analysis of the same types of products but would require the collection of some new data. To the extent that special aggregations excluding FGP activity could be calculated, this option would also allow continuous series to be created in industries with significant amounts of FGP activity. Other possibilities were to create a new manufacturing subsector for all FGPs that would include breakouts for industries that had a significant number of FGP

Table 2.1 Characteristics of Types of Manufacturing Establishments

	Integrated manufacturer	Manufacturing service provider	Factoryless goods producer
Owns intellectual property	Yes	No	Yes
Owns inputs	Yes	May or may not	May or may not
Performs transformation activities	Yes	Yes	No
Owns and sells or transfers finished product	Yes	No	Yes

SOURCE: Author's compilation.

establishments or add six-digit NAICS codes into the current manufacturing structure where warranted. If separate industries were created, it would be important that the new FGP industry product details be collected at the seven-digit product level of the manufacturing numerical list to allow for data analysis. This option would allow for the creation of continuous data series for currently existing manufacturing industries. To the extent that the creation of separate FGP industries might result in unpublishable data, it would not be a very useful distinction for data users.

2) Classification in wholesale trade

All FGP establishments could be classified in the wholesale trade sector, since the composition of labor and capital expenses for FGPs is similar to that in wholesale trade. This classification option would also be consistent with the concept that the primary economic activity of an FGP is the selling aspect of the production process. On the other hand, wholesale trade margin is for the service of goods distribution only. The margin for an FGP would include the value of the services related to design and those related to overseeing transformation in addition to goods distribution. Two possibilities were also considered within the wholesale trade classification option.

In the first possibility, FGP establishments could be classified in the appropriate merchant wholesale industry with or without separate data below that level for own-brand importers, own-brand marketers, and domestic FGPs in addition to the current breakouts for wholesale distributors. Including this additional detail supports calculations and analysis by allowing FGPs to be identified separately from traditional wholesalers; however, data may be unpublishable for some of the breakouts, which would hinder usefulness. It is unlikely that the wholesale trade detail could be expanded to match the current manufacturing detail, making comparisons between FGP and manufacturing data difficult.

A second possibility would be to classify FGP establishments in wholesale trade either in one industry or in three separate industries: 1) own-brand importers (those that arrange transformation by overseas contractor and import and distribute the final good), 2) own-brand marketers (those that arrange transformation by overseas contractor and that drop-ship the output to customers), and 3) domestic FGPs (those that arrange transformation by domestic contractors). This second possibility supports calculations and analysis by allowing FGPs to be identified separately from traditional wholesalers. The potential benefit of this method is offset by the fact that it is unlikely that the wholesale trade detail could be expanded to match the current manufacturing detail, making comparisons between FGP data and manufacturing data difficult.

3) Split classification between manufacturing and wholesale trade

This option would classify establishments according to whether they outsource overseas in wholesale trade or whether they outsource domestically in manufacturing. This option prevents goods transformed by foreign contractors from being included in domestic manufacturing when it is possible that the only domestic input was the intangible capital owned or leased by a domestic entity; however, it does not handle the situation where both domestic and international contractors are used. The production process for FGPs is exactly the same whether the transformation is contracted out domestically or internationally, so having different classifications based on the location of the contract manufacturer is inconsistent with a NAICS classification system based on production processes. In addition, switches between domestic and foreign contractors would result in classification changes that would lessen the stability of the classification system.

4) Classification in professional, scientific, and technical services

This option would classify FGPs in research and development, since this is the first step in the production process. If research and development is determined to be the primary activity of FGPs, they should be classified in this sector. However, if an FGP acquires the design of the product from another company, no research and design (R&D) activity would be performed at the establishment. Since FGPs are responsible for the sale of products, this option would require an expansion of the definition of this sector to include the selling process, and FGPs would report the value of the good as well as the value of the R&D.

5) Classification in management of companies and enterprises

This option would create a new three-digit industry code (defined as "managing the production process") within the "Management of

Companies and Enterprises" sector. Input costs for FGPs are probably similar to those associated with other establishments in this sector. If management of production is determined to be the primary activity of FGPs, they should be classified in this sector. On the other hand, this option focuses only on the management of the production process, not on the design or selling of the product. The amount of product detail would be significantly less than would be available in manufacturing, limiting its usefulness for analysis purposes.

ECPC RECOMMENDATION

The ECPC evaluated the report and used it as a basis for a January 2009 Federal Register notice that outlined the issues surrounding offshoring and described some of the available classification options. The ECPC used the Manufacturing Transformation Outsourcing Subcommittee's paper, the Federal Register responses, and an examination of international classification guidance to aid its members in forming a final classification decision.

The ECPC decided that all factoryless goods producers should be classified in manufacturing with the specific industry classification that is based on the transformation production process used by the contractor. Furthermore, the committee encouraged programs to provide breakouts for IMs, FGPs, and MSPs within each industry to support data analysis needs. The ECPC carefully considered the ISIC4 classification recommendation to base classification solely on legal ownership of material inputs, but it decided that control of the entrepreneurial aspects of the production process, including economic ownership of material inputs, was more appropriate. In doing so, it put forth the following argument:

> A strict adherence to the international recommendation to classify FGPs based solely on ownership of materials was considered and rejected as impractical. If the definition of ownership required physical possession, the ability to substitute between input sources in different countries to obtain the lowest cost could change sector classification in NAICS if the inputs were sent directly from the producer in country B to a manufacturing service provider in

> country C. The establishment that arranged for the production in country A would never take physical possession of the materials. If the definition of ownership were based on separate transactions, problems would still arise. Contracts between FGPs and their manufacturing partners change with market conditions. Payment terms and the allocation of risk can shift based on variations in the availability of credit and the market power or capacity of the individual parties. Classification of an establishment should not change simply because [that establishment has] the market power to shift the timing of payment for the inputs from the front of the process to the end of the process or because critical shortages of transformation capacity provide outsized negotiating power to a manufacturing service provider. By focusing on the entrepreneurial aspects of the process (and therefore ownership of the goods being produced) rather than ownership of materials, the ECPC eliminates the aforementioned ownership of materials issues. (ECPC 2010)

IMPLEMENTATION PLANNING

Both the U.S. and international statistical communities realized that even after all of the extensive research, outreach, and guideline update efforts had been completed, there was still a significant amount of work to do in order to implement the decisions that had been made and to continue analyzing the best methods to measure national and international transactions in a global economy. In response, implementation groups were formed both internationally and in the United States.

In 2007, the Conference of European Statisticians (CES) created an Expert Group on the Impact of Globalization on National Accounts. Specifically, the goal of this group was to analyze the impact of the updated guidelines on existing statistical measures, with a particular focus on national accounts, and to identify and propose solutions for problem areas. The group completed an extensive review of the topic and produced a detailed guide, "The Impact of Globalization on National Accounts," which was finalized in June 2011 (United Nations Economic Commission for Europe 2011). The guide documented a wide variety of issues and offered solutions to many problems; however, the authors recognized that there was still a need for additional research and included a chapter at the end outlining work still to be done. As a follow-up to this effort, the CES requested that Statistics Netherlands elaborate on the remaining issues, and this work resulted in the paper "In-Depth Review on Global Manufacturing" (Statistics Netherlands 2011). It also led to the formation by the CES of a Task Force on Global Production, which is responsible for developing guidance on unresolved issues related to SNA2008 and BPM6 and on aspects related to implementing these standards.

In early 2012, this Task Force on Global Production developed and prioritized a list of conceptual and measurement issues that needed to be addressed. In October 2012, the task force prepared an interim report that focused on the top-priority issues and presented a draft report on all issues to the Group of Experts on National Accounts in April 2012. The task force received feedback from the Group of Experts on National Accounts that there was a need for more emphasis on specific guidance and practicality, so the output will be finalized in the form of a practical guide to be used in the preparation of statistics on global-production-related activities (ECE 2013). The task force also produced a report on factoryless goods production that questioned whether ownership of material inputs is an appropriate criterion for classifying an FGP in manufacturing (Task Force on Global Production 2013). That report was presented to the Expert Group on International Statistical Classifications in May 2013.

In the United States, the ECPC recognized that the NAICS classification decisions the committee adopted would affect multiple U.S. agencies, as well as programs within those agencies. Furthermore, the ECPC realized that, as with any new concept, there would likely be some differences in interpretation across agencies during the implementation process, and that these differences might lead to data inconsistencies. As a result, the ECPC sponsored a multiagency task force to ensure consistent implementation of the inclusion of FGPs in the manufacturing sector in the 2012 NAICS. The team is composed of representatives from the Bureau of Economic Analysis (BEA), the Bureau of Labor Statistics (BLS), the Census Bureau, the Federal Reserve, and the International Trade Commission.

The FGP Implementation Planning Group began meeting in late June 2010, with the goal of defining a set of rules that agencies could use to implement the ECPC recommendation for classification of FGPs in the 2012 NAICS. The group's analysis of the issues relating to implementation of this concept indicated that these changes must first be implemented in conjunction with a quinquennial economic census in order to survey establishments in the appropriate sector. Given the complexity of the changes and the timing within the planning for the 2012 Economic Census, the group determined that it did not seem feasible to implement in 2012. The team considered partial or sequential implementation on a pilot basis by applying the new rules to only some establishments or industries or by applying only some of the rules, but it determined that this approach would be problematic since it would result in multiple series breaks over time, especially at aggregate levels. As a result, the planning group recommended that full implementation of the outsourcing redefinitions should be delayed, the new goal being to implement them for the 2017 Economic Census.

This recommendation was accepted by the ECPC and the OMB in November 2010. Implementation was deferred, and the interagency group was asked by the ECPC to continue the work of coordinating the implementation of this change. Then, in a further delay, the OMB announced in August 2014 that it was rescinding its earlier decision requiring that statistical agencies implement the classification change of assigning FGPs to the manufacturing sector by 2017, because the agencies "need an opportunity to perform additional research, testing, and evaluation." The remainder of this chapter will discuss the work of the FGP Implementation Planning Group.

U.S. IMPLEMENTATION ISSUES

Internationally, the concept of economic ownership was integral to many of the decisions made relating to the handling of transactions. The ECPC decision to classify FGPs in manufacturing did not explicitly mention the concept of economic ownership, but it did focus on control of the entrepreneurial aspects of production, which is in essence the acceptance of the risks and rewards of the production process. To be the economic owner of a product, an establishment must control the intellectual property (IP) or design, control the production process, control the sale of the product and assume entrepreneurial risk. A more detailed description of each of those four criteria, however, is required for an in-depth understanding of the concept.

Control of the IP or design means that the establishment either has developed it internally, has purchased it from another firm, or has negotiated to lease it from another firm. For a domestic establishment with a foreign affiliate, it is possible that the U.S. establishment could be leasing the IP or design from its affiliate. It is also possible that it could be leased to more than one economic owner. From a business-function standpoint, an establishment is the economic owner of the IP or design if it has the right to use it in its products, redistribute it, and can independently change the design of the final product.

There are many aspects to controlling the production process, including controlling inputs, product quality, and production levels. With respect to inputs, the economic owner can control inputs for the final product in a number of different ways. The owner could purchase the inputs and ship them to the MSP, arrange to have them shipped to the MSP from another domestic or foreign location, or merely approve the selection of input providers and the quality of the inputs. The economic owner also makes decisions about which products to produce and controls production levels and product quality. An economic owner can decide whether to add or delete product lines, expand his or her business, move into a different business, or leave the business entirely. Finally, the economic owner must also be able to report the cost of manufacturing service.

The economic owner of a product arranges to sell (or transfer in the case of an affiliate) the product to buyers (consumers, government, wholesalers, retailers, or other types of businesses, including manufacturers) and sets the price associated with the transaction. The economic owner does not need to take physical possession of the product or arrange the details of shipments to purchasers, but the owner must be able to report the value of those shipments.

There are a number of indicators that an establishment has taken on the entrepreneurial risk related to a product. The economic owner absorbs the loss for any unsold final products. It is also responsible for losses due to final products that fail to meet the customer's satisfaction, for which an unsatisfied customer would return the product to the economic owner (or a representative of the economic owner) for a refund, rather than to the establishment that performed the transformation.

Finally, it is legally responsible for legal problems related to defects or other problems in the final product.

The criteria for determining economic ownership apply in the same way whether the relationship is between a U.S. establishment and a foreign establishment that performs transformation activities or between a foreign establishment and a U.S. establishment performing transformation activities.

Defining Decision Rules

The FGP Implementation Planning Group determined that the best way to ensure a consistent understanding of how the classification decision-making process that is related to outsourcing should be implemented was to consider various scenarios and determine the appropriate classification for each. Based on these discussions of potential scenarios, the team reached conceptual agreement on classification outcomes and created an outsourcing decision tree that reflected the implementation of those concepts. In creating the scenarios, it became clear that a single establishment might perform both integrated manufacturing and manufacturing service–providing activities and at the same time have a factoryless goods production relationship with an unaffiliated transforming establishment. As a result, those possibilities are found in the decision tree. The decision tree reflects what the team considered would be the "ideal" implementation from a conceptual standpoint and is displayed in Figure 2.2.

There may be practical difficulties in implementing this ideal scenario because of external factors such as the differences between international and U.S. recommendations or issues reporting establishments might have in providing the information required to support classification decision making. There could also be internal limitations to implementation procedures related to the availability of resources within statistical agencies.

Several different agencies or programs currently make independent classification decisions for establishments. As long as a potential FGP and an MSP don't belong to the same enterprise, decision making using the decision tree is fairly straightforward and would routinely result in consistent decision making across agencies and programs. Multi-

Figure 2.2 Outsourcing Decision Tree—Ideal Definitions

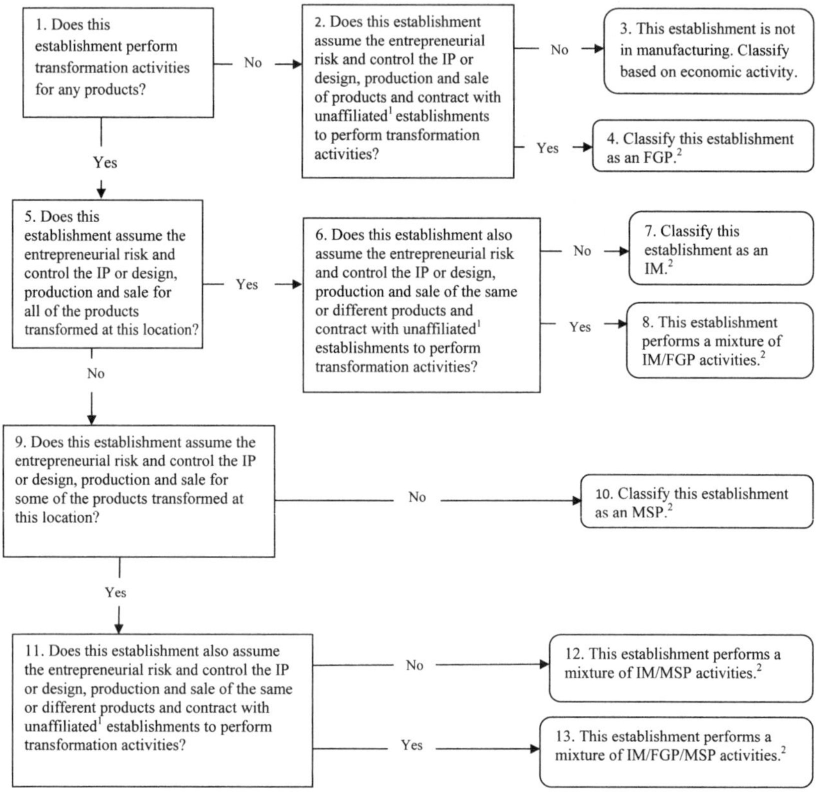

[1] All foreign establishments should be treated as unaffiliated.

[2] If an establishment performs a mixture of integrated manufacturer (IM), manufacturing service provider (MSP), and factoryless goods producer (FGP) activities, it should be classified into one of the three unique subindustries, IM, MSP, or FGP, based on where most of its activity occurs.

SOURCE: Author's compilation.

establishment enterprises in manufacturing industries generally include establishments that perform transformation activities and establishments that control or provide support to the production activities. When all of the establishments of an enterprise are in the United States, the decision-making process is still fairly straightforward, since an establishment can only have FGP activity if it assumes the entrepreneurial risk and controls the IP or design, the production, and the sale of products, and if it contracts with *unaffiliated* establishments to perform transformation activities.

The ideal definitions, however, specify that all foreign establishments should be treated as unaffiliated. Thus, there is a potential FGP/MSP relationship whenever a product is transformed by a foreign affiliate. In recent years, multinational enterprises (MNEs) have responded to improved communications and a need to manage global operations by unbundling management functions in the same way they have unbundled production functions. Global enterprises may spread typical headquarters functions across locations, even in different countries, based on local regulations and proximity to labor sources, customers, and suppliers. This can result in different locations for the financial, legal, and decision-making functions of an enterprise (Desai 2009). As a result, assigning economic ownership to a specific establishment is particularly difficult when analyzing the relationship between headquarters-type and transforming-type establishments of the enterprise. Within an enterprise, an establishment that doesn't perform transformation may meet all the criteria for economic ownership of a product, but the transaction may be recorded on another establishment's books for reasons such as tax purposes. In addition, it is possible that some of the decision-making tasks that are included in the economic ownership criteria may be split across more than one headquarters-type establishment.

The U.S. interagency group has expressed concern that the complexity of classification decisions when MNEs are involved will result in an inefficient allocation of resources if each agency or program works independently to resolve these issues, and that will make it difficult for agencies or programs to make consistent decisions about the establishments of individual enterprises, as well as to make consistent decisions across enterprises. Some of the countries in the European Union (EU) have begun to form groups to work together to ensure that the transactions of MNEs are treated consistently across national accounts and national economic statistics. The U.S. interagency group has proposed a similar approach as part of the plan for the implementation of the FGP concept, with the formation of a standing cross-agency group to make classification recommendations for the major multinational enterprises that operate in the United States. The Census Bureau, the BEA, and the BLS each collect a different set of detailed statistical data from enterprises and establishments. Analysis of the combination of those data would likely result in the best decisions related to the classification of the establishments of these enterprises and the amount of revenue that should be attributed to each. Given the organization of U.S. statistical programs, the formation of such a group would require new data-sharing agreements and potentially new funding sources, and thus this proposal might be very difficult to implement. In the meantime, efforts to develop other approaches for handling these challenges will continue.

Understanding Data Needs

There are many data interdependencies among U.S. statistical agencies and the programs within them. In order to successfully implement the manufacturing redefinition clarification, statistical agencies have some special needs related to the data inputs that they receive from one another so they can accurately calculate statistics that reflect the inclusion of factoryless goods manufacturers in manufacturing.

Integrated manufacturers, manufacturing service providers, and factoryless goods producers each have a different mix of inputs and operating constraints. As a result, it may be necessary to produce separate data for each type of operation in many statistical series, either as unpublished components of published aggregate data or as published series. In order to support these data analysis needs, statistical programs will need values for inputs and outputs broken out by type of operation.

Some statistical agencies use the customs data provided by the IMTS in the production of statistics related to imports and exports. Since IMTS2010 gave priority to the need for statistics that reflect physical border-crossing of goods, customs data provided by the IMTS differ conceptually from the ECPC definition of FGP with respect to goods for processing and the return of processed goods. In order to use customs data in compiling other statistics that follow the ECPC definition, data will need to be obtained from other sources to adjust customs data to reflect the ECPC concept.

It is important both to statistical agencies and to other data users to be able to distinguish between definitional and economic changes so that these users of the data can create continuous time series and analyze data changes over time. As a result, individual statistical programs will need access to conversion, or bridge data, for various data series in order to produce historically consistent time series.

Statistical agencies rely on businesses to provide the data required to calculate economic statistics. For this reason, the interagency group also recognized the importance of understanding the types of data that establishments involved in outsourcing would likely be able to supply. In order to obtain this information, the group met with associations and companies and analyzed publicly available company data (particularly Form 10-Ks) to determine how companies manage and record their outsourcing activities. Another method used to determine data availability was the inclusion of "special inquiry" questions on current survey forms for some statistical programs. These questions serve the dual purpose of testing potential questions and identifying establishments that would likely be classified as FGPs when the manufacturing redefinition is implemented. The results of this research will be used as input to the creation of updated data collection instruments.

EXPECTED IMPACT ON ECONOMIC STATISTICS

The classification of factoryless goods producers in manufacturing is expected to have an impact on a number of different statistical programs, some of which are listed below:

- **U.S. Census Bureau**—Economic Census, annual and monthly wholesale trade surveys, Annual Survey of Manufacturers, several other NAICS-based series.
- **Bureau of Economic Analysis**—industry accounts, international accounts, National Income and Product Accounts, regional accounts.
- **Bureau of Labor Statistics**—Current Employment Statistics program, Quarterly Census of Employment and Wages, Producer Price Index program, International Price Program, Major Sector Productivity program, and Industry Productivity program.
- **Federal Reserve**—industrial production.

General Expectations by Type of Measure

The exact impact of these changes will depend on the classification decisions that are made for individual establishments when the new rules are applied, as well as on the size of those establishments at the time the rules take effect, whenever that may be. As a result, there is currently not enough information to quantify the exact impact, and there won't be until that information becomes available. We do have enough information, however, to describe the types of changes that are expected for a number of different economic measures. These expectations are described in Table 2.2.

Impact on Specific Manufacturing Industries

Although exact impact measures cannot currently be calculated, existing data can be analyzed in an attempt to identify which industries are most likely to be affected by these changes and to make some estimates related to the size of some of the changes. The data expectations described above indicate that changes within manufacturing will be centered on specific industries. For planning purposes, it would be helpful to economic programs to identify which industries will likely be most affected by the inclusion of FGPs in manufacturing in order to support any required decision making.

In order to develop measurement statistics, I make the following four assumptions related to manufacturing industries:

1) Manufacturing industries that currently purchase a relatively large amount of contract work have a production process that is consistent with the outsourcing of transformation tasks.
2) Under current procedures, if a manufacturing establishment outsources all of the transformation for its products, the sales of those products are coded as resales. Therefore, manufacturing industries with relatively high levels of resales are likely to have FGP activity under the new rules.
3) The ratio of production employees to total employees will be lower for manufacturing industries that outsource transformation activities.
4) Manufacturing industries with relatively high levels of imports for their products are likely to be involved in outsourcing.

Based on these assumptions, data from the 2007 Economic Census and the 2002 benchmark I-O tables were examined to find measures that might help identify industries that currently have characteristics that could be indicative of FGP activity. No single measure was identified that could reflect the criteria in all four assumptions. As a result, five different measures were identified, and analysis focused on the full set of measures rather than on any individual measure. For each measure, values were calculated for each six-digit NAICS manufacturing industry along with weighted average values for all manufacturing industries. For most of the measures, values higher than the average were considered indicative of potential FGP activity. For the number of production workers divided by total employment, values lower than the averages were considered indicative of potential FGP activity. In order to further support analysis, a level was judgmentally selected for each measure to indicate a value that was significantly higher or lower than the average, so that about half of the above- or below-average industries were considered to be significantly above or below. The formulas for each measure are displayed in Table 2.3, along with the percentage level significantly above or below.

The goal of the analysis was two-pronged. At a high level, the goal was to provide a big picture of the impact of this change on the manufacturing sector. At an industry level, the goal was to provide early support for agency planning processes by systematically identifying those specific industries that are most likely to be affected by the inclusion of FGPs in manufacturing and thus may need special processing. Industries were assigned to one of three categories based on the number of measures above average and significantly above average (or, as noted earlier, below average, in the case of number of production employees divided by total employment). Although the five measures were selected because of their expected relationship to potential FGP activity, the level of each of the measures for a particular industry could be affected by other factors as well. As a result, criteria were set for the three categories, assuming that an industry with fewer than five measures above average could have a high likelihood of being affected by the inclusion of FGPs in manufacturing, while those industries with only one measure above average would be unlikely to be affected. Table 2.4 displays the exact criteria that were used to assign industries to categories, as well as statistics for each of the three categories.

Table 2.2 Expected Changes to Economic Measures

Measure	Expected change
Total U.S. employment and wages	U.S. totals will not change.
Sector U.S. employment and wages	Values will shift across sectors, with manufacturing growing and other sectors, primarily wholesale trade, shrinking. Increases in manufacturing are expected to be centered on specific industries. This will result in regional shifts within sectors, including manufacturing.
Production employees	U.S. totals will not change. Sector total changes will be minimal, since FGPs would have few, if any, production employees.
Total U.S. revenue values	The total will likely change, but the direction and amount of the change are unknown. 1. FGPs may report revenues from products that would have previously been treated as imports. 2. For an FGP manufacturing establishment previously classified in wholesale trade, revenues will increase by the difference between the wholesale trade margin and the full value of the products for some statistical measures. 3. For manufacturing establishments that are determined to be MSPs rather than IMs, revenues will decrease by the difference between the full value of the product and the value of the manufacturing service they provided.
Sector U.S. revenue values	Sector totals will change, with increases expected in manufacturing and decreases in other sectors. The manufacturing changes will likely be in specific industries.
Value of U.S. imports	The total will likely change, but the direction and amount of the change are unknown. The mix between goods and services will also change. The changes will be centered in specific product areas. For products transformed by foreign MSPs for domestic FGPs: 1. The full value of the products that the foreign MSPs transformed and returned to the U.S. FGPs will be excluded from imports.

	2. The value of the manufacturing service that they performed and any inputs they provided will be included in imports. For products transformed by U.S. MSPs for foreign FGPs: 1. The full value of the products that they transformed that remain in the U.S. are included in imports. 2. The value of any inputs that they received from the foreign FGP will be excluded from imports.
Value of U.S. exports	The total will likely change, but the direction and amount of the change are unknown. The mix between goods and services will also change. The changes will be centered on specific product areas. For products transformed by foreign MSPs for domestic FGPs: 1. The value of products that have remained in a foreign MSP's country or that were shipped by a foreign MSP to another country will be added to exports. 2. The value of the inputs that the domestic FGP provided to the MSP will be excluded from exports. For products transformed by U.S. MSPs for foreign FGPs: 1. The full value of any product that they transformed and returned to the foreign FGP will be excluded from exports. 2. The value of the manufacturing service that they performed and any inputs they provided will be included in exports.

SOURCE: Author's compilation.

Table 2.3 Industry Impact Analysis Measures

Measure	Average for all manufacturing industries (%)	Significantly above/below average level (%)
2007 Economic Census		
(Cost of contract work) / (payroll)	9.7	15
(Cost of contract work) / (cost of materials and parts)	5.9	10
(Cost of resales) / (total cost of materials)	2.3	5
(Number of production workers) / (total employment)	70.1	60
2002 benchmark I-O tables		
(Imports) / (domestic production + imports − exports)	23.2	30

SOURCE: 2007 Economic Census and 2002 benchmark input-output (I-O) tables.

In order to summarize the industry results, the industry categorization was further analyzed by aggregating the industries by subsector and calculating the percentage of each subsector's value of shipments (VOS) that is attributable to industries in each of the three categories. These percentages are displayed in the Table 2.5, along with a count of the number of industries in the category. The analysis indicates that the apparel manufacturing and computer and electronic product manufacturing subsectors had the highest portion of their VOS from industries in the highest-likelihood category. This is consistent with the generally accepted assumption that these two subsectors will be strongly affected by the manufacturing redefinition.

Analysis of Wholesale Trade for Own-Brand Importer-Marketers

The wholesale trade survey forms for the Economic Census include a question related to the type of operation. One of the operation types is, "own-brand importer-marketer." Own-brand importers-marketers deal primarily or exclusively in the parent company's own branded products manufactured outside the United States. The products are either imported into the United States and then sold, or they are sold and then drop-shipped directly from a foreign location to the U.S. customer. It is expected that many of the wholesale trade establishments categorized

Table 2.4 Results of Manufacturing Industry Impact Analysis

Category	Criteria	Number of industries	% of total manufacturing establishments	% of total manufacturing employment	% of total manufacturing VOS
Highest likelihood	4 or 5 measures above average, or 3 above average with more than one significantly above average	150	33	30	25
Medium likelihood	3 measures above average with fewer than 2 significantly above, or 2 above average	160	40	34	39
Lowest likelihood	0 or 1 measure above average	161	27	36	36

NOTE: "VOS" stands for value of shipments.
SOURCE: Author's calculations based on 2007 Economic Census and 2002 benchmark input-output (I-O) tables.

in this operation type will be classified in manufacturing using the new classification rules. In the 2007 Economic Census, about 3 percent of all wholesale trade establishments were own brand importer-marketers.[5] Those establishments accounted for about 4 percent of wholesale trade sales and employment. If all those establishments had been classified in manufacturing, the number of manufacturing establishments would have increased by about 3 percent, sales would have increased by about 4 percent, and employment would have increased by about 2 percent. The wholesale trade industry groups that have the largest proportion of their sales from own-brand importer-marketers are officially known as "Apparel, piece goods, and notions merchant wholesalers" and "Electrical and electronic goods merchant wholesalers."

Table 2.5 Analysis of the Impact of Inclusion of FGPs in Manufacturing by NAICS Subsector

		% of subsector VOS from industries by likelihood of impact			No. of subsector industries by likelihood of impact		
Sector	Title	High	Medium	Unlikely	High	Medium	Unlikely
311	Food manufacturing	3.0	20.0	76.9	2	8	37
312	Beverage and tobacco product manufacturing	0.0	52.1	47.9	0	5	4
313	Textile mills	25.2	41.7	33.1	4	4	4
314	Textile product mills	47.9	48.4	3.7	5	2	1
315	Apparel manufacturing	86.8	11.7	1.5	17	5	2
316	Leather and allied product manufacturing	43.6	56.4	0.0	5	4	0
321	Wood product manufacturing	4.1	8.3	87.6	1	2	11
322	Paper manufacturing	0.5	5.5	94.0	1	3	16
323	Printing and related support activities	21.1	65.7	13.2	4	5	3
324	Petroleum and coal product manufacturing	0.0	96.2	3.8	0	2	3
325	Chemical manufacturing	30.7	48.8	20.5	4	19	11
326	Plastics and rubber product manufacturing	0.0	13.3	86.7	0	4	13
327	Nonmetallic mineral product manufacturing	17.3	28.0	54.6	7	10	7
331	Primary metal manufacturing	40.6	24.2	35.2	2	11	13
332	Fabricated metal product manufacturing	33.1	51.4	15.5	17	19	7
333	Machinery manufacturing	46.9	38.6	14.5	27	17	5
334	Computer and electronic product manufacturing	77.4	20.3	2.3	21	7	2
335	Electrical equipment, appliance, and component manufacturing	25.1	35.9	39.0	5	9	8
336	Transportation equipment manufacturing	23.3	22.2	54.5	5	12	13
337	Furniture and related product manufacturing	17.0	35.6	47.4	4	5	4
339	Miscellaneous manufacturing	75.6	23.9	0.5	14	8	1

NOTE: "VOS" stands for value of shipments.
SOURCE: Author's calculations based on 2007 Economic Census and 2002 benchmark input-output (I-O) tables.

IMPORTANCE OF CHANGES FOR DATA USERS

Over the past 20 years, U.S. economic statistical programs recognized that there have been major changes in the way businesses operate, particularly with respect to production fragmentation and globalization, but individual agencies and programs in those agencies made different methodological decisions in response to those changes. There was not an integrated comprehensive examination of how these economic changes should be reflected in the entire set of economic statistics.

Business and governmental decision makers use a wide variety of U.S. economic statistics from different agencies and programs on a daily basis. To the extent that these statistics are inconsistent with one another or have not kept pace with changes in the economy, they may make it difficult for data users to make sound decisions. This problem has been recognized by both government and business data users and has been characterized as "using a 1950s dashboard to operate a 21st-century machine" (Karabell 2013, p. G1).

The collaborative effort of U.S. statistical agencies to reach agreement on how to identify and handle factoryless goods producers and manufacturing service providers will result in more data consistency across agencies. In addition, it will allow statistical agencies to provide data about the three different types of manufacturing establishments, at least at an aggregate level, allowing data users to see changes over time and to analyze differences across the three types of establishments. These benefits will support the need of business and government leaders to make informed decisions.

Notes

1. All views expressed in this chapter are those of the author and do not necessarily reflect the views or policies of the U.S. Bureau of Labor Statistics.
2. For a detailed description of the usual classification rules, refer to United Nations Department of Economic and Social Affairs (2008).
3. More information about the ECPC can be found at http://www.census.gov/eos/www/naics/ecpc/ecpc.html (accessed November 12, 2013).
4. The following link includes links to various sectors of the manual: http://www.census.gov/cgi-bin/sssd/naics/naicsrch?chart=2007 (accessed April 21, 2014).

5. Detailed data on wholesale trade by type of operation can be found at U.S. Census Bureau (2007).

References

Becker, Ralf, and Ivo Havinga. 2007. "Treatment of Outsourcing in the International Standard Industrial Classification (ISIC), Rev. 4." Paper presented at the OECD Structural Business Statistics Expert Meeting "Entrepreneurship and Business Statistics," held in Paris, May 10–11. http://www.oecd.org/std/business-stats/oecdstructuralbusinessstatisticsexpertmeetingparis10-11may2007.htm (accessed November 5, 2013).

Center on Globalization, Governance, and Competitiveness (CGGC). 2006. *Global Value Chains: Concepts and Tools*. Durham, NC: Center on Globalization, Governance, and Competitiveness. http://globalvaluechains.org/concepts.html (accessed November 8, 2013).

Chang, Philip, Akhmad Bayhaqi, and Bernadine Zhang Yuhua. 2012. "Concepts and Trends in Global Supply, Global Value, and Global Production Chains." Asia-Pacific Economic Cooperation (APEC) Policy Support Unit, Issues Paper No. 1. Singapore: Asia-Pacific Economic Cooperation.

Desai, Mihir A. 2009. "The Decentering of the Global Firm." *World Economy* 32(9): 1271–1290.

Economic Classification Policy Committee (ECPC). 2010. *Recommendation for Classification of Outsourcing in North American Industry Classification System (NAICS) Revisions for 2012*. Suitland, MD: U.S. Census Bureau. http://www.census.gov/eos/www/naics/fr2010/ECPC_Recommendation_for_Classification_of_Outsourcing.pdf (accessed November 7, 2013).

Economic Commission for Europe (ECE). 2013. *Report of the Twelfth Meeting of the Group of Experts on National Accounts*. Geneva: United Nations Economic and Social Council. http://www.unece.org/fileadmin/DAM/stats/documents/ece/ces/ge.20/2013/18Add16-NA.pdf (accessed November 7, 2013).

European Commission, International Monetary Fund, Organisation for Economic Co-operation and Development, United Nations, and World Bank. 2009. *System of National Accounts 2008*. New York: Joint publication by the European Commission, International Monetary Fund, Organisation for Economic Co-operation and Development, United Nations, and World Bank. http://unstats.un.org/unsd/nationalaccount/docs/SNA2008.pdf (accessed November 11, 2013).

Gereffi, Gary, John Humphrey, and Timothy Sturgeon. 2005. "The Governance of Global Value Chains." *Review of International Political Economy* 12(1):78–104.

International Monetary Fund (IMF). 2009. *Balance of Payments and International Investment Position Manual, Sixth Edition (BPM6).* Washington, DC: International Monetary Fund. http://www.imf.org/external/pubs/ft/bop/2007/pdf/bpm6.pdf (accessed November 6, 2013).

Karabell, Zachary. 2013. "It's an Old Numbers Game. What If They're Wrong?" *Washington Post*, April 19, G:1. http://articles.washingtonpost.com/2013-04-19/business/38666060_1_gdp-economic-statistics-ratio (accessed November 8, 2013).

Office of Management and Budget (OMB). 2007. *NAICS United States 2007.* Alexandria, VA: National Technical Information Service.

Statistics Netherlands. 2011. *In-Depth Review on Global Manufacturing.* Geneva: Economic Commission for Europe, Conference of European Statisticians. http://www.unece.org/fileadmin/DAM/stats/groups/tfgp/3-InDepth_Review_Global_Manufacturing.pdf (accessed November 7, 2013).

Task Force on Global Production. 2013. "Issue Paper on Classifying Factoryless Goods Producers." Geneva and New York: United Nations Department of Economic and Social Affairs. https://unstats.un.org/unsd/class/intercop/expertgroup/2013/AC267-26.PDF (accessed November 7, 2013).

United Nations Department of Economic and Social Affairs. 2008. *International Standard Industrial Classification of All Economic Activities, Revision 4.* Statistical papers, Series M, No. 4, Rev. 4. New York: United Nations. http://unstats.un.org/unsd/publication/seriesM/seriesm_4rev4e.pdf (accessed November 8, 2013).

———. 2011. *International Merchandise Trade Statistics: Concepts and Definitions 2010.* Statistics and Statistical Methods Publications Series M, No. 52, Rev. 2. New York: United Nations Department of Economic and Social Affairs, Statistics Division.

United Nations Economic Commission for Europe. 2011. *The Impact of Globalization on National Accounts.* New York and Geneva: United Nations.

United Nations Statistical Commission. 2006. "Report on the Thirty-Seventh Session." Official Records of the Economic and Social Council, 2006, Supplement No. 4. Presented at the Thirty-Seventh Session of the United Nations Statistical Commission, held in New York, March 7–10. http://unstats.un.org/unsd/statcom/doc06/Report-English.pdf (accessed November 8, 2013).

U.S. Census Bureau. 2007. *American FactFinder: Wholesale Trade: Subject Series—Misc Subjects: Detailed Type of Operation for the United States: 2007.* Washington, DC: U.S. Census Bureau. http://factfinder2.census.gov/faces/tableservices/jsf/pages/productview.xhtml?pid=ECN_2007_US_42SXSB04&prodType=table (accessed November 11, 2013).

3
Measuring "Factoryless" Manufacturing

Evidence from U.S. Surveys

Fariha Kamal
U.S. Census Bureau

Brent R. Moulton
U.S. Bureau of Economic Analysis

Jennifer Ribarsky
Organisation for Economic Co-operation and Development[1]

Globalization has created new opportunities and competitive challenges, forcing producers to seek more efficient ways to make their products. It has become increasingly common for producers seeking more efficient means of production to divide the traditional vertically integrated production model into stages or tasks (known as fragments), thus allowing them to outsource part of their production process. When the resulting production arrangement is interlinked across different countries, the measurement challenges facing national economic statistics programs increase dramatically.

Many economic forces are driving the fragmentation of production to specialized establishments, both foreign and domestic. Improvements in information technology have allowed firms to relocate production to new and often distant locations. International cost differences (such as lower relative wage costs and lower trade and transport costs), improved logistics, and improved intellectual property rights protection and contract enforcement have facilitated the use of global supply chains and global value chains, or GVCs (U.S. International Trade Commission 2011).

A supply chain is a system of organization, technology, activities, information, and resources involved in moving a good or service from supplier to customer. It can be within an enterprise, between enterprises in a local economy, or among a group of countries. The supply chain is a network where the activities involved can be grouped using the traditional broad stages of production—from upstream research and development (R&D) and design, through manufacturing, to downstream logistics, marketing, and sales. The complexity of the supply chain and the business relationship between the various stages can vary by industry and by enterprise. A global supply chain consists of a worldwide network of these activities.

A value chain refers to the value-added activities required to bring a good or service from its conception, design, production, marketing, distribution, and support to final customers.[2] It is the value added to the good or service at each stage of the network. Similar to the supply chain, the complexity of the value chain and the business relationship between the various stages can vary by industry and by enterprise. A value chain can be between enterprises in a local economy or span enterprises across a group of countries.

The fragmentation of production through the use of GVCs raises many issues for economic measurement, including classifying the firms within these chains, measuring and classifying trade in goods and services, and measuring and classifying trade in intermediate inputs. The recently updated international guidelines for compiling national and international accounts include new guidelines to better capture the impacts of GVCs on the economy.[3] The U.S. Census Bureau, the Bureau of Economic Analysis (BEA), and the Bureau of Labor Statistics (BLS) have been studying ways to classify and collect data from entities that are part of GVCs. A key element in identifying the relationship between firms that outsource the fabrication of products—while still controlling the production process—and firms that perform the processing is contract manufacturing services (CMS).

This chapter focuses on efforts to collect data on CMS and the challenges with identifying and collecting data on entities that are part of GVCs. In particular, it identifies data that the BEA and the Census Bureau are already collecting on both producers and users of CMS. In this way, the chapter not only demonstrates that it is feasible to identify and collect data on these activities but also provides a snapshot of companies that are engaged in these activities. Although the descriptive data presented in this chapter do not provide the full accounting of these activities that is recommended by the latest U.S. and international statistical guidelines, they do provide an indication of the potential scope and magnitude of the measurement task before us. The statistical agencies will use this and other information to guide their efforts to improve the measurement of these activities in order to implement the latest statistical guidelines and provide more useful data on manufacturing value chains. This will enable them to cover both the firms that outsource fabrication services and the CMS producers that provide these services.

The chapter's remaining sections describe new U.S. and international guidelines and relevant data on CMS activities. Section Two, "Classifying 'Factoryless' Manufacturers," looks at U.S. and international recommendations on the industry classification of "factoryless" manufacturers—units that entirely outsource the fabrication of their products. Section Three, "Data Collection on Contract Manufacturing Services," describes the BEA and Census Bureau surveys and discusses data collection efforts on CMS. Section Four, "Analysis of Contract Manufacturing Services on the BEA's BE-10 Survey," discusses the BEA's analysis of the CMS data reported in its surveys. Section Five, "Analysis of Contract Manufacturing Services on Census Bureau 2011 COS," treats the Census Bureau's analysis of the CMS data reported in the Report of Organization Survey. Section Six, "Future Work," concludes with a discussion of future data collection endeavors.

CLASSIFYING "FACTORYLESS" MANUFACTURERS

The North American Industry Classification System (NAICS) is an industry classification system for establishments based on a production-oriented conceptual framework in which establishments are grouped together by common production processes. A production process describes any activity in which inputs, including types of labor and related skills, capital equipment, raw and intermediate materials, and, in many cases, intangible inputs such as intellectual property, are used to fabricate a material good or to render a service.[4] Establishments are the smallest operating entity for which records provide information on the cost of resources—materials, labor, and capital—employed to produce the units of output (OMB 2007, p. 19).

With the rise of global competition, economies are becoming more integrated, and the use of global supply chains is rapidly increasing. This has complicated the application of the production function classification principle to units that control intellectual property and perform underlying entrepreneurial components of arranging the factors of production, but outsource all of the actual transformation activities to other specialized units. The Office of Management and Budget (OMB) calls these units "factoryless" goods producers, or FGPs (OMB 2010).

Units in the manufacturing sector arrange for and bring together the factors of production necessary to produce a good. They accept the entrepreneurial risk of producing and bringing goods to market. As the Economic Classification Policy Committee (ECPC) states in the 2012 NAICS manual's supporting documents,

> when individual steps in the complete process are outsourced, an establishment should remain classified in the manufacturing sector. For example: 1) a decision to produce or purchase raw materials does not change the classification; 2) a decision to use contractors or a professional employer organization (PEO) rather than a traditional employment contract does not change classification; and 3) a decision to outsource marketing and distribution to a wholesaler does not change classification. In each case, the decision to perform or outsource a function changes the establishment production function but does not change the classification. (ECPC 2010, p. 6)

The ECPC defines the characteristics of FGPs to include the following (OMB 2010, p. 4):[5]

- Owns rights to the intellectual property or design (whether independently developed or otherwise acquired) of the final manufactured product.
- May or may not own the input materials.
- Does not own production facilities.
- Does not perform transformation activities.
- Owns the final product produced by manufacturing service provider partners.
- Sells the final product.

International Recommendations

The NAICS classification, employed in the United States, does not use ownership of material inputs as a basis for industry classification. However, the International Standard Industrial Classification of All Economic Activities (ISIC), Revision 4, which is promulgated by the United Nations and forms the basis for industrial classification systems used by many other countries, bases classification of units that outsource transformation solely on ownership of material inputs. “A principal who completely outsources the transformation process should be classified into manufacturing if and only if it owns the input materials to the production process—and therefore owns the final output,” the ISIC says (United Nations Statistics Division 2008, p. 30). According to the ISIC, a unit that outsources transformation but owns the material inputs is a manufacturer; a unit that outsources transformation and does not own the material inputs is engaged in wholesale or retail trade.

The ECPC considers a strict adherence to the ownership of materials as impractical because a slight change in how the materials were acquired would change the industry classification. For example, the principal could purchase the inputs and do one of two things: 1) take physical possession of the inputs and ship them to the contract manufacturer or 2) arrange to have the inputs shipped directly to the contract manufacturer from another domestic or foreign location. Under ISIC rules, the contractual arrangement of the case in which the principal purchases the materials directly would result in the principal being classified in the manufacturing sector even if the principal did not take physical possession of the materials. However, rather than purchasing the inputs, the principal may simply approve the input providers from whom the contract manufacturer must buy and monitor the quality of the inputs acquired by the contract manufacturer. Under ISIC rules, this contractual arrangement would most likely result in the principal being classified in a trade sector because the principal did not directly purchase the material inputs. The ECPC considers controlling the production process a more important criterion than owning the material inputs.

The ISIC classification based on ownership of the material inputs is consistent with the treatment recommended in both the *System of National Accounts 2008* (referred to in this chapter as SNA 2008) and the sixth edition of the *Balance of Payments and International Invest-*

ment Position Manual (referred to in this chapter as BPM6) for goods sent abroad for processing (European Commission et al. 2009; IMF 2009).[6] According to this treatment, goods sent abroad for processing without a change in ownership should be excluded from goods trade; the processing fee charged by the manufacturing service provider should be recorded as services trade. The fee for this service is related to the difference between the value of the goods exported for processing and the value of the goods returned (imported) after processing.[7] When goods are shipped abroad for processing and subsequently sold abroad, the processed goods should be recorded as U.S. merchandise exports at the time they are sold, and any inputs purchased abroad by the U.S. firm and processed abroad should be recorded as U.S. merchandise imports.[8] The new international guidelines state that the recording of imports and exports of goods should be based on the transfer of economic ownership. For example, if a U.S. shoe company sent soles and leather to a contract manufacturer in another country for assembly of its athletic shoe, the U.S. shoe company—the principal—is importing manufacturing services from the contract manufacturer. Because the U.S. shoe company owns the soles, leather, and assembled athletic shoe, there is no international transaction; therefore, the soles and leather should not be recorded as U.S. exports and the assembled athletic shoe should not be recorded as a U.S. import.

It is important to note that although the NAICS does not base its classification of "factoryless" goods producers strictly on change in ownership, the change-in-ownership principle is still the most relevant criterion for measuring international transactions. It is desirable to define international transactions as transactions between residents and nonresidents, thus focusing on the change in ownership, regardless of whether the establishments engaged in the transactions are classified in manufacturing or in another industry. Thus, adoption of the NAICS recommendation for FGP does not preclude the adoption of the SNA 2008/BPM6 recommendation for the treatment of goods sent abroad for processing.

DATA COLLECTION ON CONTRACT MANUFACTURING SERVICES

Identifying CMS is a key element in identifying the relationship between firms that outsource the fabrication of products—while still controlling the production process—and firms that perform the processing. Through preliminary outreach conducted by the Census Bureau, respondents appear to understand the concept of CMS and the need for U.S. statistical agencies to collect the data. Collecting data, however, could be challenging. Some respondents indicated that they were generally unable to provide CMS data because either accounting or production management systems did not include a searchable characteristic that would distinguish these services.

To determine whether data collection can be robust, the Census Bureau and the BEA have added questions to their respective surveys to determine whether U.S. businesses can accurately report purchases and sales of CMS. See Table 3.1 for a list of all surveys conducted by these two agencies that contain CMS-related questions. This section describes three surveys that include questions about CMS.

Bureau of Economic Analysis Surveys

The first two surveys we cover are conducted by the Bureau of Economic Analysis; the third is done by the Census Bureau.

Benchmark Survey of U.S. Direct Investment Abroad

Every five years, the BEA conducts the Benchmark Survey of U.S. Direct Investment Abroad (BE-10) to track the economic activity of U.S. multinational companies and their foreign affiliates.[9] The BE-10 benchmark survey covers the entire universe of U.S. direct investment abroad in terms of value and is the BEA's most comprehensive survey of such investment in terms of subject matter. The survey collects detailed information on the financial structure and operations of U.S. parent companies and their foreign affiliates and on the transactions and positions between the parents and their affiliates.

Any U.S. person that had a foreign affiliate is required to report.[10] If the respondent is a U.S. corporation, the respondent reports transactions

Table 3.1 List of Surveys Containing CMS-Related Questions

Form number	Survey name	Year	Sponsoring organization	Used in this chapter?
BE-10A	Benchmark Survey of U.S. Direct Investment Abroad for U.S. Parents	2009	Bureau of Economic Analysis	Y
BE-120	Benchmark Survey of Transactions in Selected Services and Intellectual Property Products with Foreign Persons	2011	Bureau of Economic Analysis	N
NC-99001	Company Organization Survey	2011	Census Bureau	Y
MC31101–MC33975[a]	Census of Manufactures	2007, 2012	Census Bureau	N
WH42101–WH42237[a]	Census of Wholesale Trade	2007, 2012	Census Bureau	N

[a] Only industries where the CMS question is applicable.
SOURCE: Authors' compilation.

for the fully consolidated U.S. domestic enterprise, which excludes foreign branches and other foreign affiliates. The BEA defines an entity as a foreign affiliate if it meets the following criteria:

- If it is incorporated abroad, it is always considered a foreign affiliate. Most affiliates meet this criterion.
- If the entity is not incorporated, it is a foreign affiliate if it
  - is subject to a foreign income tax, has a substantial physical presence abroad as evidenced by employees permanently located abroad, etc.;
  - has separate financial records that would allow the preparation of financial statements; or
  - takes title to the goods it sells and receives revenues from the sale, or receives funds from customers for its own account for services it performs.

To understand the activity of U.S. multinationals with respect to manufacturing services, the BEA added questions on purchases and performance of contract manufacturing to the 2009 Benchmark Survey of U.S. Direct Investment Abroad for U.S. parents that are not banks (BE-10A).[11] The questions were added to identify a group of firms engaged in manufacturing services that could be used either as a sample frame for a special survey on that topic or as a way to identify firms engaged in CMS that may be linked to data collected by the Census Bureau. A data link is performed when company identification codes from the BEA files are matched to the corresponding companies in the Census Bureau files. A data link project provides access to additional data items that the BEA did not collect.

The BE-10 survey defines contract manufacturing as "contracting with a firm to process materials and components, including payments for fabricating, assembling, labeling, and packaging materials and components." Because the BEA was trying to identify a group of firms that engaged in contract manufacturing, only yes/no questions were added to the survey. The BE-10 CMS definition was broader than the international guidelines' definition of "manufacturing services" as constituting the processing of materials and components owned by others. However, the BEA requested respondents to answer the question of whether they owned some or all of the materials used by the contract manufacturers or whether they did not own the materials.

Benchmark Survey of Transactions in Selected Services and Intellectual Property Products with Foreign Persons

The BEA conducts the Benchmark Survey of Transactions in Selected Services and Intellectual Property Products with Foreign Persons (BE-120) to track U.S. imports and exports of services and intellectual property products. The BE-120 benchmark survey collects information on U.S. international trade in all types of services and intellectual property for which information is not collected on other BEA surveys and is not available to the BEA from other sources. The major types of services transactions *not* covered by the BE-120 survey are travel, transportation, insurance (except for payments for primary insurance), financial services (except for payments by nonfinancial firms), and expenditures by students and medical patients that are studying or seeking treatment in a country different from their country of residence.

The survey covers U.S. persons that have engaged in services or intellectual property transactions with foreign persons. As with the U.S. direct investment abroad reporting unit, the respondent is required to report transactions for the fully consolidated U.S. domestic enterprise. Questions separately identifying receipts and payments for CMS were added to the 2011 BE-120 survey.[12] Contract manufacturing services, as defined in the BE-120, are "manufacturing services on materials and components owned by others and covers processing, assembly, labeling, packing and so forth undertaken by businesses that do not own the goods concerned."

The BEA is in the process of collecting these data to determine whether respondents can separately identify the costs of the manufacturing service as well as the destination of the goods after processing. Reporting by companies on the contract manufacturing questions is voluntary, and initial review of these questions indicates a low response rate.

Census Bureau Surveys

To date, there are three data sources that cover explicit questions about CMS. Jarmin, Krizan, and Tang (2011) analyze the CMS-specific questions in the 2007 economic censuses, which include both the Census of Manufactures and the Census of Wholesale Trade. Fort (2013) utilizes the CMS question in the 2007 Census of Manufactures to study the role of communication technology on a firm's decision to fragment its production process within and outside national boundaries. Bayard, Byrne, and Smith (Chapter 4, this volume) present a case study of "factoryless" goods–producing firms in the semiconductor industry using the 2002 and 2007 Census of Wholesale Trade. A third survey, the 2011 Report of Organization Survey (Form NC-99001, called the Company Organization Survey, or COS), has heretofore been unexplored by researchers. This chapter will focus on analyzing the 2011 COS, which asks detailed questions about both providing and purchasing CMS.[13]

2011 Company Organization Survey

The COS covers all multiunit companies with 250 or more employees and a selection of smaller companies to support other Census Bureau surveys. Companies with fewer than 250 employees are only selected for the COS when administrative records indicate that the company may be undergoing organizational change and is adding or dropping establishments. The COS is conducted annually in the four years between economic censuses.[14] The COS is designed primarily to maintain the Business Register, a current list of business establishments in the United States that is used to conduct establishment-level economic surveys every five years.[15] Therefore, it has heretofore not directly been used to conduct economic research. However, the 2011 COS included a section that asked firms about their activities pertaining to purchasing and providing CMS.[16] These questions are some of the most detailed questions pertaining to the CMS activities of a firm from any survey currently in use. Although not nationally representative, analyzing responses to these questions furthers our understanding of the characteristics of firms engaged in CMS activities.

The survey unit in the COS is the company, which is linked to a firm identification code.[17] However, the unique identifier is the survey unit identifier. It would be useful to create a firm-level data set that can be linked to other Census Bureau data sets for further analysis. It is not possible to achieve this simply by aggregating the data by firm identifiers, since CMS activities are indicated by categorical variables. Therefore, "Y" is assigned to a firm in response to a question (that requires "Y" or

"N"—"yes" or "no") where multiple survey units under that firm identifier responded differently to the question. For example, if survey unit A responds "Y" to question 2 in the 2011 COS under Section 3D while survey unit B responds "N" (or does not respond), then "Y" is assigned to the firm to which both units belong. After the preceding adjustments have been made, the COS contains records for 34,228 unique firms.

Using the firm identifier, the firm-level data set is then linked to the 2010 Longitudinal Business Database (LBD) to identify three key firm characteristics: 1) firm age, 2) total employment, and 3) sector. The LBD is a longitudinally linked data set of all business establishments that operate in the United States except for farms, government-owned or government-operated entities, and private households (Jarmin and Miranda 2002). For multiunits or firms with multiple plants, age is calculated as the difference between the year of interest and the year of establishment of its oldest plant. Since multiunit firms may operate in several sectors of the economy, the firm is considered to be operating in the sector where the largest share of its employment is housed.[18] Since the LBD is an establishment-level data set, employment is first aggregated up to the firm level by sector. The firm is then assigned its "predominant" sector, and its employment is aggregated to the firm level.[19] Finally, the firm-level data, which now include information about firm age, total employment, and sector, are linked to the 2011 COS. Of 34,228 firms in the COS data set, 34,191 firms are linked to the LBD.

The final analysis data set is a firm-level data set that includes information about the firm's age, total employment, the sector in which it operates, and several indicator variables based on responses to the CMS-related questions.[20] The firms are categorized into four mutually exclusive categories: 1) provides CMS only, 2) purchases CMS only, 3) both provides and purchases CMS, and 4) does none of the aforementioned. Within the category of firms that purchase CMS, the analysis further distinguishes among those that purchase CMS in three ways: 1) within the United States only, 2) outside the United States only, and 3) both within and outside the United States. Among firms that purchase CMS outside the United States, it is possible to further identify whether a firm does so from its foreign affiliates. Analysis of the responses to the second part of Question 2 and Question 3d is done only for survey units that belong to a unique firm identifier, because there is no straightforward yes-or-no rule that can be implemented in this instance. There are 33,865 such observations.

The 2011 COS is further linked to the 2007 Census of Manufactures (CM) and the 2009 Linked/Longitudinal Foreign Trade Transactions Database (LFTTD) to create two separate data sets: the COS-CM and the COS-LFTTD.[21] The COS-CM provides data on the total value added and the total value of shipments of each firm in the COS that belongs to the manufacturing sector. These firms represent about 27 percent of firms in the final COS analysis data set. The COS-LFTTD provides data on the total value of exports and the total value of imports of each firm in the COS because the LFFTD links the universe of export and import transactions to firms and considers all 10-digit Harmonized Commodity Description and Coding System (commonly called Harmonized System, or HS) products. The Harmonized System is an internationally standardized system of names and numbers for classifying traded products. Approximately 33 percent of the firms in the final COS analysis data set exported in 2009, and 24 percent imported that year.

ANALYSIS OF CONTRACT MANUFACTURING SERVICES ON THE BEA's BE-10 SURVEY

The results presented in this chapter are based on reported data for 3,830 U.S. parent companies. CMS questions were only included on the parent's survey form, and no corresponding questions were included on the foreign affiliate's form. Specific examples of a firm's purchase or performance of CMS cannot be described, because the data are confidential. However, hypothetical examples of purchases of CMS include the manufacturing of Company A's computer based on specifications of the design of the computer provided by Company A, and the assembly of Company B's semiconductor chips by a foundry. In each case, a firm is contracting with another unit to process materials and components based on specifications supplied by the purchasing firm.

Each U.S. parent is classified by industry using the International Survey Industry (ISI) classification system. For the most part, the ISI classifications are equivalent to NAICS four-digit industries; at its most detailed level, the NAICS classifies industries at a six-digit level. The ISI system is less detailed than the NAICS because it is designed for classifying enterprises rather than establishments (or plants). Each U.S.

parent is classified in a sector that accounted for the largest percentage of its sales. The sector classification is chosen first because many direct investment enterprises are active in several industries; it is not meaningful to classify all their data in a single industry if that industry is defined too narrowly.[22]

The first step in the analysis was to analyze how U.S. parents responded to the question of whether they purchased or provided CMS. The respondents were asked to consider CMS activity performed by their foreign affiliates as purchasing CMS from others. As shown in Table 3.2, approximately a quarter of U.S. parents reported purchases of CMS from foreign or domestic contract manufacturers, while three-fourths reported no purchases of CMS. Only 8 percent of U.S. parents reported performing CMS for nonresidents. Not surprisingly, the majority, or 72 percent, of U.S. parents that reported purchases of CMS are classified in the manufacturing sector. As shown in Table 3.3, the other two sectors with significant purchases of CMS are wholesale (13 percent) and information (5 percent).

Table 3.4 presents the characteristics of U.S. parents who are classified within the manufacturing sector by three-digit NAICS-based ISI industry classification and by firm size (measured as total domestic employment of the U.S. parent). Table 3.4 shows that U.S. parents that purchased CMS were large firms with more than 250 employees and

Table 3.2 U.S. Parents Who Purchased or Performed Contract Manufacturing Services (CMS), 2009

	No. of respondents	% of respondents
Parents who purchased CMS:		
Yes	888	23
No	2,860	75
No response	82	2
Parents who performed CMS:		
Yes	324	8
No	3,423	89
No response	83	2

NOTE: Percentages may not sum to 100 because of rounding.

SOURCE: BEA's 2009 Benchmark Survey of U.S. Direct Investment Abroad, http://www.bea.gov/surveys/pdf/2009be10i_web.pdf.

Table 3.3 U.S. Parents Who Purchased Contract Manufacturing Services (CMS), by Sector, 2009 (%)

Manufacturing	Wholesale	Information	Professional, scientific, technical services	Other
72	13	5	1	9

NOTE: "Manufacturing" includes all two-digit NAICS industries in sectors 31–33; "Wholesale" includes NAICS industries in sector 42; "Professional, scientific, and technical services" includes NAICS industries in sector 54; "Other" includes all other industries.
SOURCE: BEA's 2009 Benchmark Survey of U.S. Direct Investment Abroad.

Table 3.4 U.S. Parents Who Purchased Contract Manufacturing Services (CMS), by Manufacturing Subsectors, 2009

	Total	Small	Med.	Large
All manufacturing industries (NAICS sectors 31–33)	642	93	104	445
Computer and electronic product mfg. (334)	153	30	32	91
Machinery mfg. (333)	82	17	14	51
Chemical mfg. (325)	80	9	13	58
Miscellaneous mfg. (339)	61	10	15	36
Transportation equipment mfg. (336)	54	2	4	48
Food mfg. (311)	36	6	3	27
Electrical equipment, appliance, and component mfg. (335)	33	2	6	25
Fabricated metal product mfg. (332)	31	7	4	20
Plastics and rubber products mfg. (326)	28	2	3	23
Primary metal mfg. (331)	22	2	1	19

NOTE: "Large" includes firms with 250 or more employees, "Medium" includes firms of between 100 and 249 employees, and "Small" includes firms of between 1 and 99 employees.
SOURCE: BEA's 2009 Benchmark Survey of U.S. Direct Investment Abroad.

were concentrated in industries that are known for outsourcing transformation activities to contract manufacturers. Examples of these industries include computer and electronic product manufacturing, machinery manufacturing, chemical manufacturing (includes pharmaceutical manufacturing), and transportation equipment manufacturing.

Because the international guidelines consider ownership of the materials used by the contract manufacturer in determining whether the contract manufacturer is selling manufacturing services or selling a good, questions were added to the BE-10 survey to determine whether U.S. parents could separately identify such transactions. U.S. parents who purchased CMS were asked to indicate whether they owned the materials used by contract manufacturers and whether the services were purchased from businesses inside or outside the United States. A respondent could answer "yes" to more than one type of arrangement; about 10 percent of U.S. parents that purchased CMS responded "yes" to all four types of arrangements, indicating that they used contract manufacturers located both in the United States and abroad and that they both owned the materials and did not own the materials used by the contract manufacturer. As shown in Table 3.5, U.S. parents were more likely to purchase CMS from U.S. contract manufacturers and to provide the material inputs to them (65 percent) than to purchase CMS from foreigners (about 37 percent). Interestingly, U.S. parents were just as likely to own the material inputs as to not own them when purchasing CMS from foreigners. Of the approximately 325 U.S. parents that reported purchasing CMS from outside the United States, nearly half of the respondents answered "yes" to both owning the material inputs and not owning the material inputs used by the contract manufacturer. This suggests that separately identifying purchases of CMS based on the ownership of the materials used by the contract manufacturer may be difficult to collect on an enterprise survey.

Table 3.5 U.S. Parents Who Purchased CMS, 2009

Category	*N*
U.S. parents who purchased CMS	888
U.S. parents who owned materials used by contract manufacturers located inside U.S.	579
U.S. parents who owned materials used by contract manufacturers located outside U.S.	330
U.S. parents who did not own materials used by contract manufacturers located inside U.S.	369
U.S. parents who did not own materials used by contract manufacturers located outside U.S.	323

SOURCE: BEA's 2009 Benchmark Survey of U.S. Direct Investment Abroad.

Table 3.6 Selected Statistics for U.S. Parents and for All U.S. Companies, by Sector, 2009

	Value-added (in $ millions)[a]	Employees (in thousands)[b]	Value-added per employee ($)
U.S. parents who purchased CMS[c]			
All industries	585,366	4,112	142,366
Manufacturing	400,369	2,413	165,910
Wholesale trade	44,286	307	144,240
Information	33,338	141	236,555
Other industries	107,374	1,251	85,859
All U.S. parents[c]			
All industries	2,595,776	22,933	113,191
Manufacturing	1,034,139	6,864	150,655
Wholesale trade	124,433	1,065	116,795
Information	287,628	1,712	168,056
Other industries	1,149,576	13,292	86,490
All U.S. companies			
All private industries	12,018,095	112,139	107,171
Manufacturing	1,540,226	11,856	129,911
Wholesale trade	768,548	5,620	136,752
Information	615,445	2,814	218,708
Other industries	9,093,876	91,849	99,009

NOTE: Figures may not sum to total because of rounding.

[a] Statistics on value-added for all U.S. companies are from the BEA's GDP by Industry series, as published in Table 3, p. 55 of Barefoot (2012).

[b] Statistics on employees for all U.S. companies are from the BEA's National Income and Product Accounts (NIPA) Table 6.4D, "Full-Time and Part-Time Employees by Industry," http://www.econstats.com/nipa/NIPA6_6_4D_.htm.

[c] Statistics for U.S. parents are from the BEA's 2009 Benchmark Survey of U.S. Direct Investment Abroad, as published in Table 3, p. 55 of Barefoot (2012).

SOURCE: See table notes a, b, and c.

Table 3.6 compares selected statistics of U.S. parents who purchased CMS with those of all U.S. parents and all U.S. companies. Table 3.6 shows that U.S. parents classified in manufacturing, wholesale trade, and information that purchased CMS had a higher value-added per employee compared to the value-added per employee of all U.S. parents and of all U.S. companies. This finding suggests that firms

Table 3.7 U.S. Trade in Goods (in $ millions) Associated with U.S. Parents, 2009

	U.S. parents who purchased CMS	All U.S. parents
Exports of goods to all foreigners	204,467	535,409
To foreign affiliates	102,768	207,479
For further manufacture	63,747	117,624
For resale without further manufacture	31,027	66,632
Other	7,993	23,223
To other foreigners	101,699	327,930
Imports of goods from all foreigners	194,879	679,521
From foreign affiliates	97,659	233,578
From other foreigners	97,220	445,943

SOURCE: BEA's 2009 Benchmark Survey of U.S. Direct Investment Abroad.

that use contract manufacturers to make their products may be more productive than firms that do not use contract manufacturers, though it is also possible that firms that use contract manufacturers have high value-added per employee by contracting out low value-added tasks, without any difference in output per quality-adjusted unit of inputs.

As was stated earlier, no corresponding CMS questions were included on the foreign affiliate's survey forms. Thus, a direct linkage cannot be made as to whether the U.S. parent purchased CMS from its foreign affiliate or from an unaffiliated foreigner. Table 3.7 shows that U.S. parents that purchased CMS exported a higher share of their total exports to their foreign affiliates (50 percent) than did all U.S. parents to their foreign affiliates (39 percent). In addition, U.S. parents that purchased CMS had a slightly higher share of export of goods sent for further processing to foreign affiliates (62 percent) than did all U.S. parents (57 percent).

ANALYSIS OF CONTRACT MANUFACTURING SERVICES ON CENSUS BUREAU 2011 COS

Table 3.8 presents the distribution of firms by various CMS activity categories in the linked COS-LBD data set. Panel A of Table 3.8 shows

Table 3.8 Percentage Distribution of Firms by CMS Activity

Panel A: All firms	
No CMS activity	92
Provide CMS only	3
Purchase CMS only	4
Provide and purchase CMS	1
Panel B: Firms that purchase CMS	
Inside U.S. only	39
Outside U.S. only	20
Inside and outside U.S.	37
Panel C: Firms that purchase CMS outside U.S.	
From affiliates	53

NOTE: This table provides the percentage share of the count of firms within each CMS activity category. Panel A is computed as a share of the total number of unique firms in the data; Panel B is computed as a share of the total number of unique firms that purchase CMS (the rows "Purchase CMS only" and "Provide and purchase CMS" from Panel A); and Panel C is computed as a share of the total number of unique firms that purchase CMS outside the United States (the rows "Outside U.S. only" and "Inside and outside U.S." from Panel B). Panel B does not add up to 100 percent because some firms did not respond and so could not be categorized.
SOURCE: Linked COS-LBD data set.

that 92 percent of the firms in the survey do not engage in any CMS activity. Among the remaining firms, there is an almost even share that either provide or purchase CMS, and only 1 percent that both provide and purchase CMS. Panel B shows that within the group of firms that purchase CMS, about 39 percent do so within the United States only, 20 percent do so outside the United States only, and 37 percent purchase CMS both inside and outside the United States. Finally, Panel C shows that of the firms that purchase CMS outside the United States, more than half of these firms do so from their foreign affiliates. Overall, a small share of firms engage in CMS activities, and among those that purchase CMS, a larger share purchase domestically. These observations are consistent with those made in Fort (2013) using the 2007 Census of Manufactures.

Table 3.9 presents two key firm characteristics associated with firms engaged in various CMS activities: size (measured as total employ-

Table 3.9 Average Firm Size and Age by CMS Activity

	Employment	Age
Panel A: All firms		
No CMS activity	1,366	23
Provide CMS only	761	26
Purchase CMS only	1,871	25
Provide and purchase CMS	4,315	25
Panel B: Firms that purchase CMS		
Inside U.S. only	1,065	25
Outside U.S. only	1,817	25
Inside and outside U.S.	4,427	24
Panel C: Firms that purchase CMS outside U.S.		
From affiliates	5, 054	25

NOTE: This table provides the average employment and age of firms within each CMS activity category; Panel A is computed for the total number of unique firms in the data; Panel B is computed for the firms that purchase CMS (the rows "Purchase CMS only" and "Provide and purchase CMS" from Panel A); and Panel C is computed for firms that purchase CMS outside the United States (the rows "Outside U.S. only" and "Inside and outside U.S." from Panel B).
SOURCE: Linked COS-LBD data set.

ment) and age. Panel A of Table 3.9 reports the average employment and age at firms within each CMS category. Firms that both provide and purchase CMS are the largest in terms of average employment, while those that provide CMS only are the smallest. Panel B shows that firms that purchase CMS both inside and outside the United States are much larger than those that purchase CMS either inside or outside the United States only. Finally, Panel C shows that firms that purchase CMS from their affiliates located abroad are the largest. An average firm in the survey is about 24 years old, and the average firm age does not vary greatly by CMS activity. The overwhelming majority of firms in the COS have been in existence for 10 or more years.

Table 3.10 provides further detail on the size distribution of firms in the survey by CMS activity. Firms with 250 or more employees are considered to be large, those with 100 to 249 employees to be medium, and those with one to 99 employees to be small. Since the COS primarily

Table 3.10 Distribution of Firm Size by CMS Activity

	Large	Medium	Small
Panel A: All firms	60	18	22
No CMS activity	61	18	22
Provide CMS only	41	34	25
Purchase CMS only	58	22	20
Provide and purchase CMS	55	24	21
Panel B: Firms that purchase CMS			
Inside U.S. only	45	27	28
Outside U.S. only	64	19	17
Inside and outside U.S.	66	20	14
Panel C: Firms that purchase CMS outside U.S.			
From affiliates	74	17	9

NOTE: This table provides the percentage share of firms in three size categories within each CMS activity category. "Large" includes firms with 250 or more employees, "Medium" includes firms of between 100 and 249 employees, and "Small" includes firms of between 1 and 99 employees.

SOURCE: Linked COS-LBD data set.

surveys large firms, the results in this table are not directly comparable to those in Table 3.4 and should be interpreted with the COS survey frame in mind. Within the group of firms that do not engage in any CMS activity, well over half the firms are large, and the remainder can be almost evenly divided between small and medium-sized firms. This pattern also holds for those that purchase CMS only or both provide and purchase CMS. Three-quarters of firms that provide CMS only are large or medium, and a quarter are small. Among firms that purchase CMS, those that do so outside the United States only and those that purchase CMS both outside and inside the United States exhibit similar firm-size distributions. As shown in Table 3.9, an overwhelming share of firms that purchase CMS from their foreign affiliates are large. However, of the firms that provide CMS only, about 40 percent are large and 30 percent are medium-sized. Firms that purchase CMS inside the United States only have a similar size distribution.

Tables 3.10 and 3.11 show the sectoral distribution of firms engaged in various CMS activities. The COS asked firms whether they operated

Table 3.11 Distribution of Firm Response to Operating a Manufacturing Facility, by CMS Activity

	% that answered "Yes"
Panel A: All firms	
No CMS activity	22
Provide CMS only	97
Purchase CMS only	77
Provide and purchase CMS	97
Panel B: Firms that purchase CMS	
Inside U.S. only	85
Outside U.S. only	77
Inside and outside U.S.	81
Panel C: Firms that purchase CMS outside U.S.	
From affiliates	85

NOTE: This table provides the percentage share of firms that responded "Yes" to Question 1 under Section 3D of the 2011 Company Organization Survey (COS) within each CMS activity category. The left-out category is "No," except for under "No CMS activity." Four percent of the responses are missing.
SOURCE: Linked COS-LBD data set.

a manufacturing facility where products are completed or partially produced. Table 3.11 reports the share of firms within various categories that responded "Y" or "N" or had missing data. Table 3.12 shows the distribution of firms within one of three broad sectors: 1) manufacturing, 2) wholesale and retail, or 3) all remaining sectors of the economy. Panel A in Table 3.11 and Panel A in Table 3.12 show that an overwhelming majority of firms that report engaging in some CMS activity also operate a manufacturing facility. Seventy-four percent of the firms that do not engage in any CMS activity report not operating a manufacturing facility; this finding is corroborated by the finding that 76 percent of these firms operate in sectors other than manufacturing, wholesale, or retail. In addition, 97 percent of the firms that provide CMS only or both provide and purchase CMS reported operating a manufacturing facility, and over 80 percent of them operate in the manufacturing, wholesale, or retail sectors. However, within the group of firms that purchase CMS only, 77 percent report operating a manufacturing

Table 3.12 Distribution of Sectors by CMS Activity

	Manu-facturing	Wholesale/ retail	Other
Panel A: All firms			
No CMS activity	18	16	76
Provide CMS only	76	7	17
Purchase CMS only	58	16	16
Provide and purchase CMS	75	7	18
Panel B: Firms that purchase CMS			
Inside U.S. only	66	10	24
Outside U.S. only	56	22	22
Inside and outside U.S.	62	15	23
Panel C: Firms that purchase CMS outside U.S.			
From affiliates	64	15	21

NOTE: This table provides the percentage share of firms in three broad sectors of the economy within each CMS activity category. "Manufacturing" includes all two-digit NAICS industries in sectors 31–33; "Wholesale/retail" includes two-digit NAICS industries in sectors 42, 44, and 45; and "Other" includes all other industries.
SOURCE: Linked COS-LBD data set.

facility and operate in the manufacturing, wholesale, or retail sectors; the share is smaller compared with firms only providing CMS or both providing and purchasing CMS.

Table 3.13 is based only on responses of survey units that have a one-to-one link to a firm identifier.[23] It shows the percentage share of revenues (costs) generated (incurred) from providing (purchasing) CMS as a share of total revenues and net sales (cost of sales from expenses). Three-quarters of the firms providing CMS report less than a quarter of total revenues and net sales originating from providing CMS. A little over three-quarters of firms purchasing CMS also report less than a quarter of the total cost of sales from expenses originating from purchasing CMS. This suggests that for most firms engaged in some CMS activity, the activity constitutes a relatively small share of total revenues or total costs.

Table 3.13 Distribution of Percentage Share of Revenue and Costs by CMS Activity

% of operating revenues and net sales (cost of sales from expenses) from (for) CMS	Provide CMS	Purchase CMS
Less than 25	75	79
25 to 49	5	9
50 to 74	4	5
75 to 99	8	5
100	8	2

NOTE: This table provides the percentage share of firms in five mutually exclusive categories in response to Questions 2 and 3d from the 2011 COS form (see Appendix 3A, Illustration 3A.1). The second column shows the percentage share of firms that receive *x* percent of operating revenues and sales from providing CMS; the third column shows the percentage share of firms that incur *x* percent of cost of sales from expenses for purchasing CMS.
SOURCE: Linked COS-LBD data set.

Finally, Table 3.14 shows the average output per employee as well as export and import values of firms by various CMS activities. The first column shows the log of value-added per employee (VA/L), and the second column shows the log of total value of shipments per employee (TVS/L). Firms that engage in some type of CMS activity exhibit both higher (VA/L) and (TVS/L) than those that do not. Among firms that purchase CMS, those that purchase both inside and outside the United States exhibit the highest average output per employee, using both measures.

The last two columns show the average export and import values, in millions of dollars, respectively. Focusing on the third column, firms that both provide and purchase CMS have higher average export value compared to all other firms in the sample. Firms that do not engage in any CMS activity and firms that provide only CMS have very similar average export values. Firms that purchase CMS inside and outside the United States have the highest average export values among firms that purchase CMS. Focusing on the last column, firms engaged in some CMS activity display much higher average firm import values compared to those that do not, and, of these, firms that both purchase and provide CMS have the highest value. Firms that purchase CMS inside and outside the United States have the highest average import value among firms that purchase CMS. Among firms that purchase CMS outside the

Table 3.14 Output per Employee and Trade Value by CMS Activity

	Log (value added/ employment)	Log (total value of shipments/ employment)	Export value (in $ millions)	Import value (in $ millions)
Panel A: All firms				
No CMS activity	4.23	4.98	29	82
Provide CMS only	4.45	5.19	30	232
Purchase CMS only	4.63	5.31	113	190
Provide and purchase CMS	4.61	5.30	241	289
Panel B: Firms that purchase CMS				
Inside U.S. only	4.58	5.27	32	104
Outside U.S. only	4.53	5.22	68	144
Inside and outside U.S.	4.73	5.40	284	327
Panel C: Firms that purchase CMS outside U.S.				
From affiliates	4.75	5.44	334	417

NOTE: The above statistics are calculated for manufacturing firms only.
SOURCE: Linked COS-CM and COS-LFTTD data sets.

United States, those that do so from their affiliates are larger traders and have higher value-added per employee than those that do not.

FUTURE WORK

This chapter analyzes existing data on firms' activities relating to providing or purchasing CMS as a means to measure "factoryless" manufacturing, where the manufacturer undertakes the entrepreneurial steps in the global supply chain but does not transform any of the material inputs. Our primary goal was to analyze the characteristics of firms that report engaging in various CMS activities to provide a preliminary glimpse into factoryless goods producers. However, comprehensive work is needed, and indeed is underway, as described below, to do three things: 1) quantify the scope of FGP activity, 2) look at how the CMS data discussed in this chapter compare to CMS data in other existing surveys, and 3) evaluate the feasibility of the proposed changes in the definitions to the manufacturing sector and import and export flows.

The recently updated international guidelines for services on physical inputs owned by others (goods for processing) are designed to better capture the impacts of GVCs on the economy. The BEA is evaluating whether implementation of the new guidelines is feasible. Successful implementation of this recommendation requires detailed information on not only the processing fees received and paid by U.S. firms for CMS but also the underlying goods transactions. Data for these transactions are currently either not available in the U.S. statistical system or not separately identifiable. Despite these data challenges, the BEA continues to investigate options for implementing this new treatment of manufacturing services.

The results from the BEA BE-120 survey will be available soon. Once the results are available, the BEA can evaluate whether the value of receipts and payments for CMS can be reported along with the destination of the goods after processing. To determine the feasibility of adjusting the merchandise trade statistics to remove goods that cross the border without a change in ownership, the BEA is also continuing to work with the Census Bureau to explore options for identifying the merchandise trade transactions of U.S. firms that purchased manufacturing services from overseas contractors or that provided manufacturing services to foreigners.

The CMS questions on the enterprise-level COS discussed in this chapter represent initial steps in determining whether further data collection is likely to be robust and whether the Census Bureau can identify "factoryless" manufacturers in its surveys. As a next step, the Census Bureau added special inquiries to the 2012 Economic Census to collect information at the establishment level that will better identify "factoryless" manufacturers and assess whether sufficient data can be collected on the value of the manufacturing service and the associated revenue on sales of products produced by contract manufacturers.[24]

An interagency effort across the Census Bureau, the BEA, and the BLS is underway to analyze census microdata in support of consistent and accurate implementation of the decision to classify FGPs in the manufacturing sector as soon as the agencies can perform the research, testing, and evaluation necessary to do so. One of the main goals of this effort is to estimate the number of establishments, the total value of shipments, and the total employment that will be moved across various sectors with the eventual implementation of the FGP concept in the Economic Census. Furthermore, comparisons will be made between the results from the special inquiry questions in the economic censuses and the COS in order to refine the questions that will be used by agencies and programs to identify FGPs on data collection instruments. The agencies must take care that as changes are made in the measurement of manufacturing activities, whether in the production of services or in the shipments of goods, these changes are implemented in a way that consistently and correctly allocates manufacturing value-added to the domestic and nonresident producers, in order to avoid overstating or understating U.S. gross domestic product.

Notes

Any opinions and conclusions expressed herein are those of the authors and do not necessarily represent the views of the U.S. Census Bureau or the Bureau of Economic Analysis. All results have been reviewed to ensure that no confidential information is disclosed. We thank Susan Houseman for helpful comments on an earlier version. We also thank Mai-Chi Hoang for preparing the BEA data tables and providing valuable feedback, Raymond Mataloni for providing guidance on the BEA data, and Anthony Caruso, C.J. Krizan, Shawn Klimek, and William Powers for helpful comments.

1. The research in this chapter was undertaken while this author was at the U.S. Bureau of Economic Analysis.
2. For more information on GVCs, see APEC Policy Support Unit (2012).
3. The *System of National Accounts 2008* (European Commission et al. 2009) provides recommendations for compiling the national accounts, and the sixth edition of the *Balance of Payments and International Investment Position Manual* (IMF 2009) provides recommendations for compiling the international accounts.
4. For more information, see the Economic Classification Policy Committee's "Issue Paper No. 1" (ECPC 1993).
5. See Doherty (Chapter 2 of this volume) for a discussion of identifying FGPs in the U.S. Statistical System.
6. The *System of National Accounts 2008*, published by five international organizations, is the international guideline for compilation of gross domestic product and other national accounts statistics (European Commission et al. 2009), and the *Balance of Payments and International Investment Position Manual*, published by the International Monetary Fund, is the international guideline for compilation of balance of payments and international investment position statistics (IMF 2009).
7. In practice, this may not hold. Maurer and Degain (2010) state that, for most cases, the value of the manufacturing service or the processing fee is not simply the difference between the value of the goods before processing and the value after processing.
8. For more information, see BPM6, Chapter 10, Sections 10.65–10.66 (IMF 2009, p. 162). For a discussion of the measurement issues related to goods for processing, see United Nations Economic Commission for Europe (2011), pp. 71–84.
9. The term "affiliated" refers to a direct investment relationship, which exists when a U.S. person has ownership or control, directly or indirectly, of 10 percent or more of a foreign business enterprise's voting securities or the equivalent, or when a foreign person has a similar interest in a U.S. business enterprise.
10. A U.S. "person" includes companies.
11. See questions 28–30 on the 2009 Benchmark Survey of U.S. Direct Investment Abroad for U.S. parents that are not banks (BE-10A) at http://www.bea.gov/surveys/pdf/be10a_web.pdf.
12. See Schedule D on the 2011 Benchmark Survey of Transactions in Selected Services and Intellectual Property with Foreign Persons (BE-120), at http://www.bea

.gov/surveys/pdf/be120.pdf, p. 12. Prior versions of the survey recorded receipts and payments for contract manufacturing services within the "other services" category.

13. The 2012 Economic Census includes a similar set of questions to those in the 2011 COS. It will provide the richest set of information at the establishment level once the data collection process is completed.
14. See http://www.bea.gov/surveys/pdf/be120.pdf. for further details.
15. The COS data are unedited and have had no adjustments for survey nonresponse.
16. Form NC-99001, Section 3D, Questions 1–3; see https://www.census.gov/econ/overview/mu0700.html for a description of the survey. Also see Appendix 3A.
17. A company is an economic unit comprising one or more establishments under common ownership or control. The COS may survey different subsidiaries of the same company, so several survey units may belong to one firm identification code.
18. Industry assignments remain qualitatively unchanged if payroll information is used instead to assign sectors.
19. Sales data are not readily available for all firms in the sample. Therefore, employment is used to assign a sector.
20. The LBD contains information on employment within the United States only; therefore, figures on employment at foreign subsidiaries of U.S. parent companies are not available in the linked LBD-COS data set.
21. The 2007 CM and 2009 LFTTD are the most recent available years. See Bernard, Jensen, and Schott (2009) for an overview of LFTTD, including match rates.
22. For more on the BE-10 U.S. Direct Investment Abroad methodology, see http://www.bea.gov/international/pdf/usdia_2004f/Text%20sections/methodology.pdf.
23. See the subsection of this chapter titled "Census Bureau Surveys," pp. 54–55, for details.
24. See Question 26 on the 2012 Economic Census manufacturing sample forms, located at http://bhs.econ.census.gov/ec12/php/census-form.php. An example of such a form is found at https://bhs.econ.census.gov/2012forms/MC31101.pdf.

Appendix 3A

Excerpts from Three Survey Forms Used in This Chapter

Questions on contract manufacturing services activities included these from the 2011 Report of Organization Survey (Form NC-99001):

Illustration 3A.1 Excerpt from Form NC-99001

❸ COMPANY ACTIVITIES - continued

D. MANUFACTURING ACTIVITIES

In 2011, did your company do any of the following activities related to manufacturing?

1. Operate manufacturing facilities (such as a factory, plant, or mill) where products are completed or partially produced?
   - 9709 ❒ Yes - *Go to line 2*
   - 9710 ❒ No - *Go to line 3*
2. Provide contract manufacturing services to other companies incorporating their patents, trade secrets, or proprietary technology?
   - 9711 ❒ Yes
   - 9712 ❒ No - *Go to line 3*

   Estimate the percent of operating revenues and net sales, as reported in ❸B, from contract manufacturing services.
   - 9713 ❒ Less than 25%
   - 9714 ❒ 25 to 49%
   - 9715 ❒ 50 to 74%
   - 9716 ❒ 75 to 99%
   - 9717 ❒ 100%
3. Purchase contract manufacturing services from other companies or foreign subsidiaries of your company incorporating your company's patents, trade secrets, or proprietary technology?
   - 9718 ❒ Yes
   - 9719 ❒ No - *Go to ❹, CERTIFICATION*

   a. Use 3rd party contract manufacturing services inside the U.S.?
   - 9720 ❒ Yes
   - 9721 ❒ No

   b. Use 3rd party contract manufacturing services outside the U.S.?
   - 9722 ❒ Yes
   - 9723 ❒ No

(continued)

Illustration 3A.1 (continued)

c. Use your company's foreign subsidiaries' or affiliates' contract manufacturing services at locations outside the U.S.?
9724 ❒ Yes
9725 ❒ No

d. Estimate the percent of the cost of sales from expenses for contract manufacturing services.
9726 ❒ Less than 25%
9727 ❒ 25 to 49%
9728 ❒ 50 to 74%
9729 ❒ 75 to 99%
9730 ❒ 100%

Questions on purchases of contract manufacturing services included these from the 2009 Benchmark Survey of U.S. Direct Investment Abroad for U.S. parents (Form BE-10A):

Illustration 3A.2 Excerpts from Form BE-10A

1. Did this U.S. reporter purchase contract manufacturing services from others (including foreign affiliates)? (Yes/No)
2. The U.S. reporter **owned** some or all of the materials used by the contract manufacturers and the companies providing the manufacturing services were:
   a. Located **inside** the U.S. (Yes/No)
   b. Located **outside** the U.S. (Yes/No)
3. The U.S. reporter **did not own** the materials used by the contract manufacturers and the companies providing the manufacturing services were:
   a. Located **inside** the U.S. (Yes/No)
   b. Located **outside** the U.S. (Yes/No)

This survey also included a question on performance of contract manufacturing services for others:

1. Did this U.S. reporter **perform** contract manufacturing services for others (including foreign affiliates) outside the U.S.? (Yes/No)

Questions on purchases of contract manufacturing services included these from the 2011 Benchmark Survey of Transactions in Selected Services and Intellectual Property Products with Foreign Persons (Form BE-120):

Illustration 3A.3 Excerpts from Form BE-120

1. Did you purchase contract manufacturing services from foreign persons in Fiscal Year 2011?
2. Are you able to report the fee you paid for contract manufacturing services?
   - If yes—enter the amount you paid foreign persons for contract manufacturing services.
3. The payments for manufacturing services in Question 2 were (check the appropriate box):
   - ❒ Based on accounting records.
   - ❒ Estimated by persons knowledgeable regarding these transactions.
4. Destination of goods produced after you purchased contract manufacturing (check the appropriate box):
   - ❒ Goods do not enter United States.
   - ❒ Goods are imported into the United States.
   - ❒ A portion of the goods remain abroad and a portion are imported into the United States.
   - ❒ Destination is unknown.

Questions on receipts for contract manufacturing services include the following:

1. Did you perform contract manufacturing services for foreign persons in Fiscal Year 2011?
2. Are you able to report the fee you received for performing contract manufacturing services?
   - NOTE: This may include the cost of the materials you purchased to perform this service.
   - If yes—enter the amount received from foreign persons for contract manufacturing services you performed on goods owned by foreign persons and go to Questions 3 and 4.
3. The receipts for manufacturing in Question 2 were (check the appropriate box):
   - ❒ Based on accounting records.
   - ❒ Estimated by persons knowledgeable regarding these transactions.
4. Destination of goods produced after you performed contract manufacturing (check appropriate box):
   - ❒ Goods remain in the United States.
   - ❒ Goods are exported from the United States.
   - ❒ A portion of the goods remain in the United States and a portion are exported from the United States.
   - ❒ Destination is unknown.

References

Asia-Pacific Economic Cooperation (APEC) Policy Support Unit. 2012. *Concepts and Trends in Global Supply, Global Value, and Global Production Chains*. Issues Paper No. 1. Singapore: Asia-Pacific Economic Cooperation.

Barefoot, Kevin B. 2012. "U.S. Multinational Companies: Operations of U.S. Parents and Their Foreign Affiliates in 2010." *Survey of Current Business* 92(11): 51–74. https://bea.gov/scb/pdf/2012/11%20November/1112MNCs.pdf (accessed December 13, 2013).

Bernard, Andrew B., J. Bradford Jensen, and Peter K. Schott. 2009. "Importers, Exporters, and Multinationals: A Portrait of Firms in the U.S. That Trade Goods." In *Producer Dynamics: New Evidence from Micro Data*, Timothy Dunne, J. Bradford Jensen, and Mark J. Roberts, eds. NBER series on Studies in Income and Wealth, Vol. 68. Chicago: University of Chicago Press, pp. 513–552.

Economic Classification Policy Committee (ECPC). 1993. "Issues Paper No. 1." *Federal Register*, March 31, 16991–17000. Washington, DC: U.S. Census Bureau, Economic Classification Policy Committee. http://www.census.gov/eos/www/naics/history/docs/issue_paper_1.pdf (accessed May 5, 2014).

———. 2010. *Economic Classification Policy Committee (ECPC) Recommendation for Classification of Outsourcing in North American Industry Classification System (NAICS) Revisions for 2012*. Supporting Documents: North American Industry Classification System—Update for 2012; Notice May 12, 2010. Washington, DC: U.S. Census Bureau, Economic Classification Policy Committee. http://www.census.gov/eos/www/naics/fr2010/ECPC_Recommendation_for_Classification_of_Outsourcing.pdf (accessed June 5, 2014).

European Commission, International Monetary Fund, Organisation for Economic Co-operation and Development, United Nations, and World Bank. 2009. *System of National Accounts 2008*. New York: United Nations Statistics Division.

Fort, Teresa C. 2013. "Breaking Up Is Hard to Do: Why Firms Fragment Production across Locations." CES Paper No. 13-35. Hanover, NH: Dartmouth College, Tuck School of Business. http://www2.census.gov/ces/wp/2013/CES-WP-13-35.pdf (accessed December 13, 2013).

International Monetary Fund (IMF). 2009. *Balance of Payments and International Investment Position Manual*. 6th ed. (BPM6). Washington, DC: International Monetary Fund.

Jarmin, Ron S., C. J. Krizan, and John Tang. 2011. "Outsourcing, Offshoring, and Trade: Identifying Foreign Activity across Census Data Products." *Survey of Current Business* 91(2): 121–139.

Jarmin, Ron S., and Javier Miranda. 2002. "The Longitudinal Business Database." Center for Economic Studies Discussion Paper No. CES-WP-02-17. Suitland, MD: U.S. Census Bureau, Center for Economic Studies.

Maurer, Andreas, and Christophe Degain. 2010. "Globalization and Trade Flows: What You See Is Not What You Get!" Staff Working Paper ERSD-2010-12. Geneva: World Trade Organization, Economic Research and Statistics Division.

Office of Management and Budget. 2007. *North American Industrial Classification System, United States*. Washington, DC: Executive Office of the President, Office of Management and Budget.

———. 2010. *Economic Classification Policy Committee (ECPC) Recommendation for Classification of Outsourcing in North American Industry Classification System (NAICS) Revisions for 2012*. Washington, DC: Bureau of Economic Analysis. https://www.bea.gov/about/pdf/ECPC_Recommendation_for_Classification_of_Outsourcing_1.pdf (accessed December 13, 2013).

United Nations Economic Commission for Europe. 2011. *The Impact of Globalization on National Accounts*. New York and Geneva: United Nations.

United Nations Statistics Division. 2008. *International Standard Industrial Classification of All Economic Activities (ISIC), Rev. 4*. Statistical papers, Series M, No. 4, Rev. 4. New York: United Nations, Department of Economic and Social Affairs, Statistics Division. http://unstats.un.org/unsd/publication/seriesM/seriesm_4rev4e.pdf (accessed December 13, 2013).

U.S. International Trade Commission. 2011. *The Economic Effects of Significant U.S. Import Restraints.* Seventh update. Special Topic: Global Supply Chains. Washington, DC: U.S. International Trade Commission. http://www.usitc.gov/publications/332/pub4253.pdf (accessed December 13, 2013).

4
The Scope of U.S. "Factoryless Manufacturing"

Kimberly Bayard
David Byrne
Federal Reserve Board of Governors

Dominic Smith
University of Minnesota

The "factoryless manufacturing" (FM) business model is employed by a rising share of U.S. firms. Factoryless manufacturers outsource the fabrication of products but maintain control of the production process, own the associated intellectual property, and bear the entrepreneurial risk. FM is an important component in the role of U.S. firms in global manufacturing value chains. Currently, U.S. Census Bureau programs assign establishments engaged in factoryless manufacturing, known as factoryless goods producers (FGPs), to the wholesale trade sector. U.S. statistical agencies are considering classification of FGPs in the manufacturing sector in the future, if collecting data on FM is shown to be feasible.

This chapter estimates the scope of U.S. factoryless manufacturing using three approaches. First, we use financial reports for S&P 500 companies to show that FM is prevalent and increasing in the United States and that FM, once only common in the production of apparel, electronics, toys, and pharmaceuticals, has spread to a broader array of products. Second, we use Economic Census microdata to estimate that manufacturing value-added would have been 5 to 20 percent greater for 2007 if all FGPs were reclassified to manufacturing. Third, using a list of FM semiconductor companies matched to Economic Census microdata, we estimate that value-added would be 20 to 30 percent greater for semiconductor manufacturing, an industry where FM is especially prevalent, if FGPs were included. These results suggest that outsourcing and offshoring of product fabrication by U.S. firms is coupled with significant domestic production management. Thus, identifying FGPs in economic data is important for the study of fragmentation and globalization.

In the next section, "Defining and Measuring Factoryless Manufacturing and Factoryless Goods Producers," we define factoryless manufacturing (a company concept) and discuss the treatment of factoryless goods producers (an establishment concept) in U.S. economic statistics. In the third section, "The Extent of U.S. Factoryless Goods Production," we look at the extent of FM using company reports, and we examine the prevalence of FGPs using Economic Census establishment data. The fourth section, "The Structure of Factoryless Manufacturing Firms in the Semiconductor Industry," presents a close look at the establishment structure of FM firms in the semiconductor industry. Alternative estimates of the size of the manufacturing sector when FGPs are included are found in the fifth section, "U.S. Manufacturing with Factoryless Goods Producers Included," with a particular focus on semiconductor manufacturing. In Section Six, "Selected Effects of Reclassification and Relevance for Economic Analysis," we speculate on the effects of reclassifying FGPs for selected economic measures, and we discuss the role that better data on factoryless manufacturing may play in the study of economic issues. Section Seven offers a conclusion.

DEFINING AND MEASURING FACTORYLESS MANUFACTURING AND FACTORYLESS GOODS PRODUCERS

In 1997, the Office of Management and Budget (OMB) introduced the North American Industry Classification System (NAICS), an approach to classifying establishments into industries "according to similarity in the processes used to produce goods or services" (OMB 1998, p. 13).[1] NAICS defines the manufacturing sector to be the set of establishments "engaged in the mechanical, physical, or chemical transformation of materials, substances, or components into new products." Yet NAICS acknowledges that the relevant transformation may happen outside the establishment: "Manufacturing establishments may process materials or may contract with other establishments to process their materials for them. Both types of establishments are included in manufacturing" (OMB 1998, p. 105)

Since the introduction of NAICS in 1997, the outsourcing of processing materials into products—hereafter, "fabrication" for convenience—has risen dramatically, elevating the importance of consistent treatment of this practice across statistical programs. The Economic Classification Policy Committee (ECPC) of the OMB studied the issue and defined three types of establishments:

1) Integrated manufacturers (IMs)

2) Manufacturing service providers (MSPs)

3) Factoryless goods producers (FGPs)

FGPs have the following characteristics (OMB 2009): They

- own the rights to the intellectual property or design (whether independently developed or otherwise acquired) of the final manufactured product,
- may or may not own the input materials,
- do not own production facilities,
- do not perform transformation activities,
- own the final product produced by MSP partners, and
- sell the final product.

In contrast, IMs and MSPs own production facilities and perform transformation activities, and MSPs do not own the intellectual property or the final product.

In the absence of clear guidance from NAICS, the approach used to classify FGPs has differed across statistical agencies. U.S. Census Bureau practice has been to classify such establishments in the "Wholesale trade" sector.[2] In contrast, the Bureau of Labor Statistics' (BLS) Producer Price Index (PPI) program collects prices from FGPs for use in some manufacturing PPIs, and the BLS's Current Employment Statistics (CES) program classifies some reporting FGP establishments in the "Management of companies and enterprises" sector.[3] In 2011, the OMB adopted the ECPC's proposal to classify FGP establishments in the manufacturing sector "beginning no later than 2017" (OMB 2011); however, in August 2014 the OMB backed off from that decision, say-ing that "agencies need an opportunity to perform additional research, testing, and evaluation." U.S. statistical agencies are currently studying the feasibility of this proposal.[4]

As noted above, the NAICS definition of the manufacturing sector is flexible enough to allow for a manufacturing establishment to be "engaged" in fabrication even if the fabrication takes place at another establishment. But the notion that an establishment can be in manufacturing if no fabrication takes place on-site is somewhat controversial (OMB 2011).[5] The BLS's Business Processes and Business Functions (BPBF) classification system provides a helpful framework for considering the characteristics that distinguish manufacturing establishments from those in other sectors. The manufacturing "operations" business process includes the tasks of producing goods, assembling products, and fabricating components, as well as those of managing production and conducting quality assurance (Brown 2008).[6] In this scheme, FGPs perform the production management and quality assurance portions of manufacturing operations. In addition, other business processes may be performed by the FGPs as well, such as product design and development.[7]

For the purpose of characterizing *companies* (groups of establishments under common ownership), we define the term "factoryless manufacturing" (FM) to be the use of contract manufacturing to produce some or all of the final products sold by a company, provided the company controls the intellectual property or design. We expect that at least one of the establishments of an FM company will be an FGP.

Factoryless manufacturing emerged in the U.S. apparel sector in the 1950s when U.S. companies shifted fabrication to Japan (Gereffi 2002). In the 1970s, FM became common for consumer goods, especially toys (Steiner 1995).[8] The role of contract manufacturing in the production of final goods in electronics has risen dramatically over time as well—in particular, the revenue of major offshore final electronics MSPs has risen markedly over the past 10 years (Figure 4.1).[9] Finally, the use of factoryless manufacturing has surged for semiconductors: The share of semiconductor sales accounted for by FM firms, predominantly U.S. companies, climbed from 3 percent in 1993 to 25 percent in 2012 (Figure 4.2).

Figure 4.1 Sales of Selected Taiwanese Contract Electronics Manufacturers

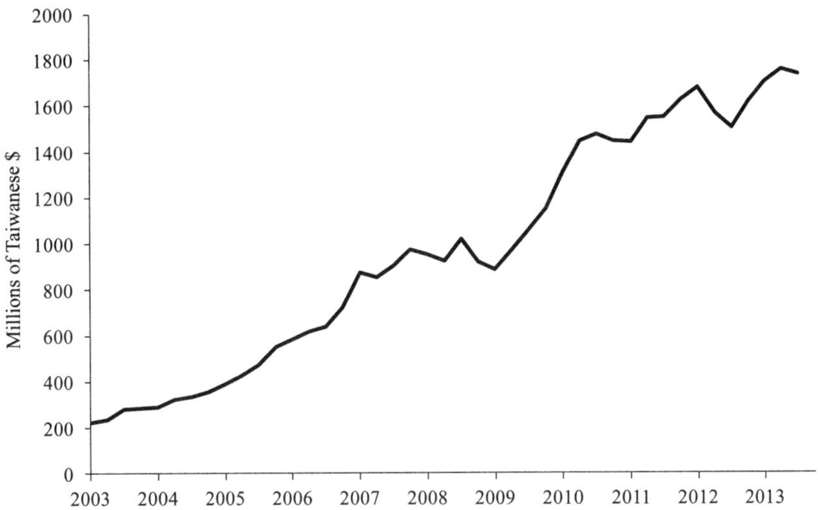

SOURCE: Authors' calculations based on public financial reports. Companies included are contract electronics firms traded on the Taiwan Stock Exchange: Hon Hai (Foxconn), Quanta, Compal, HTC, Inventec, WNC, and ASUS.

THE EXTENT OF U.S. FACTORYLESS GOODS PRODUCTION

Evidence from Company Financial Reports

In financial reports filed with the Securities and Exchange Commission (SEC), manufacturing companies often indicate that they use factoryless manufacturing for some or all of their production.[10] For example, the 2012 annual report for Nike Inc. notes, "Our principal business activity is the design, development, and worldwide marketing and selling of high quality footwear, apparel, equipment, accessories, and services" and that "virtually all of our footwear is produced by factories we contract with outside of the United States." Similarly, the 2012 annual report for electronics manufacturer Juniper Networks Inc. states, "Our manufacturing is primarily conducted through contract

Figure 4.2 Share of Global Industry Shipments for Factoryless Manufacturing of Semiconductors

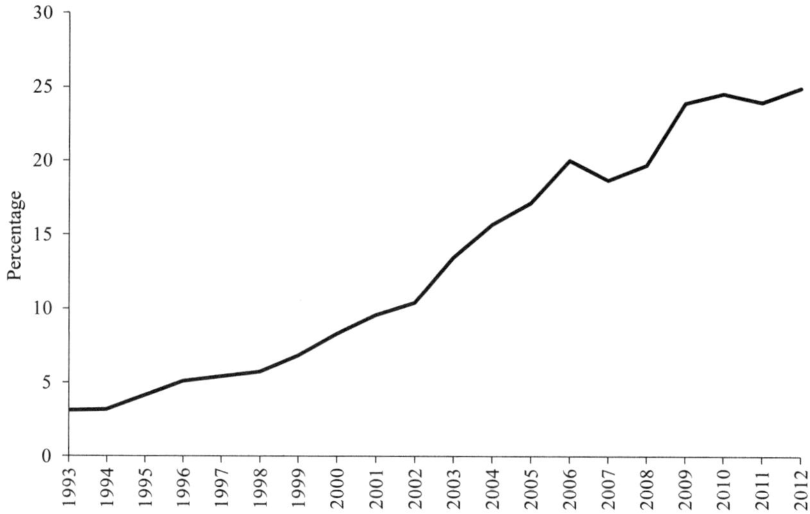

SOURCE: Global Semiconductor Alliance.

manufacturers," and goes on to say that Juniper employees "manage relationships with contract manufacturers, manage our supply chain, and monitor and manage product testing and quality." These companies report that they outsource some or all of their fabrication activity, but that they manage production and perform product design in-house. Other examples are shown in Table 4.1.

To get a sense of the breadth of factoryless manufacturing by U.S. companies, we searched for evidence of FM activity in the annual reports of all firms in the Standard and Poor's (S&P) 500 for both 2002 and 2012.[11] Specifically, we reviewed the reports for references to the use of contract manufacturing for fabrication of the companies' final products.[12] Table 4.2 summarizes the results of our review of the annual reports. For 2012, we find that about half (46 percent) of firms reporting manufacturing of any kind use FM. This is substantially higher than the 31 percent share observed for 2002. About four-fifths of the FM companies use MSPs for only a portion of their output, and approximately one-fifth rely exclusively on MSPs for fabrication.

Table 4.1 Selected S&P 500 Companies Reporting Factoryless Goods Production, by Primary Product Grouping, 2012

Toys and games
Hasbro Inc.
Mattel Inc.
Apparel
Abercrombie & Fitch Co.[a]
Nike Inc.[a]
Electronics
Advanced Micro Devices Inc. (semiconductors)[a]
Qualcomm Inc. (semiconductors)[a]
Amazon.com Inc. (electronic readers)[a]
Apple Inc. (computing, communications, consumer)
Cisco Systems Inc. (communications)[a]
Pharmaceuticals
Bristol-Myers Squibb Co.
Eli Lilly and Co.
Chemicals excluding pharmaceuticals
Clorox Co.
Colgate-Palmolive Co.
Food, beverage, and tobacco
Campbell Soup Co. (food)
Monster Beverage Corp. (beverage)[a]
Philip Morris International (tobacco)
Paper, plastic, and wood products
Avery Dennison Corp. (paper products)
Newell Rubbermaid Inc. (plastics products)
Electrical equipment
General Electric Co.
Machinery
Applied Materials Inc.
Transportation equipment
Delphi Automotive
Medical supplies excluding pharmaceuticals
Boston Scientific Corp.

[a] Company using FGP exclusively—i.e., a company with no integrated manufacturing activity.

SOURCE: Classification based on authors' analysis of 2012 annual reports filed with the Securities and Exchange Commission.

Table 4.2 Prevalence of Factoryless Manufacturing among Companies in the S&P 500 Index with Manufacturing Activity

	2002		2012	
	Count	Share (%)	Count	Share (%)
No factoryless manufacturing	172	70	120	54
Any factoryless manufacturing	74	30	104	46
Exclusively factoryless manufacturing	12	16	21	20
Mixed factoryless and integrated manufacturing	62	84	83	80
	$n = 246$		$n = 224$	

SOURCE: Classification based on authors' analysis of annual reports filed with the Securities and Exchange Commission.

As we expected from the evidence reviewed at the end of Section Two, in both 2002 and 2012, factoryless manufacturing was used by a very high share of firms manufacturing toys, apparel, and most electronic products (Table 4.3). For example, in both 2002 and 2012, all companies in the "Toys and games" category of the S&P 500 employed FM practices. Firms in the "Toys and games" sector represented 2 percent of all manufacturing companies in the index in both years. The FM business practice is also quite common among firms producing pharmaceuticals and medicine.

Also of note is the degree to which factoryless manufacturing spread to a broader array of goods from 2002 to 2012. For example, only 9 percent of large cap firms in the "Food, beverage, and tobacco" sector used FM in 2002, but the share had soared to 52 percent by 2012. Several other industries also experienced strong growth in the share of firms using FM over the past decade: notable gains were recorded for the sectors "Paper, plastic, and wood products," "Chemicals excluding pharmaceuticals," "Transportation equipment," and "Electrical equipment."

Evidence from Economic Census Data

The Economic Census collects extensive information on U.S. *establishments* every five years, and questions on the 2002 and 2007 Economic Censuses shed light on the prevalence of FGPs. Wholesale trade establishments were asked whether they sold products manufac-

Table 4.3 S&P 500 Sector Distribution and Share of Companies Using Factoryless Manufacturing (%)

	Share of companies using factoryless manufacturing[a]		Sector share of total S&P manufacturing	
Sector	2002	2012	2002	2012
Toys and games	100	100	2	2
Apparel	86	100	3	4
Electronic components (including semiconductors)	77	94	9	7
Computers and communications equipment	70	82	11	8
Pharmaceuticals and medicine	48	70	10	9
Food, beverage, and tobacco products	9	52	10	14
Paper, plastic, and wood products	6	45	7	5
Chemicals excluding pharmaceuticals	15	37	8	8
Other final electronics (industrial, defense, aerospace, etc.)	15	37	5	8
Medical excluding pharmaceuticals (including electromedical equipment)	10	23	4	6
Transportation equipment	0	22	7	4
Electrical equipment	0	17	3	3
Machinery	6	17	8	11
Metal, nonmetallic mineral, and petroleum products	6	0	7	8
Unclassified (conglomerates, miscellaneous production)	43	33	6	3

[a] Includes companies employing a mix of factoryless manufacturing and integrated manufacturing.

SOURCE: Authors' classification based on company reports filed with the Securities and Exchange Commission.

tured for them by contract manufacturers and whether they engaged in product design.[13] We consider an affirmative answer to either question to be supporting evidence for classifying the establishment as an FGP, though the questions are not definitive.[14] More than 30 percent of establishments answered "yes" to at least one of these questions in a majority of wholesale industries in 2002 (Tables 4.4 and 4.5).

Table 4.4 Performance of Product Design/Engineering and Use of Contract Manufacturing Services Share of Merchant Wholesale Establishments, 2002 (%)

NAICS Code	Industry description	Design/ engineer products sold	Purchase contract manufacturing services	Both	Either
	Durable goods				
4231	Motor vehicles and parts	8	13	3	18
4232	Furniture and home furnishings	25	26	10	41
4233	Lumber and other construction materials	14	20	4	30
4234	Professional and commercial equip. and supplies	19	18	7	30
4235	Metal and mineral	15	26	5	36
4236	Electrical and electronic goods	21	20	7	34
4237	Hardware, plumbing, heating equip. and supplies	15	17	4	28
4238	Machinery, equip. and supplies	19	22	7	34
4239	Miscellaneous durable goods	25	21	10	36
	Nondurable goods				
4241	Paper and paper products	22	25	10	37
4242	Drugs and druggist sundries	22	26	11	37
4243	Apparel, piece goods, and notions	42	35	21	56
4244	Grocery and related	13	14	4	23
4245	Farm product raw material	6	6	1	11
4246	Chemical and allied products	24	24	8	40
4247	Petroleum and petroleum products	3	8	1	10

4248	Beer, wine, distilled alcoholic beverages	5	14	1	18
4249	Miscellaneous nondurable goods	21	17	7	31
	Total, durable and nondurable	18	20	6	32
	Memo:				
	Establishments of FGP semiconductor companies	51	22	18	55
	Firms of FGP semiconductor companies	67	56	48	75

NOTE: Response rate was approximately 50 percent. Special question was on all Census of Wholesale Trade forms in 2002. Establishments reclassified to wholesale trade during census processing did not receive a survey form with this question.
SOURCE: 2002 Census of Wholesale Trade.

Table 4.5 Performance of Product Design/Engineering and Use of Contract Manufacturing Services Share of Merchant Wholesale Establishments, 2007 (%)

NAICS Code	Industry description	Design/ engineer products sold	Purchase contract manufacturing services	Both	Either
	Durable goods				
4231	Motor vehicles and parts	6	8	3	11
4233	Lumber and other construction materials	12	16	4	24
4234	Professional and commercial equip. and supplies[a]	23	20	12	31
4235	Metal and mineral	13	23	5	31
4236	Electrical and electronic goods	15	16	7	24
4238	Machinery, equipment, and supplies[a]	15	15	7	23
4239	Miscellaneous durable goods	18	17	8	27
	Nondurable goods				
4241	Paper and paper products	17	16	7	26
4242	Drugs and druggist sundries	22	27	14	35
4243	Apparel, piece goods, and notions	35	29	16	48
4244	Grocery and related	13	12	4	21
4245	Farm product raw material	5	6	1	10
4248	Beer, wine, distilled alcoholic beverages	4	5	2	7
4249	Miscellaneous nondurable goods[a]	17	12	6	23
	Total, durable and nondurable	15	15	7	23

Memo:				
Establishments of FGP semiconductor companies	52	40	35	57
Firms of FGP semiconductor companies	68	42	47	63

NOTE: 2007 response rate was approximately 53 percent for establishments receiving forms. Survey forms for some wholesale trade industries did not include these questions. Statistics are shown for covered six-digit industries within each four-digit industry group. Industry groups marked with an asterisk have omitted industries. Industry groups with no coverage are 4232, 4237, 4246, and 4247. Establishments reclassified to wholesale trade during census processing did not receive a survey form with this question. The "Purchase contract manufacturing services" column combines results for separate questions on domestic and foreign CMS.

SOURCE: 2007 Census of Wholesale Trade.

Prevalence among pharmaceutical and apparel wholesalers is particularly high, as we expected in light of our company report analysis. Interestingly, "Electrical and electronics wholesaling" is not among the industries with the highest prevalence of FGPs. However, when we matched known semiconductor FM companies to census firm records (as discussed in the next section), we found that 75 percent have at least one wholesale establishment reporting design or use of contract manufacturing.[15]

Results for prevalence of contract manufacturing use and product design by industry were similar in 2007 to what they were in 2002; unfortunately, the questions asked were somewhat different in the two years, making it hard to discern trends. Furthermore, in 2007 the questions were not asked of establishments in all industries, as they had been in 2002 (Bernard and Fort 2013).

Estimates in Related Work

Other studies have estimated the scope and scale of factoryless manufacturing using the Economic Census and other data. No survey contains an ideal set of questions for identifying FM, and consequently approaches in studies of FM have varied significantly.

Doherty (Chapter 2 of this volume) focuses on wholesalers who reported their type as "own-brand importer-marketer" (OBM), a term that is similar to FGP, but one that only applies to the use of offshore contract manufacturing. In the 2007 Economic Census, 3 percent of wholesale establishments self-identified as OBMs, which is a reasonable lower bound on FGP prevalence. However, because domestic outsourcing is much more common than offshore outsourcing (Fort 2011), FGPs are likely to be substantially more common than OBMs. Kask, Kiernan, and Friedman (2002) note that the OBM share of wholesalers was 3 percent for the 1997 Economic Census as well. In light of other evidence on the rising prevalence of offshore MSPs between 1997 and 2007, the stable share for OBMs is somewhat puzzling.

Jarmin, Krizan, and Tang (2011) look at outsourcing and offshoring using the same Economic Census special questions used in this study, but they employ a different FGP classification rule, which requires that establishments report "resales" as their primary activity in addition to reporting use of contract manufacturing and performance of product design. Conditioning on resale—the sale of products *bought* and sold without further processing—is problematic in that we expect that FGPs may contract for the service provided by the MSP, rather than purchasing the good itself. Also, as noted above, creating the product design is sufficient to establish ownership of the intellectual property, but not necessary—designs can be purchased or licensed by FGPs. Jarmin, Krizan, and Tang estimate that FGPs account for 1 percent of establishments within the manufacturing and wholesale trade sectors combined.

Bernard and Fort (2013) use a definition of FGP that differs from the ECPC standard in that a wholesale establishment that fabricates products on-site and does not use contract manufacturing can be counted as an FGP. We view reports of fabrication at wholesale trade establishments as evidence of one of two possibilities: 1) misclassification of an IM to wholesale trade, or 2) an FGP establishment with secondary IM activity. Despite the conceptual differences, Bernard and Fort find that the inclusion of FGPs in manufacturing leads to an increase in gross output ranging from 5.2 to 19.4 percent—estimates that are similar to ours. The range in Bernard and Fort depends on the assumptions made about respondents who did not answer the key questions.

Kamal, Moulton, and Ribarsky (Chapter 3 of this volume) examine company-level data from surveys conducted by the Census Bureau and the Bureau of Economic Analysis (BEA) and report results broadly consistent with ours, in that they find that the use of contract manufacturing is common in a wide array of industries and that companies with a mixed FGP/IM approach are far more common than pure FM companies.[16]

THE STRUCTURE OF FACTORYLESS MANUFACTURING FIRMS IN THE SEMICONDUCTOR INDUSTRY

Semiconductor manufacturing is a prominent example of an industry with extensive factoryless manufacturing—in 2012, 25 percent of global semiconductor sales came from FM companies (Figure 4.2).[17] By matching directories of FM firms in the semiconductor industry to Economic Census microdata, we are able to study the establishment structure of FM firms for this industry.[18] In this section, we discuss the results of that matching exercise.

We find that the footprint of semiconductor FM firms in the Economic Census is complex. Single-unit firms account for about 90 percent of the company observations in our data, and of these, only about 30 percent are located in the wholesale trade sector (Table 4.6).[19] This is a surprising result in light of the Census Bureau directive to treat FGPs as wholesalers. However, the classification process depends on a broad review of an establishment's activities. The sole establishment of a single-unit firm would likely be engaged in multiple business processes in addition to production management, such as product, process, and technology development; marketing and sales; strategic management; and any general management "back office" operations that have not been outsourced. If one of these other activities is the primary activity of the establishment, as "determined by its relative share of current production cost and capital investment," the establishment may be classified to an industry outside of "Wholesale trade" (OMB 1998, p. 17). Still, establishments in the wholesale trade sector account for two-thirds of the value of sales for these firms for 2007 (Table 4.7). About one-half of the 2007 employment for FM semiconductor firms is found in the wholesale trade sector. Among the smaller number of multiunit firms, the majority have units in multiple sectors (Table 4.6).

The establishments of these FM firms are highly concentrated in a few key information technology industries, corroborating our matching process (Table 4.8). Many units are found outside of the whole-

Table 4.6 Firms by Establishment Structure

Category	2002	2007
Total	525	525
Single-unit	450	470
Manufacturing	105	100
Wholesale	130	120
Services	220	245
Multi-unit	70	55
3 Sectors	15	10
2 Sectors	25	20
1 Sector	30	20

NOTE: Excludes management establishments. Rounded to nearest 5. Numbers may not sum to totals because of rounding.
SOURCE. Economic Census, 2002 and 2007.

Table 4.7 Sector Distribution of Semiconductor FM Firm Activity

Sector	Sales ($ billions)	Employment (000s)
	2002	
Total	22	55
Wholesale	15	27
Services	2	10
Manufacturing	5	18
	2007	
Total	26	55
Wholesale	19	29
Services	2	12
Manufacturing	5	14

NOTE: Sales and employment rounded to whole numbers. Numbers may not sum to totals because of rounding.

SOURCE: Matched Economic Census and company data, 2002 and 2007. See data appendix.

sale trade sector, but note that while Census Bureau practice is to classify FGPs (establishments) in wholesale trade, establishments of FM companies may have primary activity in other sectors and be properly classified there. Wholesale trade establishments for the FM firms are almost exclusively in "Other electronic parts and equipment wholesalers" (which includes semiconductor wholesalers) and in "Computers, peripherals, and software wholesalers." The service establishments for these firms are predominantly in "Custom computer programming and systems design services," in "Physical, engineering, and life sciences R&D services," and in "Engineering services." Manufacturing establishments for the FM firms are heavily concentrated in "Semiconductor and related device manufacturing," with a small but notable share in other electronics manufacturing industries. These manufacturing establishments are an indication that the associated company employs a hybrid FGP/IM approach to production.

Focusing on establishments in the two key wholesale industries, we find that semiconductor FGPs are significantly larger with respect to the value of revenue and the number of employees than non-FGPs within these industries (Table 4.8).[20, 21] The difference in log revenue between FGPs and non-FGPs is 1.5, and the difference in average log

Table 4.8 Mean Establishment Characteristics by Firm Type and Sector, 2002

	Sector	
	Wholesale trade[a]	
	FM firm	Other
Log revenue ($ 000s)	8.7	7.2
Log employment	2.4	1.8
Log avg. earnings ($ 000s)	4.4	3.7
	Services[b]	
	FM firm	Other
Log revenue ($ 000s)	7.8	5.8
Log employment	2.9	1.5
Log avg. earnings ($ 000s)	4.4	3.7
	Manufacturing[c]	
	FM firm	Other
Log revenue ($ 000s)	9.6	7.9
Log employment	4.2	2.8
Log avg. earnings ($ 000s)	4.1	3.8

[a] Dominant industries (and their NAICS codes) for the wholesale trade sector include "Other electronic parts and equipment" (423690) and "Computers, peripherals, and software" (423430).

[b] Dominant industries (and NAICS codes) for the services sector include "Custom computer programming services" (541511) and "Computer systems design" (541512).

[c] Dominant industries (and NAICS codes) for the manufacturing sector include "Semiconductor and related device manufacturing" (334413) and other industries within "Computer & electronic product manufacturing" (334).

SOURCE: 2002 Matched Economic Census and company data. See data appendix.

employment is 0.6. The average earnings for employees of FM firms is substantially higher as well—the mean of the log earnings distribution is 4.4 for FGPs and 3.7 for non-FGPs. We speculate that FGPs are more likely than conventional wholesalers to employ engineers and other technical professionals with relatively high earnings and are less likely to employ lower-skilled laborers, such as those devoted to managing warehouse inventories.

Establishments of the semiconductor FM firms in the two wholesale industries identified in the previous paragraph and in superscript note [a] of Table 4.8 display a striking tendency to cluster geographically. Approximately two-thirds of wholesale revenue for semiconductor FGPs comes from plants located in just three metropolitan statistical areas (MSAs), and the top 10 MSAs for FGP activity account for 87 percent of FGP revenue (Table 4.9). In contrast, the other establishments within the two key wholesale trade industries are more geographically diverse. The top three MSAs account for only 26 percent of revenue, and the top 10 MSAs account for only 56 percent. We conjecture that in contrast to wholesalers as conventionally defined—a warehouse or sales office—which are drawn to centers of business activity and transportation hubs, FMs locate FGPs close to other establishments in their industry to benefit from active local markets for specialized labor and other inputs. Silicon Valley for electronics and New York City for apparel are well-known examples (Porter 1998).

The composition of employment in the semiconductor manufacturing industry would be much different with FGPs included in its scope. The mean of the log earnings distribution is 4.4 for FGPs in "Wholesale trade," noticeably greater than the 3.8 average for log earnings in the "Electronics manufacturing" sector (NAICS 334), excluding semiconductor FGPs.

Table 4.9 Geographic Concentration of Wholesale Sales, 2002

FM semiconductor firms		Other firms	
MSA	Sales share	MSA	Sales share
1	43	1	10
2	11	2	8
3	11	3	8
4	6	4	7
5	3	5	6
6	3	6	5
7	3	7	3
8	3	8	3
9	2	9	3
10	2	10	3
Total	87	Total	56

NOTE: MSA rankings generated separately for FM and non-FM companies. "FM" stands for "factoryless manufacturing." See text for definition.
SOURCE: 2002 Matched Economic Census and company data. See data appendix.

U.S. MANUFACTURING WITH FACTORYLESS GOODS PRODUCERS INCLUDED

Total Manufacturing Using Economic Census Special Questions

As noted in the section beginning on p. 82, the OMB has encouraged economic statistical agencies to assess the feasibility of classifying FGPs in the manufacturing sector. What remains unknown, however, is the effect of this reclassification on the size of the sector. The 2002 and 2007 Economic Censuses of Wholesale Trade both include two questions on contract manufacturing and design that offer an opportunity to assess the difference that classifying FGPs to manufacturing would make. For 2007, we estimate that if one reclassified to manufacturing those establishments answering “yes” to both questions, the value-added for the sector would be greater by $96 billion, or 4 percent (Table 4.10).[22] Using a more lenient assumption—that an affirmative answer to either question suffices to identify an establishment as an FGP, manufacturing value-added would be greater by $303 billion, or 13 percent. For 2002, manufacturing would be 3 percent greater using the strict definition, and 14 percent greater using the lenient definition. Unfortunately, response rates for these questions are quite low, and these results implicitly assume nonresponse is a negative answer. We imputed answers for nonrespondents and found manufacturing value-added would have been 5 to 20 percent higher in both years, which we take to be our most plausible estimate.[23]

Semiconductor Manufacturing Using Matched FM Company Data

Next, we narrow our focus to the semiconductor industry, and we use the matched company-establishment data. We count sales of the wholesale establishments of FM firms as manufacturing revenue and estimate that the value of shipments for the semiconductor industry in 2007 would have been $92 billion—26 percent higher than the $75 billion reported in the 2007 Economic Census. The share of the (broader) semiconductor industry accounted for by plants of FM firms (including those already in manufacturing) would have been 28 percent.[24]

Table 4.10 Total Value-Added for Establishments Reporting Product Design, Use of Contract Manufacturing, or Both ($ billions)

Levels	2002	2007
Baseline		
Either CMS or design	260	303
Both	60	96
Baseline + imputed response		
Either CMS or design	364	413
Both	94	152
Total manufacturing value added	1,888	2,383
Increase to manufacturing (%)		
Baseline		
Either CMS or design	14	13
Both	3	4
Baseline + imputed response		
Either CMS or design	19	17
Both	5	6

NOTE: Selected wholesale trade industries (423690, 423430). Manufacturing value-added from the Census of Manufacturers.
SOURCE: Economic Census, 2002 and 2007.

Interestingly, the FGP share of industry shipments for 2002 is little different from its share for 2007. Consequently, semiconductor industry shipments, including shipments from FGPs, rose 3.7 percent (annual rate) between 2002 and 2007, an increase only slightly greater than the 3.4 percent reported under the current classification system. Meanwhile, the FM portion of the global semiconductor industry ballooned from $15 billion in 2002 to $54 billion in 2007 (Figure 4.2). Because U.S. companies account for a very large share of global FM revenue, this could suggest that U.S. FM companies were expanding rapidly during this period, but that the expansion was primarily at offshore establishments. However, such a scenario could be the result of companies keeping earnings overseas for tax avoidance purposes.

SELECTED EFFECTS OF RECLASSIFICATION AND RELEVANCE FOR ECONOMIC ANALYSIS

Because the impact of the NAICS guidance for FGP classification will reflect not only the effect of conceptual differences but also the significant measurement challenges faced by statistical programs in adopting the change, no definitive analysis can be made of its effect on measures of economic activity. Nevertheless, for the sake of discussion we provide a speculative assessment of the effect on some key economic measures.

Manufacturing Value-Added

To begin with, estimates in this chapter and in other work suggest that classification of FGPs to the manufacturing sector will materially increase that sector's value-added. However, it is important to note that the total nominal value-added of the economy should not change, because the increase in manufacturing will be offset by decreases in other sectors. The expansion of the scope of the manufacturing sector beyond establishments engaged in fabrication on-site will introduce an appreciable discontinuity in statistics for the manufacturing sector. That said, the change has the appeal of introducing continuity in the treatment of production management activities and product development. When those tasks are colocated with fabrication, their value-added is counted as manufacturing, and the outsourcing of fabrication arguably should not move their value-added out of that sector. To quote from the OMB decision on the issue, "Goods producers arrange for and bring together all of the factors of production necessary to produce a good. . . . When individual steps in the complete process are outsourced, an establishment should remain classified in the manufacturing sector." That goal will be served by classifying FGPs in the manufacturing sector, but it would be desirable to also report economic statistics that allow for analysis of manufacturing with FGPs excluded.[25]

In addition, classifying FGPs to manufacturing will change the industry composition of the sector because FGPs are not evenly prevalent across wholesale trade industries (Tables 4.4 and 4.5). For example, we expect the change will temper the long decline in U.S. production of electronics. We consider a provocative example for illustration: Value-added in the "Electronic computer manufacturing" industry (NAICS Industry 334111), as reported by the Census Bureau's Annual Survey of Manufacturers (ASM), dropped from $26 billion to $9 billion between 2008 and 2010, and it fell further, to $3 billion, in 2011. In addition to the economy-wide effects of the recent recession, such as businesses postponing computer investment, the decline can be partially attributed to a shift in the composition of household computer spending toward tablet computers, especially the iPad, produced by Apple Inc., a company that relies primarily on offshore MSPs for fabrication.

To the extent that offshore iPad fabrication is managed by domestic FGPs, a portion of value-added for this type of product will be counted in the U.S. computer industry under the new classification rules. According to Apple annual reports, Apple's global iPad revenue surged from $5 billion to $20 billion between 2010 and 2011. Assuming Apple's gross margin share of overall revenue, approximately 40 percent, applies to sales of iPads, and assuming for the sake of argument that half of that margin is value-added at domestic Apple FGPs, under the new NAICS guidance $6 billion in value-added at these FGPs would be counted in the manufacturing sector and would roughly offset the $6 billion decline in domestic computer manufacturing reported in the ASM. This somewhat fanciful example illustrates how the new classification approach may have first-order effects and change the narrative for some industries where FM is prevalent.

Trade

It is also worth noting that the new treatment of FGPs has the potential to cause significant changes in the composition of U.S. trade flows, though net trade is in principle unaffected. An FGP that purchases contract manufacturing will record as its own production the product fabricated by the MSP. If the MSP is located abroad and the product is delivered to a foreign market, the sale will be treated as a U.S. export, even though the finished good did not cross the U.S. border. In contrast, if the product is shipped to the U.S. market from the foreign MSP, it will not be treated as a U.S. import, even though the good did cross the U.S. border. In both cases, an import of manufacturing services will be recorded. Thus, the relative importance of services and goods in total trade may differ under the new system. The new treatment of FGPs has the potential to cause significant changes in the composition of U.S. trade as recorded in the National Income and Product Accounts (NIPAs), though net trade is in principle unaffected.

Measurement Effects

In addition to the conceptual changes mentioned above, we note two ways in which aggregates conceptually unaffected by the change in treatment of FGPs may nevertheless be affected as measured. First, the accuracy of economic statistics whose construction relies on the combination of data generated by different statistical programs, such as industrial production and labor productivity, will be aided by the better alignment of FGP classification practices. Such statistics are at risk of inadvertent mismeasurement if differences with respect to current FGP classification are not taken into account. The added clarity with regard to the treatment of FGPs will serve to reduce the risk of such errors.

Second, measurement of the prices needed to deflate nominal value-added and trade flows for FGPs and MSPs will require significant attention. Byrne, Kovak, and Michaels (2013) study prices for manufacturing services in the semiconductor industry and find that the well-known challenges faced in quality-adjusting product prices also exist for semiconductor manufacturing services. If the composition of trade shifts from goods to services, the relative quality of price measures for services will affect the resulting real balance of trade.[26]

Economic Issues

Deeper understanding of the use of the FM business model may lead to insights into important economic questions. Among these are the following four:

1) What is the effect of offshoring on domestic activity—do management and design follow fabrication offshore, or does offshoring enhance that domestic activity through gains from trade?[27]
2) What is the impact of this shift in manufacturing approach on manufacturing employment—does the loss of production

worker jobs to offshoring coincide with a gain in domestic knowledge-worker jobs?[28]

3) How much of the substantial contribution of information technology (IT) production to productivity growth can be attributed to FGP activity, and how much to fabrication?[29]
4) What is the role of FGPs in global "trade in tasks"? Can FGP data lead to more appropriate input-output tables for use in the burgeoning work on decomposing product value into contributions from different economies through value-added trade?[30]

CONCLUSION

Using company data, we document our premise that factoryless manufacturing is becoming more prevalent and is employed in the production of an increasingly wide variety of goods. With Census Bureau establishment microdata, we find evidence that factoryless goods producers are present in a broad mix of industries in the wholesale trade sector. We present a case study of the semiconductor industry using a data set constructed by matching company data and census establishment data. Here, we find that FGPs are larger in terms of revenue and employment, have higher average earnings, and cluster markedly more than conventional wholesale trade establishments. Finally, we estimate that shifting FGP activity from wholesale trade to manufacturing may increase manufacturing value-added by 5 to 20 percent. In the case of semiconductors, we find that value-added in 2007 would be 26 percent higher if census data were used. We provide examples of anticipated effects on economic statistics from the clarification of the treatment of FGPs and note several areas of economic study that may benefit from the change.

Implementing the OMB guidance on the treatment of FGPs presents substantial challenges for U.S. statistical agencies going forward (Doherty, Chapter 2 of this volume). As was noted earlier, factoryless manufacturing is far from new, and looking backward, there is the daunting task of building a history consistent with the clarified scope of manufacturing, which will be needed to fully exploit the data. However, bearing in mind the evident size of the FGP phenomenon and the role that better measures of FGPs may play in discussion of pressing economic issues, we consider the clarification of the treatment of factoryless goods producers to be a welcome effort to update the U.S. statistical system.

Notes

This chapter stems from a paper that was prepared for presentation in 2013 at the "Measuring the Effects of Globalization" conference, organized by the Progressive Policy Institute and the W.E. Upjohn Institute for Employment Research and funded by the Alfred P. Sloan Foundation. We are grateful for the feedback we received from participants at the conference. We also benefited from additional feedback from Maureen Donoghue, Teresa Fort, Susan Houseman, Javier Miranda, John Murphy, Bill Powers, Jennifer Ribarsky, Falan Yinug, and participants in a workshop at the U.S. Census Bureau. The Global Semiconductor Alliance and IHS iSuppli provided data, and we also appreciate their guidance on the semiconductor industry. Remaining errors are our own.

All results have been reviewed by the Census Bureau to ensure that no confidential information is disclosed. References to specific companies are based exclusively on purchased data, public financial reports, and news accounts, not on confidential census information. The views expressed are not the views of the Census Bureau.

Affiliation for Bayard and Byrne is the Federal Reserve Board of Governors. The views expressed should not be attributed to the Board of Governors or other members of the Federal Reserve staff. Affiliation for Smith is the University of Minnesota Department of Economics. Direct correspondence can be addressed to the following: david.m.byrne@frb.gov.

1. An establishment is a company unit, such as a plant, warehouse, or office. The Office of Management and Budget defines it this way: "The establishment . . . is the smallest operating entity for which records provide information on cost of resources . . . employed to produce the units of output. . . . The establishment . . . is generally a single physical location" (OMB 1998).
2. A summary of a recent study of the FGP classification issued by the Economic Classification Policy Committee noted, "To the extent that FGPs can be identified, the Census Bureau statistical programs classify them to wholesale trade" (Murphy 2009). However, this guidance does not apply to apparel. (John Murphy, chair of the ECPC, in discussion with author Byrne, September 2013.)
3. Presentation by the FGP Implementation Planning Group at the Semiconductor Industry Association's annual meeting, September 11, 2012. The group's presentation was titled "Redefining Manufacturing in NAICS 2012: The Factoryless Goods Producer (FGP)."

4. For a discussion of the deliberations leading to this decision and the alternatives considered, see Doherty (2013).
5. The *Federal Register* notice from August 17, 2011 (found in *Federal Register* 76[159]: 51240–51243), describes the announced NAICS classification standard for FGP establishments as a clarification, but it also acknowledges that "the inclusion of revenues from FGP activities in manufacturing will effectively change the traditional definition of manufacturing."
6. Although the Business Processes and Business Functions classification system was not referenced in the FGP classification deliberations, it provides a useful framework for thinking about the nature of factoryless manufacturing. BPBF is based on the concepts developed for the Global Value Chains Initiative and was employed in the BLS's Mass Layoff Statistics Program, which was discontinued in June 2013 (Sturgeon 2002; Sturgeon and Gereffi 2008).
7. The NAICS manual notes that "almost all manufacturing has some captive research and development or administrative operations, such as accounting, payroll, or management" (OMB 1998).
8. Steiner (1995, 1997) was an early advocate for modifying classification practices to account for FM activity, though the term "factoryless goods producer" had not been coined at the time. Steiner notes that in the 1970s, for a "host of consumer goods," manufacturing moved offshore but the companies "did the research and development, the production engineering, and were responsible for quality control."
9. In the electronics sector, the complicated web of component production, design, and management cannot always be simplified to an FGP-MSP relationship. (See Dedrick and Kraemer [2002]; Grunwald and Flamm [1985]; and Sturgeon and Lee [2001].)
10. Under Regulation S-K of the U.S. Securities Act of 1933, annual reports to the SEC on Form 10-K are required to include discussion of risks "likely to result in registrant's liquidity increasing or decreasing in a material way."
11. Because the S&P 500 is constructed to be representative of the "large cap" segment of the U.S. equities market, these results do not apply to smaller firms. Small and medium-sized firms are an important topic for further study. One potential benefit of decoupling production management from fabrication and the associated fixed costs may be that smaller-scale enterprises are more viable, thus promoting firm creation. That being said, Kamal, Moulton, and Ribarsky (Chapter 3 of this volume) find that two-thirds of firms reporting the use of MSPs or the provision of contract manufacturing are large—they have 250 or more employees.
12. References to contract manufacturing of components of the final product, purchase of "private label" merchandise, licensing of company designs, and provision by the company of contract manufacturing services to others were not treated as evidence of factoryless manufacturing.
13. The survey forms for the Census of Wholesale Trade are included in Appendix 4B.
14. Specifically, the 2002 question asked whether fabrication was "performed for this establishment by another company," but offshore fabrication by another establish-

ment of the same company would be sufficient to meet the definition of FGP. The 2007 contract manufacturing question is also not a perfect match. With regard to design, to be an FGP, the establishment must own the rights to the design, but it may be independently developed or otherwise acquired.

15. A negative response to both of these questions by an establishment of an FM firm need not be erroneous. For example, a pure sales office for an FM firm would properly be classified in "Wholesale trade."
16. Kamal, Moulton, and Ribarsky use the Company Organization Survey, conducted by the Census Bureau, and the BEA's Benchmark Survey of U.S. Direct Investment Abroad as well as its Benchmark Survey of Transactions in Selected Services and Intellectual Property Products with Foreign Persons.
17. For a detailed discussion of FGPs and MSPs in the semiconductor industry, see Byrne, Kovak, and Michaels (2013). To avoid confusion, we do not use the industry-specific term "fabless" for FM firms or the term "foundries" for manufacturing service providers.
18. See Appendix 4A for a description of the sources and matching process.
19. A handful of these single-unit firms have a second establishment in the management sector. These establishments are omitted from the firm structure calculations. Results for the management sector did not meet Census Bureau standards for disclosure.
20. Most firms have no more than one establishment in these wholesale industries, and the results are little changed by treating each establishment separately.
21. Note that our "other" group may contain establishments of FM companies producing products other than semiconductors. We believe this would lead us to understate the differences between our semiconductor FGPs and true wholesale establishments.
22. We focus on value-added for now because of issues involved in double-counting gross output if an FGP purchases contract manufacturing services from a domestic establishment already in the scope of manufacturing. The value-added approach has limitations as well. We calculate value-added in the wholesale sector as sales minus the cost of merchandise and change in inventory. These results will be biased downwards if the reported cost of merchandise reflects the value of product design or of the management of the fabrication process performed at the FGP—for example, if its valuation on import includes the FGP's value-added.
23. For each question, we predict the probability that each nonresponding establishment would answer "yes" based on observable characteristics. We then add the value-added of the establishment, weighted by the predicted probability, to the manufacturing sector, in addition to the full value-added for the respondents in our baseline estimates. In unreported results, we also use the weighting scheme developed by Fort (2011) to develop predicted probabilities of answering a question conditional on observables. We then multiply value-added for an establishment that answered both questions by the inverse of the predicted probability. This methodology yields estimates that differ by only a few percentage points from the

results reported. Our estimates of the magnitude of the proportional increment to manufacturing gross output are similar as well.

24. Because very little MSP activity for the semiconductor industry was located domestically in 2007, the magnitude of double-counting when using gross output is unlikely to be significant.
25. At the time of this writing, it has not been determined whether such detail will be made available in U.S. economic statistics.
26. On the importance of prices for imported intermediates for productivity measurement, see Houseman et al. (2011).
27. Levinson (2013) notes the relevance for policymakers of the question of whether manufacturing is becoming "hollowed out"—that is, whether a greater share of value-added is taking place offshore.
28. Helper, Krueger, and Wial (2012) note the dwindling role of the manufacturing sector as a source of "high-wage jobs, especially for workers who would otherwise earn the lowest wages."
29. Byrne, Oliner, and Sichel (2013) note that the contribution from factoryless goods production is an important area for extension of the contribution of IT in productivity.
30. On "trade in tasks," see Grossman and Rossi-Hansberg (2008). On developments in the measurement of value-added trade, see Ahmad (Chapter 6 of this volume), Timmer et al. (2013), and Yao, Ma, and Pei (Chapter 7 of this volume).

Appendix 4A

Data Construction

For the case study of the semiconductor industry, we linked company directory entries to the Census Business Register.[1] The Business Register is a database of U.S. business establishments and companies that serves as a sampling frame for Census Bureau firm and establishment surveys.[2] For each establishment in the Business Register there are identifiers that allow the establishment to be linked to corresponding records in Census Bureau economic surveys. In addition, the Business Register contains a firm identifier for each establishment, which enables us to locate other establishments within the same firm.

To generate our list of census firm identifiers corresponding to FGP companies, we began with a list of 1,579 FGP semiconductor companies created from a directory published by Gartner, a high-tech consultancy, and a directory published by the Global Semiconductor Alliance (GSA), a trade association representing a wide variety of companies involved in semiconductor design and fabrication. Gartner provided a worldwide directory of semiconductor FGP companies active in 2001. The GSA provided a worldwide directory of all semiconductor FGP companies active as of 2012 and a supplemental list of mergers and acquisitions between 2005 and 2012.[3] The supplemental list proved critical because of the high frequency of firm birth and firm death in the industry. We reviewed public records for these companies to amend incomplete records. Eliminating companies that we believed were not operational in either 2002 or 2007 based on a review of public records left us with a list of 1,475 companies (Table 4A.1). The list contains the name, headquarters address, and year of occurrence for major events (establishment, dissolution, merger, acquisition) for each company.

Table 4A.1 Match Statistics

Company list	1,475
Matched to business register	1,050
Total Firm IDs	1,125
Matched to 2002 EC establishments	525
Matched to 2007 EC establishments	525
Matched to either 2002 or 2007	750

NOTE: Rounded to nearest 25.
SOURCE: Company data matched to Economic Census (EC) data for 2002 and 2007. See Appendix 4A.

First, for 2002 and 2007, we matched all companies in operation in either census year to a three-year window of the Business Register ending in the census year. For this first stage, we only exploit the company name, by finding the name or names in the Business Register that match the greatest number of leading characters for the FGP company name. We then reviewed a randomly selected set of 1,000 of the approximately 40,000 potential matches generated, and we judged whether the entries were a match when considering both full-name information and address variables. This set of matches was used to estimate the importance of all available match-quality variables using a probit. Variables included an indicator of state match, number of leading digits of the zip code in common, company name-spelling distance, address-spelling distance, and whether the establishment operated in a high-tech industry. The estimated index function was then used to rank possible matches for each company on our list from most to least probable. Then we reviewed by hand the matches for each company in descending order until we judged that we had either found a match or there was no match for the company.

Using this name-matching procedure, we located 71 percent of these FGP companies in the Census Business Register files (Table 4.6).[4] Sometimes, however, we could not find in the Economic Census firm identifiers that had appeared in the Business Register. In the end, we were able to locate establishments for about 50 percent of the companies on our list of FGP firms in the Economic Census microdata for 2002 and 2007. Once we link firms from the GSA and Gartner directories to the census data, we identify all establishments connected to those firms and include them in our final data set.

Appendix Notes

1. For more detail on the matching process, see Smith (2013).
2. See Jarmin and Miranda (2002).
3. Both the GSA and Gartner directories contained companies from around the world. We attempted to find matches for both foreign and domestically headquartered companies because we assumed many of the foreign companies would have a U.S. presence. For the foreign companies we were forced to rely on only name-matching characteristics.
4. It is important to note that our list contains many firms headquartered abroad that may have no U.S. presence.

Appendix 4B

Census of Wholesale Trade Forms

Form WH-42103

28 ESTABLISHMENT ACTIVITIES

A. Indicate activities that were performed by this establishment or were performed for this establishment by another company during 2002.
(Mark "X" ALL that apply.)

	This activity was performed by this establishment	This activity was performed for this establishment by another company	This activity was not provided by this establishment
1. Product Development			
a. Product design/engineering	0921 ☐	0941 ☐	0961 ☐
b. Materials fabrication/processing/assembly/blending	0922 ☐	0942 ☐	0962 ☐
2. Order Fulfillment			
a. Bundling or kitting (combining multiple items into a prepackaged product)	0923 ☐	0943 ☐	0963 ☐
b. Pick and pack (taking goods from inventory and packaging them to fill orders)	0924 ☐	0944 ☐	0964 ☐
c. Warehousing	0925 ☐	0945 ☐	0965 ☐
d. Breaking bulk (reducing large shipments into smaller portions for customers)	0926 ☐	0946 ☐	0966 ☐
e. Local delivery (within a city, town, or other local area, including adjoining towns and suburban areas)	0927 ☐	0947 ☐	0967 ☐
f. Long distance delivery (beyond local areas and commercial zones)	0928 ☐	0948 ☐	0968 ☐
g. Less than truckload	0929 ☐	0949 ☐	0969 ☐
3. Other Services			
a. Customs brokerage (providing the services of a licensed customs broker)	0930 ☐	0950 ☐	0970 ☐
b. Logistics consulting (providing advice and expertise)	0931 ☐	0951 ☐	0971 ☐
c. Processing of returned merchandise	0932 ☐	0952 ☐	0972 ☐

B. During 2002 did this establishment:

1. Manage inventory owned by this establishment AND held at this location? . . . 0936 ☐ Yes 0937 ☐ No

2. Manage inventory owned by this establishment BUT held at a customer's location? . . . 0956 ☐ Yes 0957 ☐ No

3. Manage inventory owned by another company BUT held at this location? . . . 0976 ☐ Yes 0977 ☐ No

4. Manage inventory owned by another company AND held somewhere other than at this location? . . . 0994 ☐ Yes 0995 ☐ No

Form WH-42311 (12/04/2006)

If not shown, please enter your 11-digit Census File Number (CFN) from the mailing address.

26 SPECIAL INQUIRIES - Continued

C. OTHER ESTABLISHMENT ACTIVITIES

1. Did this establishment design, engineer, or formulate the manufactured products that it sold, produced, or shipped?

0318 ☐ Yes

0319 ☐ No

2. Which of the following best describes this establishment's primary activity? *(Mark "X" only ONE box.)*

0362 ☐ Providing contract manufacturing services for others

0363 ☐ Transforming raw materials or components into new products that this establishment owns or controls

0364 ☐ Reselling goods manufactured by others (with or without minor final assembly)

0365 ☐ Other - *Specify*

0366

3. Did this establishment purchase contract manufacturing services from other companies or other establishments of your company to process materials or components that this establishment owns or controls?

0496 ☐ Yes, primarily with establishments WITHIN the 50 States and the District of Columbia

0497 ☐ Yes, primarily with establishments OUTSIDE of the 50 States and the District of Columbia

0498 ☐ No

27-29 Not Applicable.

REMARKS *(Please use this space for any explanations that may be essential in understanding your reported data.)*

30 CERTIFICATION - This report is substantially accurate and was prepared in accordance with the instructions.

Is the time period covered by this report a calendar year?		Month	Year		Month	Year
☐ Yes ☐ No - Enter time period covered →	FROM			TO		

Name of person to contact regarding this report	Title

Telephone	Area code	Number	Extension	Fax	Area code	Number
		-				-

Internet e-mail address	Date completed	Month	Day	Year

Thank you for completing your 2007 ECONOMIC CENSUS form.

PLEASE PHOTOCOPY THIS FORM FOR YOUR RECORDS AND RETURN THE ORIGINAL.

Form **WH-42311** (02-02-2012)

26 SPECIAL INQUIRIES - Continued

C. PURCHASE OF CONTRACT MANUFACTURING

1. Did this establishment **purchase** contract manufacturing services from other companies or foreign plants of your company in 2012?

Include:

- *Products for which the manufacturing (i.e., transforming or otherwise processing materials or components based on specifications provided by your company) was outsourced to other companies.*
- *Products for which the manufacturing was performed by your company's foreign plants.*

Exclude:

- *Services for packaging and assembling.*
- *Purchases of merchandise for resale (sale of products bought and sold without further processing or transformation).*

1011 ☐ Yes - *Go to line 2*

1012 ☐ No - *Go to* **30**

		2012		
		$ Bil.	Mil.	Thou.
2. Report the costs incurred by this establishment for contract manufacturing purchases in 2012	1013			
3. Report the value of sales, shipments, receipts, or revenue generated in 2012 from products whose purchases were reported as contract manufacturing costs in line 2	1015			

27-**29** Not Applicable.

REMARKS *(Please use this space for any explanations that may be essential in understanding your reported data.)*

30 CERTIFICATION - This report is substantially accurate and was prepared in accordance with the instructions.

Is the time period covered by this report a calendar year?

☐ Yes ☐ No - Enter time period covered ⟶ FROM Month Year TO Month Year

Name of person to contact regarding this report	Title

	Area code	Number	Extension		Area code	Number
Telephone				Fax		

E-mail address		Month	Day	Year
	Date completed			

Thank you for completing your 2012 ECONOMIC CENSUS form.

PLEASE PHOTOCOPY THIS FORM FOR YOUR RECORDS AND RETURN THE ORIGINAL.

References

Bernard, Andrew B., and Teresa C. Fort. 2013. "Factoryless Goods Producers in the U.S." NBER Working Paper No. 19396. Cambridge, MA: National Bureau of Economic Research.

Brown, Sharon P. 2008. "Business Processes and Business Functions: A New Way of Looking at Employment." *Monthly Labor Review* 131(12): 51–70.

Byrne, David M., Brian Kovak, and Ryan Michaels. 2013. "Price and Quality Dispersion in an Offshoring Market: Evidence from Semiconductor Production Services." Finance and Economics Discussion Series Working Paper No. 2013-06. Washington, DC: Board of Governors of the Federal Reserve System.

Byrne, David M., Stephen D. Oliner, and Daniel E. Sichel. 2013. "Is the Information Technology Revolution Over?" *International Productivity Monitor* 25(Spring): 20–36.

Dedrick, Jason, and Kenneth L. Kraemer. 2002. *Globalization of the Personal Computer Industry: Trends and Implications*. Irvine, CA: Center for Research on Information Technology and Organizations, University of California, Irvine.

Fort, Teresa C. 2011. "Breaking Up Is Hard to Do: Why Firms Fragment Production across Locations." Job Market Paper. College Park: University of Maryland, Department of Economics.

Gereffi, Gary. 2002. "Outsourcing and Changing Patterns of International Competition in the Apparel Commodity Chain." Paper presented at the conference "Responding to Globalization: Societies, Groups, and Individuals," held in Boulder, CO, April 4–7.

Grossman, Gene M., and Esteban Rossi-Hansberg. 2008. "Trading Tasks: A Simple Theory of Offshoring." *American Economic Review* 98(5): 1978–1997.

Grunwald, Joseph, and Kenneth Flamm. 1985. *The Global Factory: Foreign Assembly in International Trade*. Washington, DC: Brookings Institution.

Helper, Susan, Timothy Krueger, and Howard Wial. 2012. *Why Does Manufacturing Matter? Which Manufacturing Matters? A Policy Framework*. Metropolitan Policy Program at Brookings. Washington, DC: Brookings Institution.

Houseman, Susan, Christopher Kurz, Paul Lengermann, and Benjamin R. Mandel. 2011. "Offshoring Bias in U.S. Manufacturing." *Journal of Economic Perspectives* 25(2): 111–132.

Jarmin, Ron S., C. J. Krizan, and John Tang. 2011. "Outsourcing, Offshoring, and Trade: Identifying Foreign Activity across Census Data Products." *Survey of Current Business* 91(2): 121–139.

Jarmin, Ron S., and Javier Miranda. 2002. "The Longitudinal Business Database." Center for Economic Studies Discussion Paper No. CES-WP-02-17. Suitland, MD: U.S. Census Bureau, Center for Economic Studies.

Kask, Christopher, David Kiernan, and Brian Friedman. 2002. "Labor Productivity Growth in Wholesale Trade, 1990–2000." *Monthly Labor Review* 125(12): 3–14.

Levinson, Marc. 2013. *"Hollowing Out" in U.S. Manufacturing: Analysis and Issues for Congress*. CRS Report for Congress 7-5700. Washington, DC: Congressional Research Service.

Murphy, John. 2009. *Classification of Units that Outsource Manufacturing Transformation Activities*. Washington, DC: U.S. Census Bureau.

Office of Management and Budget (OMB). 1998. *North American Industry Classification System: United States, 1997*. Blue Ridge Summit, PA: Bernan Press.

———. 2009. "2007 North American Industry Classification System (NAICS)—Updates for 2012." *Federal Register* 74(4): 764–768.

———. 2011. "North American Industry Classification System; Revision for 2012; Notice." *Federal Register* 76(159): 51240–51243.

Porter, Michael E. 1998. "Clusters and the New Economics of Competition." *Harvard Business Review* 76(6): 77–90.

Smith, Dominic. 2013. "Probabilistic Name and Address Matching." Working paper. Washington, DC: Federal Reserve Board of Governors.

Steiner, Robert L. 1995. "Caveat! Some Unrecognized Pitfalls in Census Economic Data and the Input-Output Accounts." *Review of Industrial Organization* 10(6): 689–710.

———. 1997. "The 'Own-Brand Marketer' Debuts in the 1997 Census." *Review of Industrial Organization* 12(5–6): 809–816.

Sturgeon, Timothy J. 2002. "Modular Production Networks: A New American Model of Industrial Organization." *Industrial and Corporate Change* 11(3): 451–496.

Sturgeon, Timothy J., and Gary Gereffi. 2008. *The Challenge of Global Value Chains: Why Integrative Trade Requires New Thinking and New Data.* Report prepared for Industry Canada. Durham, NC: Duke University, Center on Globalization, Governance, and Competitiveness.

Sturgeon, Timothy J., and Ji-Ren Lee. 2001. "Industry Co-Evolution and the Rise of a Shared Supply-Base for Electronics Manufacturing." MIT Working Paper IPC-01-003. Cambridge, MA: Massachusetts Institute of Technology, Industrial Performance Center.

Timmer, Marcel P., Bart Los, Robert Stehrer, and Gaaitzen J. de Vries. 2013. "Fragmentation, Incomes, and Jobs: An Analysis of European Competitiveness." *Economic Policy* 28(76): 613–661.

Part 2

Global Supply Chains

5
Incomes and Jobs in Global Production of Manufactures

New Measures of Competitiveness Based on the World Input-Output Database

Marcel P. Timmer
Bart Los
Gaaitzen J. de Vries
University of Groningen

OVERVIEW

It is frequently argued that globalization has entered a second phase. In the early twentieth century, rapidly falling transport costs ended the need for colocation of production and consumption. Competitiveness of countries in the first phase was determined by domestic clusters of firms, mainly competing sector to sector. More recently, fostered by rapidly falling communication and coordination costs, the production process itself was unbundled, as the various stages of production need not be performed near each other anymore. In this new phase, international competition increasingly plays itself out at the level of tasks within firms, rather than at the level of products. And trade in goods is increasingly replaced by trade in tasks (Baldwin 2006). This creates new challenges for the way in which the competitiveness of nations is analyzed.

Traditional measures indicate that China and other emerging countries have rapidly improved in competitiveness since the late 1990s, both in quantity and in quality, as attested to by booming exports of technologically sophisticated products. But recent product case studies suggest that European, Japanese, and U.S. firms still capture major parts of these value chains, as they specialize in high-value-added activities such as software, design, branding, and system integration. China and other emerging countries are mainly involved in the assembling, testing, and packaging activities, which are poorly compensated. A typical finding is that China keeps less than 4 percent of a product's export value as income for its labor and capital employed in the production process of electronic goods (Ali-Yrkkö et al. 2011; Dedrick, Kraemer, and Linden 2010). To reflect this new reality, a new measure of competitiveness is needed that is based on the value added in production by a country, rather than the gross output value of its exports. Or, as put by Grossman and Rossi-Hansberg (2006, pp. 66–67), "Such measures are inadequate to the task of measuring the extent of a country's international integration in a world with global supply chains. . . . We would like to know the sources of the value-added embodied in goods and the uses to which the goods are eventually put."

Recently, Timmer et al. (2013) introduced a new concept that allows one to analyze the value that is added in various stages of regionally dispersed production processes. It is defined as the income generated in a country by participating in global manufacturing production, abbreviated by the term "GVC income" (for global value chain income). Compared to traditional competitiveness indicators such as a country's share in world exports, this new metric has three advantages. First, it indicates to what extent a country can compete with other nations in terms of *activities* related to global manufacturing, rather than by competing in manufacturing *products* as measured by exports. These activities take place in manufacturing industries but also in services industries. Second, it is a reflection of an economy's strength to compete in both domestic and global markets. Third, income and employment effects of trade in tasks for separate groups of workers (such as low- and high-skilled) can also be determined in the same unified framework, referring to the concept of "GVC jobs."[1]

The main aim of this chapter is to establish a series of stylized facts on GVC incomes and jobs that can serve as a starting point for deeper analysis of the causes of global manufacturing production. Whereas Timmer et al. (2013) focused their analysis on trends in European competitiveness, this chapter takes a more global view and provides analyses for 20 major countries in the world, including the United States, Japan, major economies in Europe, Brazil, China, India, and Russia.

In the remainder of this chapter, we first outline our methodology for slicing up global value chains (in the next section, Section Two—"GVC Incomes and Jobs: Methodology") and introduce the concepts of GVC income and GVC jobs. We identify GVCs by tracing the flow of goods and services across industries and countries as described in a world input-output table. Using a decomposition technique that is built upon the original insights by Leontief (1949), we slice up the value of manufacturing expenditure into incomes for labor and capital in various countries. These are the incomes of factors that are directly and indirectly needed for the production of the final manufacturing goods. The empirical analysis is based on a new database, called the World Input-Output Database (WIOD), which combines national input-output tables, bilateral international trade statistics, and data on production factor requirements. A crucial characteristic of this database is the explicit measurement of national and international trade in intermediates. In Section Three, "The World Input-Output Database (WIOD)," we discuss the major features of this database.

Section Four, "Trends in Manufactures' GVC Incomes," provides trends in GVC income shares across regions and major countries in the world. The analysis is based on demand for final manufacturing products, and we show the dependency of countries on domestic and foreign sources of demand. We also show that only about half of the GVC income originates in the manufacturing sector itself, which indicates the importance of interindustry linkages in the production of manufacturing goods. In Section Five, "Manufactures' GVC Income by Production Factor," we focus more in-depth on the role of different factors of production. We show how in advanced countries GVC income generated by capital and high-skilled labor is increasing, while incomes for medium- and low-skilled workers in manufactures production are declining. In Section Six, "Manufactures' GVC Jobs," we study the number of jobs involved in GVC production of manufactures and find a strong difference between Europe and the United States. Low- and medium-skilled jobs are on the decline in all advanced countries, but whereas in Europe and Japan high-skilled job opportunities have increased, they have declined in the United States since 1995.

GVC INCOMES AND JOBS: METHODOLOGY

In this section we outline the method to slice up GVCs, as introduced by Timmer et al. (2013). The basic aim of this empirical analysis is to decompose expenditure on a final product into a stream of factor incomes around the world. By modeling the world economy as an input-output model in the tradition of Leontief, we can use his famous insight, which links up changes in consumption to changes in the distribution of factor income both within and across countries. Basically, we will provide the macroeconomic equivalent of famous product case studies that suggest a new division of labor and value in electronics, such as Dedrick, Kraemer, and Linden (2010) for iPods and electronic notebooks and Ali-Yrkkö et al. (2011) for a study of mobile phones. These studies suggest a division of activities between mature and emerging economies where the former concentrate on activities that require skilled labor and capital (in particular, intangibles), while the latter mainly contribute through unskilled labor.

The GVC income metric provides a macroeconomic complement to the product case studies described above. It covers a wide set of products and analyzes not only the first-tier suppliers but also second-tier and higher-order suppliers. The method provides a full decomposition of the value of consumption in a country and traces the associated income flows for labor and capital in various regions in the world. We model the global production system through input-output tables and international trade statistics. The approach follows the seminal insight from Leontief (1949) and traces the amount of factor inputs needed to produce a certain amount of final demand. Value is added at various stages of production through the utilization of production factors such as labor and capital. These links between expenditure and income are illustrated in Figure 5.1.

The arrows in Figure 5.1 indicate flows of products and factor services, which are mirrored by payments that flow in the opposite direction. The central link between income and consumption is the production process, in which value is added through the deployment of labor and capital in the various stages of production. This production process can be highly fragmented, as the case study of the iPod illustrates. Through international trade, consumption in Country B will lead to income for

Figure 5.1 Links between Expenditure, Production, and Income

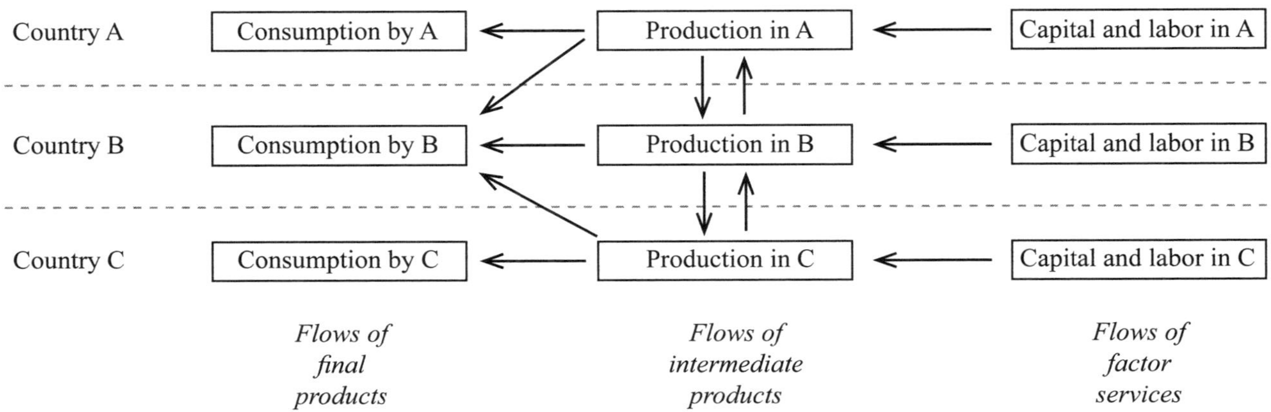

SOURCE: Authors' construction.

production factors in other countries, either through importing final goods, or through the use of imported intermediates in the production process of Country B. Through these indirect linkages, consumption in Country A will generate income in Country C even though Country C does not trade directly with Country A. These indirect effects are sizable, as international trade in intermediate goods is high.

To model the international production linkages, we use a world input-output model that obeys the identity that at the global level consumption is equal to all value-added generated.[2] Below we will outline how this identity can be used to consistently decompose the value of consumption by a country into income in any country in the world. To do this we rely on the fundamental input-output identity introduced by Leontief (1949), which states that $Q = BQ + C$, where Q denotes outputs, C is consumption, and B is an input-output matrix with intermediate input coefficients. B describes how a given product in a country is produced with different combinations of intermediate inputs. The identity states that a good produced is either used as an intermediate input in another production process or is consumed. It can be rewritten as $Q = (I - B)^{-1}C$, with I being an identity matrix.[3] $(I - B)^{-1}$ is famously known as the Leontief inverse. It represents the total production value in all stages of production that is generated in the production process of one unit of consumption.

To see this, let Z be a vector column, with the first element representing the global consumption of iPods produced in China, which is equal to the output of the Chinese iPod industry, and the rest zeros. Then BZ is the vector of intermediate inputs, both Chinese and foreign, needed to assemble the iPods in China, such as the hard-disc drive, battery, and processors. But these intermediates need to be produced as well. B^2Z indicates the intermediate inputs directly needed to produce BZ, and so on. Thus

$$\sum_{n=1}^{\infty} B^n Z$$

represents all intermediate inputs needed for the iPod production. Then the total gross output value related to the production of Z is given by

$$Z + \sum_{n=1}^{\infty} B^n Z = (I - B)^{-1} Z .$$

Using this insight, we can derive production factor requirements for any vector Z. Let F be the direct factor inputs per unit of gross output. An element in this matrix indicates the share in the value of gross output of a production factor used directly by the country to produce a given product. These are country- and industry-specific—one example would be the value of low-skilled labor used in the Chinese electronics industry to produce one dollar of output and to add up to value-added by construction in our data. The elements in F are direct factor inputs in the industry, because they do not account for value embodied in intermediate inputs used by this industry. To include the latter as well, we multiply F by the total gross output value in all stages of production that is generated in the production process defined above, so that

$$(5.1) \quad K = F(I - B)^{-1}C ,$$

in which C indicates the levels of consumption[4] and K is the matrix of amounts of factor inputs attributed to each consumption level. A typical element in K indicates the amount of a production factor f from country i, embodied in consumption of product g in country j. By the logic of Leontief's insight, the sum of all elements in a column of K will be equal to the consumption of this product. Thus we have completed our decomposition of the value of consumption into the value-added by various production factors around the world.[5]

For the purpose of this chapter, we are also interested in the effects of foreign versus domestic final demand for growth in GVC income and jobs. For a particular country i, we define foreign final demand (C^{FOR}) and domestic final demand (C^{DOM}) so that $C^{FOR} + C^{DOM} = C$. Substituting this in the linear system given above, one can now derive the gross output generated because of final demand from home country i, and that generated because of final demand from other countries, so that

$$(5.2) \quad K = F(I - B)^{-1}C^{DOM} + F(I - B)^{-1}C^{FOR} = K^{DOM} + K^{FOR} .$$

In this equation, we have decomposed the amount of factors used in each sector of the home economy as given by K into the amount used to satisfy domestic final demand (K^{DOM}) and the amount used to satisfy foreign demand (K^{FOR}). The latter measures *value-added exports*, defined by Johnson and Noguera (2012) as the amount of value-added produced in a given source country that is ultimately embodied in final products absorbed abroad.

In Table 5.1 we provide an example of a GVC decomposition for final expenditures in the United States on electrical machinery in 1995 and 2008. The expenditure value is given at the basic price concept. A key distinction in the System of National Accounts is between a value at basic prices and at purchasers' prices. The latter is the price paid by the final consumer and consists of the basic price plus trade and transport margins in the handling of the product and any (net) product taxes. The basic price can thus be considered as the price received by the producer of the good. In 1995, the share of the value added in the United States was over 50 percent, but this swiftly dropped in the period following that year. Instead, value was increasingly added in other parts in the world, both within NAFTA and outside. China in particular benefited from U.S. demand for electrical machinery and captured more than 20 percent of the value in 2008. Partly this was by exporting final goods to the United States that had been produced in China (direct contribution), but also it was accomplished indirectly through the production of intermediates (such as parts and components) that are used in the United States and elsewhere to produce final goods destined for the U.S. mar-

Table 5.1 Value-Added in Final Expenditure on Electrical Products in United States (billions of 1995 US$)

	1995	2008	Change
Total expenditure in US$, of which	217	253	36
Domestic value-added	119	106	−13
Foreign value-added, of which	98	147	49
Canada and Mexico	10	15	5
China	7	53	46
East Asia	37	24	−13
EU 27	19	28	9
Other	25	27	2

NOTE: Table shows breakdown of final expenditure by households, firms, and government in the United States on electrical machinery products (ISIC Rev. 3 industries 30 to 33) into value-added in regions at basic prices, excluding domestic trade and transport margins, and in billions of U.S. dollars, deflated to 1995 prices with the overall U.S. CPI. "East Asia" includes Japan, South Korea, and Taiwan. "EU 27" includes all countries of the European Union.

SOURCE: Authors' calculations based on World Input-Output Database, April 2012.

ket. The decline in value-added in Japan, South Korea, and Taiwan is illustrative of the major shifts that occurred in production stages across Asia as China was increasingly used as a production location by East Asian multinationals (Fukao, Ishido, and Ito 2003), an issue we will return to later.

THE WORLD INPUT-OUTPUT DATABASE (WIOD)

To implement the new GVC metrics, one needs to have a database with linked consumption, production, and income flows within and between countries. For individual countries, this type of information can be found in input-output tables. However, national tables do not provide any information on bilateral flows of goods and services between countries. For this type of information, researchers have to rely on data sets constructed on the basis of national input-output tables in combination with international trade data. Various alternative data sets have been built in the past, of which the Global Trade Analysis Project (GTAP) database is the most widely known and used (Narayanan and Walmsley 2008). Other data sets are constructed by the Organisation for Economic Co-operation and Development (OECD; see Ahmad, Chapter 6 of this volume; IDE-JETRO (2006); and Yamano and Ahmad [2006]). However, all these databases provide only one or a limited number of benchmark year input-output tables, which preclude an analysis of developments over time. And although they provide separate import matrices, there is no detailed breakdown of imports by trade partner.

For this chapter, we use a new database, called the World Input-Output Database (WIOD), that aims to fill this gap. The WIOD provides a time series of world input-output tables from 1995 onwards, distinguishing between 35 industries and 59 product groups. The construction of the world input-output tables will be discussed in the following subsection. Another crucial element for this type of analysis comes from detailed value-added accounts that provide information on the use of various types of labor (distinguished by educational attainment level) and capital in production. This is discussed in the subsection titled "Factor Input Requirements."

World Input-Output Tables: Concepts and Construction

In this subsection we outline the basic concepts and construction of our world input-output tables. Basically, a world input-output table (WIOT) is a combination of national input-output tables in which the use of products is broken down according to their origin. In contrast to the national input-output tables, this information is made explicit in the WIOT. For each country, flows of products both for intermediate and final use are split into domestically produced or imported. In addition, for imports, the WIOT shows which foreign *industry* produced the product. This is illustrated by the schematic outline for a WIOT in Table 5.2. It illustrates the simple case of three regions: 1) Country A, 2) Country B, and 3) the rest of the world. In the World Input-Output Database we will distinguish between 40 individual countries and the rest of the world, but the basic outline remains the same.

The rows in the WIOT indicate the use of output from a particular industry in a country. This can be intermediate use either in the country itself (use of domestic output) or by other countries (in which case it is exported). Output can also be for final use,[6] either by the country itself (final use of domestic output) or by other countries (in which case it is exported). Final use is indicated on the right side of the table, and this information can be used to measure the C matrix defined in Section Two, "GVC Incomes and Jobs: Methodology." The sum of all of the uses is equal to the output of an industry, denoted by Q in Section Two.

A fundamental accounting identity is that total use of output in a row equals total output of the same industry, as indicated in the respective column in the left-hand part of the table. The columns convey information on the technology of production, as they indicate the amounts of intermediate and factor inputs needed for production. The intermediates can be sourced from domestic industries or imported. This is the B matrix from Section Two. The residual between total output and total intermediate inputs is value-added. This is made up by compensation for production factors. It is the direct contribution of domestic factors to output. We prepare the F matrix from Section Two on this information after breaking out the compensation of various factor inputs as described in the next subsection, "Factor Input Requirements."

As building blocks for the WIOT, national supply-and-use tables (SUTs) were used; these are the core statistical sources from which

Table 5.2 Schematic Outline of World Input-Output Table (WIOT), Three Regions

	Intermediate industry			Final domestic			
	Country A	Country B	Rest of world	Country A	Country B	Rest of world	Total
Country A industry	Intermediate use of domestic output	Intermediate use by B of exports from A	Intermediate use by RoW of exports from A	Final use of domestic output	Final use by B of exports from A	Final use by RoW of exports from A	Output in A
Country B industry	Intermediate use by A of exports from B	Intermediate use of domestic output	Intermediate use by RoW of exports from B	Final use by A of exports from B	Final use of domestic output	Final use by RoW of exports from B	Output in B
Rest of world (RoW) industry	Intermediate use by A of exports from RoW	Intermediate use by B of exports from RoW	Intermediate use of domestic output	Final use by A of exports from RoW	Final use by B of exports from RoW	Final use of domestic output	Output in RoW
	Value-added	Value-added	Value-added				
	Output in A	Output in B	Output in RoW				

SOURCE: Authors' compilation.

national statistical institutes (NSIs) derive national input-output tables. In short, we derive time series from national SUTs. Benchmark national SUTs are linked over time through the use of the most recent National Accounts statistics on final demand categories, as well as through the use of gross output and value-added by detailed industry. This ensures both intercountry and intertemporal consistency of the tables. As such, the WIOT is built according to the conventions of the System of National Accounts and obeys various important accounting identities. National SUTs are linked across countries through detailed international trade statistics to create so-called international SUTs. This is based on a classification of bilateral import flows by end-use category (intermediate, consumer, or investment), in which intermediate inputs are split by country of origin. These international SUTs are used to construct the symmetric world input-output of the industry-by-industry type. See Timmer (2012) for a more elaborate discussion of construction methods, practical implementation, and detailed sources of the WIOT. Dietzenbacher et al. (2013) provide an in-depth technical discussion.

The construction of the WIOT has a number of distinct characteristics. First, we rely on national supply-and-use tables rather than input-output tables as our basic building blocks. SUTs are a natural starting point for this type of analysis, as they provide information on both products and industries. A supply table provides information on products produced by each domestic industry, and a use table indicates the use of each product by an industry or final user. The linking with international trade data, which is product-based, and with factor use, which is industry-based, can be naturally made in an SUT framework.[7]

Ideally, we would like to use official data on the destination of imported goods and services. However, in most countries these flows are not tracked by statistical agencies. Nevertheless, for imports, most do publish an input-output table constructed with the import proportionality assumption, applying a product's economy-wide import share for all use categories. For the United States, researchers have found that this assumption can be rather misleading, in particular at the industry level (Feenstra and Jensen 2012; Strassner, Yuskavage, and Lee 2009). Therefore, we are not using the official import matrices but instead use detailed trade data to make a split. Our basic data are the bilateral import flows of all countries covered in WIOD from all partners in the world at the HS6-digit product level, taken from the UN Comtrade database.

Based on the detailed description, products are allocated to three use categories: 1) intermediates, 2) final consumption, and 3) investment, effectively extending the UN Broad Economic Categories (BEC) classification. We find that import proportions differ widely across use categories and, importantly, also across country of origin. For example, imports by the Czech car industry from Germany contain a much higher share of intermediates than imports from Japan. This type of information is reflected in our WIOT by using detailed bilateral trade data. The domestic use matrix is derived as total use minus imports.

Another novel element in the WIOT is the use of data on trade in services. As yet, no standardized database on bilateral service flows exists. These flows have been collected from various sources—including the OECD, Eurostat, the International Monetary Fund (IMF), and the World Trade Organization (WTO)—checked for consistency, and integrated into a bilateral service trade database.

Clearly, the validity of the findings in this chapter relies heavily on the quality of the databases used. The WIOD has been constructed with the aim of making maximum use of the publicly available data on national input-output tables, international trade statistics, and production factor incomes. In the process of consolidating these separate databases, inconsistencies have been found and compromises made to arrive at an internally consistent world input-output table. For example, the well-known inconsistency between mirror trade flows in the UN Comtrade data was resolved by focusing on import flows only. Other issues relate to reexports of goods and trade in services that are not very well reflected in today's trade statistics. It is clear that present-day statistical systems are lagging behind the developments in today's world. In particular, trade in services and intangibles such as royalties and licences are still poorly reflected (see, e.g., Feenstra et al. [2010]; Houseman and Ryder [2010]). This should have priority in the future development of international trade statistics.

Factor Input Requirements

For factor input requirements, we collected country-specific data on detailed labor and capital inputs. This includes data on hours worked and on compensation for three labor types, as well as data on capital stocks and compensation. Labor types are distinguished on the basis of educational attainment levels, as defined in the International Standard Classification of Education (ISCED) (low-skilled: ISCED 1 + 2; medium-skilled: ISCED 3 + 4; and high-skilled: ISCED 5 + 6). These series are not part of the core set of national accounts statistics reported by NSIs, and additional material has been collected from employment and labor force statistics. For each country covered, we chose what we considered the best statistical source for consistent wage and employment data at the industry level. In most countries, this was the labor force survey (LFS). In most cases this needed to be combined with an earnings survey, as information on wages is often not included in the LFS. In other instances, an establishment survey or social security database was used. Care has been taken to arrive at series that are time-consistent, as most employment surveys are not designed to track developments over time, and breaks in methodology or coverage frequently occur.

Labor compensation of self-employed persons is not registered in the National Accounts, which, as emphasised by Krueger (1999), leads to an understatement of labor's share. This is particularly important for less advanced economies, which typically feature a large share of self-employed workers in industries like agriculture, trade, business, and personal services. We make an imputation by assuming that the compensation per hour of self-employment is equal to the compensation per hour of employees. For most advanced countries, labor data is constructed by extending and updating the EU KLEMS database (www.euklems.net) using the methodologies, data sources, and concepts described in O'Mahony and Timmer (2009). For other countries additional data has been collected according to the same principles.

Capital compensation is derived as gross value-added minus labor compensation, as defined above. It is the gross compensation for capital, including profits and depreciation allowances. Being a residual measure, it is the remuneration for capital in the broadest sense, including tangible capital (such as machinery and buildings), intangible (such as research and development [R&D], software, database development, branding, and organizational capital), mineral resources, land, and financial capital.

TRENDS IN GVC INCOMES OF MANUFACTURES

In this section, we explore trends in the distributions of value in global production chains using the decompositions introduced in Section Two. We decompose global expenditure on manufacturing products into compensation for factor services that are directly or indirectly needed in the production of these products. Throughout the chapter we use the phrase "global manufacturing" to indicate the set of all production activities directly or indirectly needed in producing final manufacturing goods. Note that this includes not only activities in the manufacturing sector but also production activities in all other sectors, such as agriculture, utilities, business services, and so on, that provide inputs in any stage of the production process. Next, we define "GVC income" as the income of all production factors that have been directly and indirectly used in the production of final manufacturing goods. World GVC income is the GVC income summed over all countries; it will be equal to world expenditure on manufacturing goods as we model all regions in the world in our empirical analysis. By definition, any dollar spent on final goods must end up as income for production factors somewhere in the world.

The share of a country in world GVC income is a novel indicator of the competitive strength of a nation. Compared to traditional competitiveness indicators like a country's share in world exports, it has three advantages. First, it indicates to what extent a country can compete with other nations in terms of *activities* related to global manufacturing, rather than competing in manufacturing *products* as measured by exports. Second, it is a reflection of an economy's strength to compete in both domestic and global markets. Countries might gain income by serving foreign demand, but might at the same time lose income in production for the domestic market. The income share of a country in global manufacturing measures the combined net effect. Third, income and employment effects of trade in tasks for separate groups of workers (such as low- and high-skilled) can also be determined in the same unified framework, as shown later on.

Throughout the chapter we will focus on GVC income in the production of final manufacturing goods. We denote these goods by the term "manufactures." Production systems of manufactures are highly prone to international fragmentation, as activities have a high degree of international contestability: They can be undertaken in any country with little variation in quality. It is important to note that GVCs of manufactures do not coincide with all activities in the manufacturing sector; neither do they coincide with all activities that are internationally contestable. Some activities in the manufacturing sector are geared toward production of intermediates for final nonmanufacturing products and are not part of GVCs of manufactures. On the other hand, GVCs of manufactures also include value-added outside the manufacturing sector (such as business services, transport, and communication and finance) and value-added in raw materials production. These indirect contributions will be explicitly accounted for through the modeling of input-output linkages across sectors.

Ideally, to measure competitiveness one would like to cover value-added in all activities that are internationally contestable, and not only those in the production of manufactures.[8] GVCs of services cannot be analyzed, however, as the level of observation for services in our data is not fine enough to zoom in on those services that are heavily traded, such as consultancy services. The lowest level of detail in the WIOD is "business services," which for the most part contains activities that are not internationally traded, and hence are much less interesting to analyze from a GVC perspective. This is all the more true for other services, such as personal or retail services. They require a physical interaction between the buyer and the provider of the service, and a major part of the value-added in these chains is effectively not internationally contestable. More detailed data on trade in, and production of, services is needed before meaningful GVC analyses of final services can be made.

GVC Incomes of Manufactures

Figure 5.2, Panel A, provides a comparison of the GVC incomes in advanced and emerging regions in the production of final manufacturing goods. The GVC income share of advanced countries (East Asia plus the United States, Canada, Australia, and the EU15) has declined from almost three-quarters in 1995 to just above half of world GVC income today. Emerging regions have rapidly increased their shares, and almost all of this increase was realized after 2003. Since 2004 the increase in the GVC income of emerging countries has always been higher than that of advanced countries, reaching a peak in 2008 at a time when advanced countries' GVC income stalled. The drop in the crisis year of 2009 was large for all countries, but recovery occurred much faster in the emerging economies (Figure 5.2, Panel B).

One might hypothesize that shifts in the composition of global manufacturing demand in terms of the type of products being demanded might also be a determinant of the decline of the advanced nations in global manufacturing production. However, the product structure of global demand remained stable over the period 1995 to 2009. Following Engel's law, the expenditure shares of food and other nondurable goods, such as apparel, shoes, furniture, and toys, were on a long-term declining trend. Expenditure on machinery and transport equipment was relatively stable, around 16 percent of the total, as increasing consumer and investment demand from emerging markets was counteracted by declining demand from mature economies. Also, demand for electrical machinery was stagnant in the long run. The only clear upward trend is found for chemical products—including gasoline, cosmetics, and medicines—demand for which has steadily increased around the world, going from 12 percent of global manufacturing expenditures in 1995 to 15 percent in 2008. But these global demand shifts are too small to account for the decline in advanced nations' GVC income. Instead, this decline is due to losses in the amount of value-added in each product's GVC. This will be analyzed in more detail in the remainder of this section.

In Figure 5.3 we show the shares of regions in world GVC income in the production of manufactures for the period from 1995 to 2011. The figure plots measures for five groups of countries: 1) members of the North American Free Trade Agreement (NAFTA) (Canada, Mexico, and the United States); 2) the European Union (EU), consisting of the 27 EU member states; 3) East Asia, consisting of Japan, South Korea, and Taiwan; 4) China; and 5) BRIIAT, which includes Brazil, Russia, India, Indonesia, Australia, and Turkey. In Table 5.3, additional data for 20 major individual economies can be found for 1995 and 2008. It should be kept in mind that international competition is not a zero-sum game, and declining shares in global GVC do not necessarily mean an absolute decline in GVC income in a region. On the contrary, in real

Figure 5.2 GVC Incomes in Advanced and Emerging Countries, All Manufactures, 1995–2011

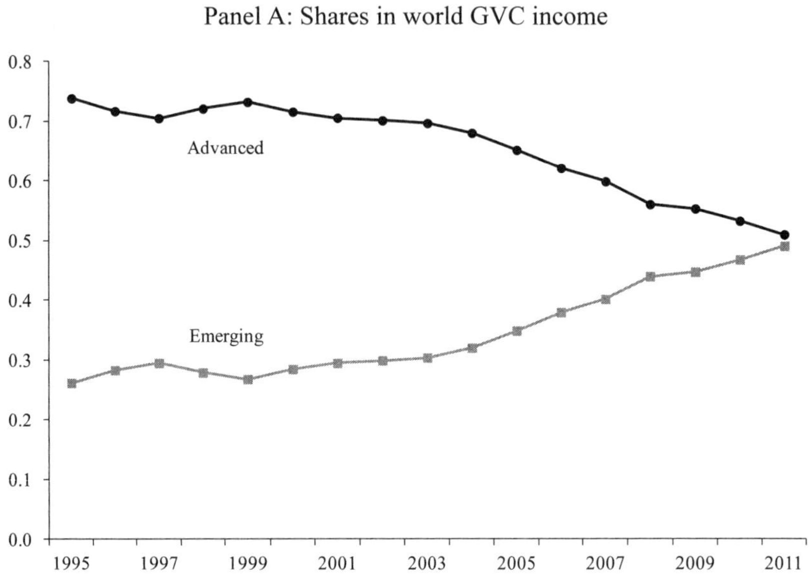

terms, world GVC income on manufactures (deflated by the U.S. Consumer Price Index) rose by about one-third over the period 1995–2008.

Figure 5.3 illustrates that the share of the NAFTA countries in world GVC income increased during the ICT bubble years, climbing as high as 30 percent, at which point their share was even higher than that of the EU. But it rapidly declined after 2001, reaching a low of 20 percent in 2008. The decline of the advanced nations taken as a whole is particularly due to the demise of East Asia, whose share has been dropping rapidly since the mid-1990s. While the shares of South Korea and Taiwan are still increasing, the GVC income share of Japan has been declining precipitously. In contrast, the EU's GVC income share has been relatively stable, only declining slowly over the period from 1995 to 2008. France, Italy, and the United Kingdom slowly lost some shares. The German share dropped rapidly in the latter 1990s but stabilized afterwards. These drops were compensated for by increasing shares for other EU countries, in particular the new member states. As is well known, the aftermath of the global financial crisis hit Europe par-

Figure 5.2 (continued)

Panel B: Annual change (in billions of 1995 US$)

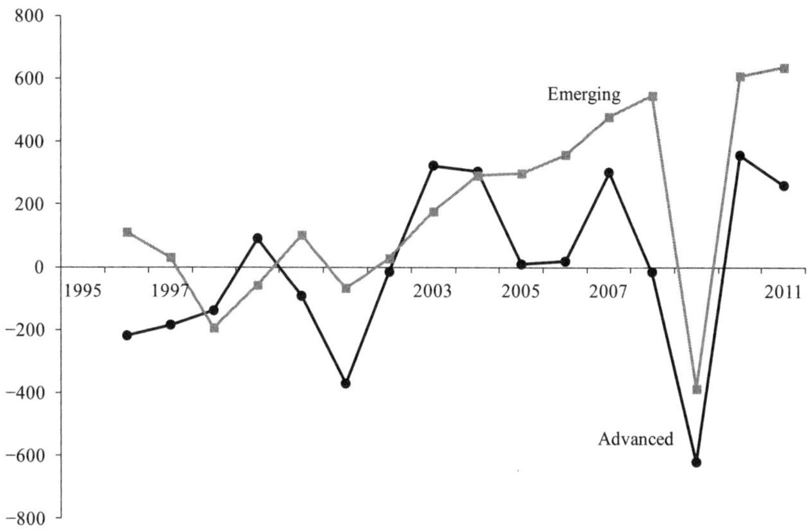

NOTE: "Advanced" nations include the EU15, Japan, Korea, Taiwan, Australia, Canada, and the United States. "Emerging" nations include all other countries in the world. National currencies have been converted to U.S. dollars with official exchange rates, deflated to 1995 prices with the U.S. Consumer Price Index (CPI). World GVC income is equal to world expenditures on manufacturing products at basic prices.
SOURCE: Authors' calculations based on World Input-Output Database. Series updated to 2011 in April 2012.

ticularly hard, and its share dropped sharply, from 32 percent in 2003 to 24 percent in 2011. On the flip side, the share of other regions in the world rapidly increased. China is mainly responsible for the increase of the emerging countries' share, because its share accelerated after its ascension to the WTO in 2000. In 2007 it overtook East Asia in terms of share. In 2009 the Chinese GVC income share overtook that of the combined countries of BRIIAT. And in 2011 its share was almost equal to that of the NAFTA region.[9]

One might argue that these shifts in regional GVC income shares are unsurprising, given the faster growth of China and other emerg-

Figure 5.3 Regional Shares in World GVC Income, All Manufactures, 1995–2011 (%)

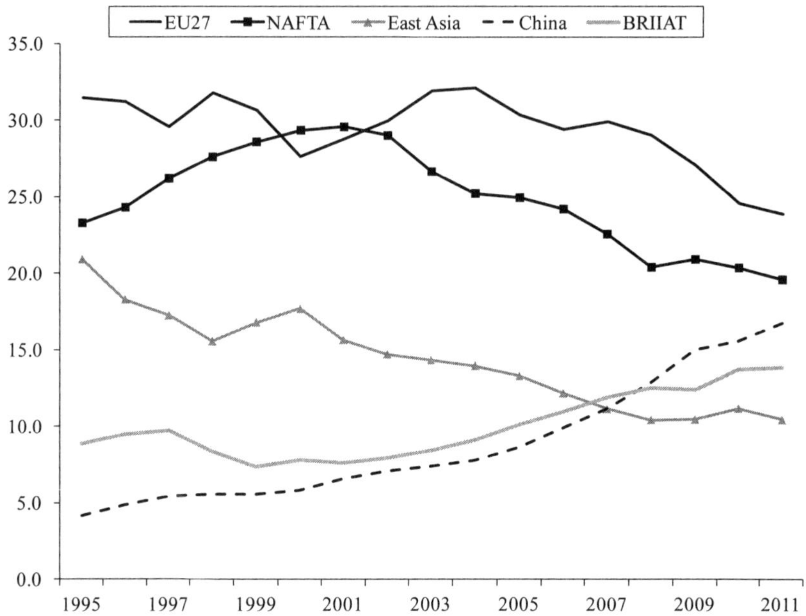

NOTE: Figure shows value-added by regions in the production of final manufacturing goods. "East Asia" includes Japan, South Korea, and Taiwan. "BRIIAT" includes Brazil, Russia, India, Indonesia, Australia, and Turkey. "EU27" includes all countries that have joined the European Union. "NAFTA" includes Canada, Mexico, and the United States. Shares do not add up to 100 percent, as the remainder is the share of all other countries in the world.

SOURCE: Authors' calculations based on World Input-Output Database, April 2012, updated to 2011.

ing economies vis-à-vis advanced regions. Higher consumption in the home economy would naturally lead to higher GVC incomes. But this is only true to the extent that demand for manufactures has a strong home production bias—that is, a bias mainly geared toward goods with a high level of domestic value-added. Given the high tradability of manufacturing goods, this home bias is not obvious, however. Increased Chinese demand for, say, chemicals or electronic equipment can be as easily served by imports as by Chinese domestic production. And in the latter case, a sizable share could still be captured by advanced countries

Table 5.3 Real GVC Income, All Manufactures (in billions of 1995 US$)

Country	1995	2008	Change
Advanced nations			
United States	1,312	1,373	62
Japan	1,154	676	−478
Germany	618	664	46
France	292	330	37
United Kingdom	254	260	6
Italy	289	353	64
Spain	126	171	44
Canada	124	190	66
Australia	68	112	45
South Korea	142	157	15
Netherlands	94	119	25
Other 10 advanced	390	459	69
Total 21 advanced	4,863	4,864	1
Emerging nations			
China	277	1,114	837
Russian Federation	80	246	166
Brazil	164	265	101
India	114	229	115
Mexico	99	208	109
Turkey	73	122	49
Indonesia	83	113	30
Poland	33	86	52
Czech Republic	14	41	27
Rest of world	786	1,396	610
Total emerging countries	1,723	3,820	2,097
World	6,586	8,684	2,098

NOTE: Real GVC indicates the value-added in countries to global output of final manufactures. It includes all manufactures and is in constant 1995 prices using the U.S. Consumer Price Index (CPI) as the deflator. Some numbers in "Change" column may be off by 1 because of rounding.

SOURCE: Authors' calculations based on World Input-Output Database, April 2012.

through the delivery of key intermediate inputs and services. The occurrence of falling shares in global GVC income for advanced regions in Figure 5.2 indicates that these regions failed to capture a large part of the value of the increased market for manufacturing goods in emerging economies. At the same time, the domestic value-added content of their own production declined. Both trends can be interpreted as a loss of competitiveness.

A number of caveats are in order. Shares in world GVC income are expressed in U.S. dollars using current exchange rates. For income changes over time, we deflate incomes in U.S. dollars to the 1995 U.S. dollar value using the U.S. Consumer Price Index (CPI). Exchange rates have fluctuated over the period considered: The dollar-to-euro rate[10] declined sharply over 1995–2001, followed by a steep rise, which by 2007 had returned it to near its 1995 value. The yen-to-dollar rate fluctuated around a long-term constant for this period. The yuan-to-dollar rate was effectively constant over this period, slightly appreciating at the end of the 2000s. The choice of the U.S. dollar as numéraire has no impact on the GVC income measure of a country relative to other countries. For example, expressing GVC income shares in yen or euros would give identical results. But it *will* affect the absolute levels of GVC incomes and hence comparisons over time within a country.

Second, one has to keep in mind that the location where the value is being added is not necessarily identical to where the generated income will eventually end up. The building of global production chains is not only through arms-length trade in intermediate inputs; it also involves sizable flows of investment, and part of the value-added in emerging regions will accrue as income to multinational firms headquartered in advanced regions through the ownership of capital. What is needed is to analyze capital income on a national rather than a domestic basis, as this chapter does in its data on foreign ownership. This type of information is notoriously hard to acquire, not least because of the notional relocation of profits for tax accounting purposes. Hence, further research is needed in this area (Baldwin and Kimura 1998; Lipsey 2010). The decline in East Asian GVC income is likely overestimated, as it is also related to the offshoring of activities to China, which effectively became the assembly place of East Asia. Income earned by East Asian capital is allocated to the place of production (in this case China) and not by ownership, as discussed in Section Two. This difference is probably larger for East Asian countries than for NAFTA or the EU, which have larger FDI flows within the region, so that they net out in regional aggregate numbers.

The Role of Domestic and Foreign Demand

By splitting the final demand vector in the decomposition given in Equation (5.2), we can analyze the importance of domestic versus foreign final demand in the generation of GVC income in a country. The GVC income due to foreign demand is identical to what Johnson and Noguera (2012) refer to as "exports of value-added."[11] Table 5.4 provides the share of GVC income of manufactures due to foreign demand for 20 major economies in the world. The overriding conclusion is that all countries have become increasingly dependent on foreign demand

Table 5.4 Percentage of Real GVC Income Due to Foreign Demand, All Manufactures

Country	1995	2008	Change
Advanced nations			
United States	25.9	33.0	7.1
Japan	24.6	41.8	17.2
Germany	46.3	69.9	23.6
France	53.1	60.0	7.0
United Kingdom	52.6	68.5	15.8
Italy	45.2	52.8	7.6
Spain	39.1	53.3	14.2
Canada	65.8	65.8	0.0
Australia	43.9	55.3	11.3
South Korea	45.2	67.8	22.6
Netherlands	79.3	87.8	8.5
Emerging nations			
China	35.3	48.7	13.5
Russian Federation	42.6	47.3	4.7
Brazil	15.7	26.0	10.3
India	17.7	29.3	11.6
Mexico	32.9	36.5	3.5
Turkey	22.5	35.3	12.8
Indonesia	28.5	38.7	10.2
Poland	42.7	63.0	20.3

NOTE: Numbers represent real GVC income for all manufactures and in constant 1995 prices using the U.S. Consumer Price Index (CPI) as a deflator. Some numbers in the "Change" column may be off by 0.1 because of rounding.

SOURCE: Authors' calculations based on World Input-Output Database, April 2012.

to generate GVC income of manufactures, with the exception of Canada. For all major mature economies, increases in foreign demand have been a necessary spur for slow or even negative growth in their value-added shares in domestic demand. Domestic demand was not a source of growth in the United States, and it contributed strongly to negative growth in Japan, as import substitution took place against a backdrop of stagnating domestic demand. The direction of this trend for advanced countries was to be expected, as the income elasticity of demand for manufactures is low, and in most countries domestic demand is increasingly served through imports with high foreign value-added. But this domestic decline was more than counteracted by a rapid increase in exports of value-added. The most extreme example of this shift toward foreign demand dependence is to be found in Germany, given the large size of its domestic market. In 1995, 46 percent of its GVC income was due to foreign final demand, and by 2008 this had increased to 70 percent. Also, dependence upon foreign demand in Japan, South Korea, Spain, and the United Kingdom rapidly increased over this period.

For emerging economies, changes in foreign demand have been important, but they also have strongly benefited from growth in domestic expenditure on manufacturing. In China, the share of GVC income due to foreign demand increased from 35 percent to 49 percent—which is high, but not outstanding when compared to that of countries of comparable size such as Japan or Germany. The share of foreign demand in Mexico and Russia did barely increase over this period; also, the share for India, while growing, is still at a relatively low level, indicating that the integration of these major emerging economies into world markets is still limited.

Sectoral Origin of GVC Income of Manufactures

The production of manufacturing goods involves a wide variety of activities, which do not take place only in the manufacturing sector. Using the decomposition technique outlined above, one can trace not only the country but also the sector in which value is added during the production process. Typically, the value that is added through activities in the manufacturing sector itself is around half the basic price value of a good, and declines over time. In Table 5.5 we provide for each country the share of a sector in the total value added by the country in

Table 5.5 Sectoral Shares in Total GVC Income, All Manufactures (% of total)

	Natural resources		Manufacturing		Services	
Country	1995	2008	1995	2008	1995	2008
Advanced						
United States	0.06	0.09	0.56	0.52	0.38	0.39
Japan	0.04	0.03	0.65	0.62	0.31	0.35
Germany	0.03	0.02	0.61	0.56	0.36	0.42
France	0.07	0.04	0.48	0.45	0.46	0.51
United Kingdom	0.07	0.07	0.60	0.48	0.34	0.45
Italy	0.05	0.03	0.57	0.52	0.38	0.44
Spain	0.09	0.05	0.54	0.51	0.37	0.43
Canada	0.12	0.19	0.54	0.44	0.34	0.37
Australia	0.20	0.26	0.42	0.34	0.37	0.39
South Korea	0.10	0.04	0.62	0.67	0.28	0.29
Netherlands	0.11	0.12	0.49	0.42	0.40	0.45
Emerging						
China	0.21	0.17	0.58	0.57	0.22	0.26
Russian Federation	0.20	0.21	0.42	0.39	0.38	0.40
Brazil	0.13	0.17	0.55	0.46	0.32	0.37
India	0.22	0.18	0.42	0.41	0.35	0.40
Mexico	0.21	0.22	0.49	0.49	0.30	0.29
Turkey	0.09	0.13	0.64	0.52	0.27	0.36
Indonesia	0.22	0.30	0.61	0.54	0.18	0.16
Poland	0.15	0.10	0.53	0.49	0.32	0.42

NOTE: The numbers represent the share of that sector in total value-added by a country's production of final manufacturing products. "Natural resource" includes the agriculture and mining industries (ISIC Rev. 3 industries A to C), "manufacturing" includes all manufacturing industries (D), and "services" all other industries (E to Q).
SOURCE: Authors' calculations based on World Input-Output Database, April 2012.

global manufacturing expenditure. This is done for 20 major economies in 1995 and 2008, distinguishing between three broad sectors: 1) natural resources, including the agriculture and mining industries (ISIC Rev. 3 industries A to C), 2) manufacturing, including all manufacturing industries (D), and 3) services including all other industries (E to Q). The table shows that the share of manufacturing has declined between 1995 and 2008 in all countries except South Korea and Mexico. The unweighted average share across all 20 countries declined from 54 percent to 50 percent. This partly reflects a shift away from traditional manufacturing activities, such as those carried out by blue-collar production workers, but also the outsourcing of white-collar activities by manufacturing firms to domestic services firms. Contributions from the natural resources sector are high and have increased over the 1995–2008 period in countries such as Australia, Canada, Indonesia, Mexico, Russia,[12] and Turkey. This pattern of value-added suggests that for resource-abundant countries, activities within manufacturing production networks are reinforcing their comparative advantage. Given India's low level of development, services contribute relatively much in that country, reflecting its well-developed business services sector, which delivers intermediate services to both domestic and foreign manufacturing firms. In China, the share of natural resources is declining, and activities in the services sector are starting to contribute more, but the level is still well below the contributions of services in Europe and the United States.

GVC INCOME OF MANUFACTURES BY PRODUCTION FACTOR

Our income data on labor and capital allow us to study which production factors have benefited from the changes in the regional distribution of global value-added. Increasing trade and integration of world markets have been related to increasing unemployment and stagnating relative wages of low- and medium-skilled workers in developed regions. On the other hand, those factors have offered new opportunities in developing regions for countries to employ their large supply of low-skilled workers. To study these trends, we decomposed value-added into four parts: 1) income for capital and income for labor, further split into 2) low-, 3) medium- and 4) high-skilled labor. High-skilled labor is defined as workers with a college degree or above. Medium-skilled workers have secondary schooling or above, including professional qualifications but below a college degree, and low-skilled have below secondary schooling. An estimate for the income of self-employed workers is included in labor compensation. The income for capital is the amount of value-added that remains after subtracting labor compensation. It is the gross compensation for capital, including profits and depreciation allowances. As a residual measure, it is the remuneration for capital in the broadest sense, including tangible, intangible, mineral resources, land, and financial capital.

In Figure 5.4 and Table 5.6 we provide a breakdown of GVC income by labor and capital for major regions. This is a breakdown of the GVC income discussed in the previous section, "Trends in Manufactures' GVC Incomes." At the global level, the share of GVC income that goes to labor is coming down, while the share of capital is increasing. In all regions, the compensation for capital is increasing relative to labor. Particularly in emerging regions, this increase is important and occurs faster than the labor income increase. This might be related to the low wage/rental ratios in these regions, which are still characterized by an abundant surplus of low-skilled workers from agricultural and informal urban sectors. In advanced regions, the increasing importance of capital might be a reflection of the increased investment in so-called intangible assets, which are becoming increasingly important for growth in advanced nations (Corrado and Hulten 2010).

It is important to note that the share captured by capital in emerging markets is known to be overestimated. Our approach is based on domestic production accounting for the location of the production factor and is silent on the ownership, as discussed before. In the case of labor income, this is unproblematic, since for most countries cross-border labor migration is relatively minor. Hence, labor income paid out in a particular country mostly benefits the workers of the country in which production takes place.

Worldwide, medium- and low-skilled workers are losing out to high-skilled workers, as the latter's share of GVC income is increasing. As expected, GVC income for low-skilled workers has increased strongly in China and in other emerging economies while declining in the advanced regions. In the United States and East Asia, the decline was particularly pronounced for medium-skilled workers. Within Europe, medium-skilled workers in Germany lost the biggest share, and in other European countries the income share going to low-skilled workers also declined. Income for high-skilled workers related to global manufacturing went up in most EU countries. This is not simply the result of a strong supply of higher-skilled labor replacing medium-skilled workers

Figure 5.4 GVC Income by Production Factor (in millions of 1995 US$), Change between 1995 and 2008

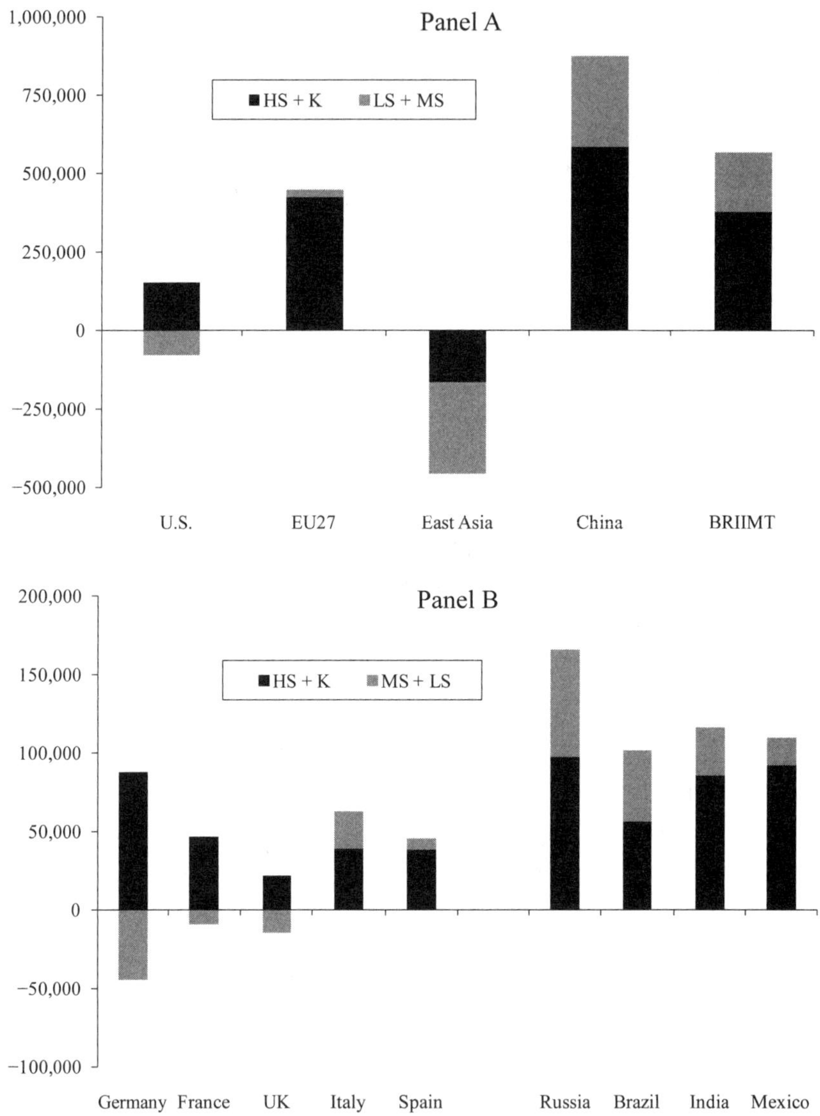

NOTE: Figure shows factor income earned by high-skilled labor and capital (HS + K) and by medium- and low-skilled labor (MS + LS). "EU27" includes all countries in the European Union. "BRIIMT" includes Brazil, Russia, India, Indonesia, Mexico, and Turkey.
SOURCE: Authors' calculations based on World Input-Output Database, April 2012, updated to 2011.

Table 5.6 GVC Income by Production Factor and Region (shares in world GVC income)

	Value-added by labor		Value-added by capital		Value-added total	
	1995	2008	1995	2008	1995	2008
EU27	21.5	18.9	9.7	9.8	31.2	28.7
United States	12.8	9.5	7.4	6.7	20.2	16.2
East Asia	12.9	6.1	8.1	4.6	21.0	10.7
China	2.0	5.2	2.1	7.8	4.2	13.0
BRIIMT	4.1	6.1	5.1	7.4	9.3	13.5
Other	6.4	7.3	7.9	10.6	14.3	17.9
World	59.7	53.1	40.3	46.9	100.0	100.0
Advanced	47.1	34.4	25.5	21.2	72.6	55.5
Emerging	12.6	18.8	14.9	25.7	27.4	44.5
	Value-added by high-skilled		**Value-added by medium-skilled**		**Value-added by low-skilled**	
	1995	2008	1995	2008	1995	2008
EU27	4.8	6.0	10.0	8.9	6.6	4.0
United States	4.3	4.1	7.4	4.9	1.1	0.5
East Asia	3.2	2.1	7.2	3.3	2.5	0.6
China	0.1	0.4	0.7	1.8	1.3	3.0
BRIIMT	0.8	1.4	1.7	3.0	1.7	1.7
Other	0.8	1.5	2.3	2.9	3.4	3.0
World	14.0	15.5	29.1	24.8	16.6	12.8
Advanced	12.4	12.2	24.8	17.2	10.0	5.0
Emerging	1.6	3.3	4.3	7.6	6.6	7.8

NOTE: "East Asia" includes Japan, South Korea, and Taiwan. "EU27" designates the countries that had joined the EU as of January 1, 2013. "BRIIMT" includes Brazil, Russia, India, Indonesia, Mexico, and Turkey. "Other" is the rest of the world. Skill categories classify workers by their educational attainment levels. World income is equal to world expenditures on manufacturing products at basic prices. Some numbers may not sum to total because of rounding.

SOURCE: Authors' calculations based on World Input-Output Database, April 2012.

but essentially carrying out the same activities; if this were the case, the wages for high-skilled workers should have dropped and the increase in GVC income for high-skilled workers would be limited. However, relative wages for high-skilled workers did not show this pattern (see Timmer et al. 2013).

GVC JOBS IN MANUFACTURES

Many policy concerns surrounding globalization issues are ultimately about jobs—good jobs in particular. The disappearance of manufacturing jobs in advanced nations is occasionally linked to production fragmentation and the associated offshoring of activities; see Bardhan, Jaffee, and Kroll (2013) for an overview. It is thus useful to look at the structure of employment in global value chains and analyze the changes in the characteristics of workers directly and indirectly involved in the production of manufacturing goods—in short, GVC jobs in manufactures.[13] For each country, we will measure the number of workers involved in the domestic territory. As the mobility of labor is much lower than that of capital, GVC jobs will be closer to a national concept than GVC income. We will characterize GVC workers by sector of employment and level of skills. In the next subsection, "The Shift toward Service Jobs in GVCs of Manufactures," we show that only about half of the workers in manufacturing GVCs are actually employed in the manufacturing sector. The other half are employed in nonmanufacturing industries delivering intermediates, and this share is growing. In most countries, GVC job increase in services is even higher than job loss in manufacturing. In the subsection titled "Specialization in High-Skilled Activities in Advanced Countries," on p. 154, we analyze the skill structure of GVC workers and find that there has been a shift away from low-skilled toward high-skilled workers for advanced nations. This increase is faster than the trend in the overall economy, suggesting increased specialization of advanced countries in GVC activities performed by high-skilled workers. This is in line with broad Heckscher-Ohlin predictions of which countries will see a comparative advantage when possibilities for international production fragmentation increase.

The Shift Toward Service Jobs in GVCs of Manufactures

By using the number of workers rather than value-added per unit of output in each industry-country as the requirement vector in Equation (5.1), we can trace the number of workers directly and indirectly involved in the production of manufacturing goods, and their sector of employment. Developments in the 20 main countries over the period from 1995 to 2008 are shown in Table 5.7. The first two columns indicate the share of manufacturing GVC workers as a percentage of the overall workforce in the economy. In the next columns the sectoral structure of employment of these workers is shown. Three sectors are considered—1) agriculture, 2) manufacturing and 3) services (which also include mining, construction, and utilities)—followed by a fourth column for "All sectors." The first set of four columns refers to the absolute number of GVC workers by sector in 2008, while the latter set of four columns refers to the change over the period 1995–2008. Two main facts clearly stand out:

1) The declining importance of global production of manufactures for overall employment in most advanced nations
2) The strong shift in the sector of employment of these workers away from the manufacturing sector toward the services sector

The first two columns of Table 5.7 show the decline in importance of GVCs of manufactures in providing jobs in the economies of all countries except China and Turkey. The job losses in Japan and the United States are major, around 2.9 and 4.6 million, respectively. Also, job loss in the United Kingdom stands out, as more than 1.6 million GVC jobs disappeared in that country alone. The only exception to this trend in advanced countries is Germany: In 2008, 26 percent of German employment was involved in the global production of manufactures, which is the highest share across all advanced countries.

Another important finding on the basis of Table 5.7 is the strong shift toward service jobs in the global production of manufactures since 1995. Faster growth (or slower declines) in service jobs than in manufacturing can be seen in all major advanced countries. As a result, in 2008, the manufacturing sector accounted for about half of the total number of GVC jobs in manufactures in advanced countries. The other

Table 5.7 GVC Workers in Manufactures, 1995 and 2008

	GVC workers in manufactures, as share of all workers in the economy (%)		GVC workers in manufactures in 2008 (in thousands), employed in				Change in GVC workers in manufactures between 1995 and 2008 (in thousands), employed in			
	1995	2008	Agriculture	Manufacturing	Services	All sectors	Agriculture	Manufacturing	Services	All sectors
Advanced										
United States	16.0	11.1	1,143	8,837	6,892	16,872	−331	−3,144	−1,138	−4,612
Japan	22.6	19.4	1,298	6,491	4,417	12,207	−794	−2,225	148	−2,871
Germany	26.8	26.4	400	5,481	4,766	10,647	−161	−666	1,388	561
France	22.0	18.7	303	2,195	2,355	4,853	−96	−423	368	−151
United Kingdom	20.1	12.6	115	1,946	1,931	3,992	−128	−1,148	−347	−1,624
Italy	29.1	25.5	333	3,553	2,559	6,444	−192	−234	517	91
Spain	23.2	17.5	271	1,827	1,494	3,592	−97	185	353	440
Canada	20.8	16.0	157	1,138	1,482	2,777	−102	−136	193	−45
Australia	18.2	14.5	165	641	855	1,661	−48	3	196	150
South Korea	29.7	22.8	655	2,646	2,077	5,378	−468	−735	524	−679
Netherlands	22.8	19.0	89	643	929	1,661	−42	−87	158	29
Emerging										
China	31.7	33.3	121,342	87,568	49,468	258,378	9,963	20,508	11,965	42,436
Russian Federation	24.7	21.9	4,259	6,749	6,228	17,237	−1,403	−2,120	2,198	−1,325
Brazil	29.6	28.7	8,347	9,490	9,823	27,660	−705	2,450	4,118	5,863
India	27.9	27.3	57,926	41,933	26,483	126,343	2,118	10,896	7,025	20,039
Mexico	30.3	24.4	2,817	6,128	3,205	12,150	−400	1,403	1,121	2,124

Turkey	27.1	30.4	1,778	3,115	1,554	6,446	−341	620	584	863
Indonesia	32.1	25.6	13,921	7,427	5,725	27,073	−1,899	−425	1,380	−944
Poland	31.0	28.8	917	2,278	1,347	4,542	−468	81	368	−19
Czech Republic	30.8	30.9	93	990	553	1,636	−59	74	35	50

NOTE: GVC workers are workers directly or indirectly involved in the production of manufacturing goods. Columns 3 through 6 indicate the total number of GVC workers by sector in 2008; columns 7 through 10 indicate the change in the number of GVC workers by sector between 1995 and 2008. The last column shows the change in the total number of workers in the economy for that period. Some numbers in the "All sectors" columns may be off by 1 because of rounding.

SOURCE: Authors' calculations based on World Input-Output Database, April 2012.

half of those jobs are found in agriculture and even more so in services—workers who are involved in the production of intermediate goods and services used in the manufacturing process. These findings testify to the increasing intertwining of manufacturing and service activities.

Following Baumol's cost disease hypothesis, one might argue that this shift in the sectoral distribution of the GVC jobs might be interpreted as the result of differential productivity growth in manufacturing and services. But while there is clear evidence that productivity growth in manufacturing is higher than in services overall, this does not necessarily hold for the service activities in GVCs of manufactures. These only form a subset of the services sector, and they involve in particular intermediate services such as wholesaling, transportation, finance, and several business services.[14] These activities are generally open for international competition and likely to have much higher rates of innovation and productivity growth than service activities for domestic demand, which are dominated by personal services, education, health, and public administration. Hence, it seems more likely that our findings are indicative of a fundamental shift in the type of activities carried out by advanced countries in the global production of manufactures—a shift away from blue-collar manufacturing to white-collar service activities. This hypothesis is confirmed when one analyzes the skill content of GVC jobs, as is done in the next subsection.

In the major emerging economies, most of the jobs are still added in the manufacturing sector, as is to be expected. For China, India, Mexico, and Turkey, job increases in manufacturing outnumber those in the services sector. In Brazil, however, services job growth appears to be more important. Even more strongly, in Indonesia and Russia the number of jobs in the production of manufactures has declined. These countries actually lost jobs overall for the period 1995–2008 and seem to have entered a premature deindustrialization phase.

Specialization in High-Skilled Activities in Advanced Countries

In a world with international production fragmentation, the broad Heckscher-Ohlin predictions will still hold: Countries will carry out activities for which local value-added content is relatively intensive amongst their abundant factors. In fact, increased opportunities for international production fragmentation may have the tendency to magnify the comparative advantage of countries, as suggested by Baldwin and Evenett (2012). A simple example will illustrate. Assume two goods, A and B, which are both produced with two activities: a low-skilled (LS) and a high-skilled (HS) activity. Before unbundling, Goods A and B are bundles of production activities with different skill intensities. Assume that Good A is on average more skill-intensive than Good B, as the HS activity is more important in the production of A than of B. A relatively skill-abundant country would specialize in the production of A, and a skill-scarce country in the production of B. After unbundling, each nation specializes in specific production activities. The skill-abundant country will specialize in the HS activities in the production of both goods, and the skill-scarce country in the LS activities for those goods. As a result, the potential range of comparative advantages across countries in activities will be greater than in the final products (see, e.g., Deardorff [2001]).[15]

To test this prediction, we analyze the number of workers by skill type needed in GVCs of manufactures using Equation (5.1) in combination with a skill requirement vector. This vector is based on a characterization of workers in each industry and country by their observable educational attainment levels, as described in Section Three, "The World Input-Output Database (WIOD)." This delivers the number of low- (LS), medium- (MS) and high-skilled (HS) GVC workers for a particular year. Results are given in Table 5.8. We find that during 1995–2008, in all advanced countries combined, the increase in high-skilled jobs was 4.6 million. Medium-skilled jobs declined by nearly 3.8 million, and the drop in low-skilled jobs was even bigger—9.7 million. This pattern of high-skilled jobs growing faster (or declining slower) than medium- and low-skilled jobs can be found for most countries. But there are some regional differences. In the United States, employment in global production of manufactures dropped for all workers, in particular the medium-skilled. This is a well-known phenomenon that characterizes a broader segment of the U.S. economy and has been extensively studied (see, e.g., Autor [2010]). More surprising is the finding that the number of high-skilled jobs has also declined. This is in stark contrast to Japan and the major EU countries: There, less-skilled jobs also dwindled, but this was at least in part compensated for by increasing opportunities for high-skilled jobs.

Table 5.8 Change in Number of Workers in Global Production of Final Manufactures by Skill Type, 1995 and 2008 (in thousands)

Country	Low	Medium	High	Total
United States	−1,125	−3,286	−201	−4,612
Japan	−1,834	−1,399	361	−2,871
Germany	−168	115	614	561
France	−768	52	566	−151
United Kingdom	−1,236	−560	172	−1,624
Italy	−1,201	853	439	91
Spain	−507	391	556	440
Canada	−118	−105	177	−45
Australia	−84	141	94	150
South Korea	−1,110	−335	766	−679
Netherlands	−119	−54	202	29
Other 10 advanced	−1,441	425	840	−176
Total 21 advanced	−9,711	−3,762	4,587	−8,886
All other countries	56,214	64,370	19,393	139,977
World	46,503	60,607	23,981	131,091

NOTE: Figures represent changes in the number of workers (including both employees and self-employed) involved in global production of final manufactures between 1995 and 2008, split into the number of low-skilled, medium-skilled, and high-skilled workers based on educational attainment. Some numbers may be off by 1 because of rounding.

SOURCE: Authors' calculations based on World Input-Output Database, April 2012.

CONCLUSION

A global-value-chain perspective has profound implications for how one thinks of competitiveness and growth. It highlights the importance of global production networks and the increasing interrelation of consumption, production, and income across national boundaries through the trade of goods and services. Enhancing competitiveness and growth is increasingly about capturing a larger share of global value chains—in particular, of products for which global demand is growing (Porter 1990). This rise of global value chains (GVCs) is also posing new challenges to analyses of international trade and measures of countries' competitiveness.

In this chapter, we take a macro perspective and analyze the value-added of production for a wide set of manufacturing product groups. This is done through a newly developed accounting method in which we build upon an input-output modeling of the world economy in the tradition of Leontief (1949). The novelty of our approach is that we trace the value added by all labor and capital that is directly and indirectly used for the production of final manufactures. We call this "GVC income." We also introduce the related concept of "GVC jobs," which connotes the number of jobs directly and indirectly needed in the production of final goods. To measure GVC incomes and jobs for a wide set of countries in the world, we use the global input-output tables and supplementary labor accounts from the World Input-Output Database, available at www.wiod.org and described in Timmer (2012).

The chapter presents new evidence on the main changes in GVC income and jobs across both mature and developing countries. Taken together, the results show that international fragmentation in the production of manufactures has been accompanied by a rapid shift toward higher-skilled activities in advanced nations. These activities are increasingly carried out in the services sector and no longer in the manufacturing sector itself. As such, the shift contributes to the so-called job polarization in advanced economies, as the displaced manufacturing workers are likely to be absorbed into personal and distributional services, where low-skilled employment opportunities are still growing (Goos, Manning, and Salomons 2011). Emerging economies are taking up increasing shares in global GVC income; much of this increase has been driven by rapid growth in China after its accession to the WTO in 2001. We also find increasing intertwining of manufacturing and services activities, which argues against a myopic view of manufacturing jobs in discussions on GVC issues. Rather than focusing on the particular sector in which jobs are lost or created, the discussion should be led by a view toward the activities that are carried out in GVCs, irrespective of the sector in which they are ultimately classified. Thinking in terms of sectors is basically a relic of a world where fragmentation of production, both domestically and internationally, had not progressed far.

Although the model to measure GVC income and jobs is relatively straightforward, it is clear that the validity of the findings relies heavily on the quality of the database used. The WIOD is a prototype database developed mainly to provide a proof-of-concept, and it is up to the statistical community to bring international input-output tables into the realm of official statistics. The development work done by the OECD (Ahmad, Chapter 6 of this volume) is certainly a step in the right direction. Various weak areas in data remain, particularly in the measurement of trade in services and intangibles. In addition, because of the lack of firm-level data matching national input-output tables, one currently has to rely on the assumption that all firms in an industry have a similar production structure. If various types of firms, in particular exporters, have a different production technology and input sourcing structure (i.e., they import larger shares), more detailed data might reveal a bias in the results presented here. More information on the ownership of capital income, which is currently measured on a domestic basis rather than on a national basis, is also desirable. This is far from easy, though, and in pursuing this line of investigation one needs to trace not only the nationality of the firms involved but also the nationality of the ultimate claimants of residual profits.

Arguably the most important area where more study is needed is in tracing where in the value chain the profits from lead firms are realized, as well as how these are recorded in the current statistical system. For example, the product case studies by Dedrick, Kraemer, and Linden (2010), among others, suggest that the profits made by the lead firms in the chains can only be inferred by comparing the final purchase and exfactory prices of the product, which include the trade margins (see also Gereffi 1999). The use of brand names, software, knowledge systems, and other intangibles of the lead firm by other firms in the chain is typically not compensated for by a direct money flow from the users. Rather, the compensation is realized indirectly through the ability of the lead firm to have the exclusive right to sell the particular product with a premium through its own (or through other tightly controlled) sales channels. This indirect compensation takes place in value chains that are completely within a multinational enterprise, but it also arises in chains that are to a large extent organized through arm's-length transactions. When the residual profits are realized—in other words, when manufacturing firms sell to final consumers—this is picked up in our GVC income measure. But alternative value-chain arrangements are feasible.

One particular example is the existence of so-called factoryless goods producers (FGPs), which are proliferating in the United States.

These are firms that are manufacturer-like in that they perform many of the tasks and activities found in manufacturing establishments themselves, except for the actual manufacturing production process. In the current U.S. statistical system they are classified in wholesaling, and their output is recorded as a wholesale margin rather than as manufacturing sales. The value-added of these firms should clearly be part of GVC incomes of manufactures but are currently not picked up, since GVC income is measured at basic prices, which means that trade and transport margins associated with final consumption are not included in GVC incomes. This might bias downwards the total GVC income for the United States compared to other countries to the extent that FGP production is more prominent in this country than in other countries. The scope for this bias is not particularly large, however. Bernard and Fort (2013) suggest that reclassifying the FGPs to the manufacturing sector would increase reported U.S. manufacturing output in 2007 by about 5 percent in a conservative estimate and by a maximum of 17 percent using a more liberal set of assumptions. A deeper understanding of the workings of global value chains is clearly needed before our measurement systems will adequately reflect all of their intricacies.

Notes

A draft version of this chapter was prepared for the conference "Measuring the Effects of Globalization," held February 28–March 1, 2013, in Washington, D.C., and organized by the W.E. Upjohn Institute for Employment Research. It is a spin-off from the work done under the World Input-Output Database (WIOD) project, which was funded by the European Commission's Directorate-General for Research and Innovation as part of the Seventh Framework Programme, Theme 8: Socio-Economic Sciences and Humanities, Grant Agreement No. 225 281. We gratefully acknowledge the helpful comments we received from the conference participants and in particular from Susan Houseman, Michael Mandel, Carol Corrado, Brad Jensen, and Robert Koopman.

1. Additional applications of the GVC income concept and analysis of fragmentation can be found in Timmer et al. (2014) and Los, Timmer, and de Vries (2014).
2. This identity does not hold true at the country level, as countries can have current account imbalances driving a wedge between value-added produced and final consumption value.
3. See Miller and Blair (2009) for an introduction to input-output analysis.
4. Throughout the paper, we analyze final expenditure, including private and government consumption, and investment.

5. Variations of this approach are also used in the burgeoning literature on trade in value-added, and our approach is related to the work by Koopman, Wang, and Wei (2014) and in particular the work by Johnson and Noguera (2012). But rather than using Leontief's insight to analyze factor content of trade flows, we focus on analyses of global value distributions.
6. Final use includes consumption by households, government and nonprofit organizations, and gross capital formation.
7. Because industries also have secondary production, a simple mapping of industries and products is not feasible.
8. When considering all goods and services produced, the GVC income of a country is equal to gross domestic product when final demand for all goods and services in the world economy are taken into account. Hence, for a meaningful analysis, one has to limit the group of products, and we focus on those products for which production processes are most fragmented and which can be analyzed with the data at hand.
9. We do not show the value-added by the "Rest of the World," consisting of all countries not covered individually in the world input-output database but for which an estimate has been made as a group (see Section Three, "The World Input-Output Database [WIOD]"). Its share in global GVC income rose from 14 percent in 1995 to 17 percent in 2008.
10. The euro was introduced in 2001. For the period before 2001, we are referring to the Deutsche Mark.
11. Johnson and Noguera (2012) focused on foreign final demand for all goods and services, not only on final manufactures as we do here.
12. The share of the natural resource sector in Russia is severely underestimated, since part of the oil and gas production is classified under wholesale services rather than under mining in the Russian national accounts. Adding the wholesale sector would almost double the natural resource share in 2008.
13. We will use the term "jobs" instead of "number of workers" as shorthand. But the underlying data pertains to number of workers rather than jobs. Ideally, one would like to measure hours worked.
14. It should be noted that these numbers exclude any jobs involved in the retailing of manufacturing goods, as we analyze final demand at the basic price concept.
15. Following this traditional international trade theory, having a greater range of comparative advantages across countries would generate higher welfare improvements from trade. These models are essentially comparative, static of nature, and they disregard any dynamic effects. In the innovation and business literature, it has been recently argued that the separation of high-skilled, innovative activities in advanced countries from production in emerging economies will in the long run lead to a decline of innovation activity. In this literature, the spillovers from manufacturing and innovation activities are central (see, e.g., Pisano and Shih [2012]).

References

Ali-Yrkkö, Jyrki, Petri Rouvinen, Timo Seppälä, and Pekka Ylä-Anttila. 2011. "Who Captures Value in Global Supply Chains? Case Nokia N95 Smartphone." Keskusteluaiheita Discussion Paper No. 1240. Helsinki: Elinkeinoelaman Tutkimuslaitos: The Research Institute of the Finnish Economy.

Autor, David. 2010. *The Polarization of Job Opportunities in the U.S. Labor Market: Implications for Employment and Earnings*. Washington, DC: Center for American Progress and the Hamilton Project.

Baldwin, Richard E. 2006. "Globalisation: The Great Unbundling(s)." In *Globalisation Challenges for Europe: Report by the Secretariat of the Economic Council*. Helsinki: Office of the Prime Minister of Finland, pp. 11–54.

Baldwin, Richard E., and Simon J. Evenett. 2012. "Value Creation and Trade in 21st Century Manufacturing: What Policies for UK Manufacturing?" In *The UK in a Global World: How Can the UK Focus on Steps in Global Value Chains That Really Add Value?*, David Greenaway, ed. London: Centre for Economic Policy Research, pp. 71–128.

Baldwin, Robert E., and Fukunari Kimura. 1998. "Measuring U.S. International Goods and Services Transactions." In *Geography and Ownership as Bases for Economic Accounting*, Robert E. Baldwin, Robert E. Lipsey, and J. David Richardson, eds. Studies in Income and Wealth 59. Chicago: University of Chicago Press, pp. 9–48.

Bardhan, Ashok, Dwight M. Jaffee, and Cynthia A. Kroll. 2013. *The Oxford Handbook of Offshoring and Global Employment*. Oxford: Oxford University Press.

Bernard, Andrew B., and Teresa C. Fort. 2013. "Factoryless Goods Producers in the U.S." NBER Working Paper No. 19396. Cambridge, MA: National Bureau of Economic Research.

Corrado, Carol A., and Charles R. Hulten. 2010. "How Do You Measure a 'Technological Revolution?'" *American Economic Review* 100(2): 99–104.

Deardorff, Alan V. 2001. "Fragmentation across Cones." In *Fragmentation: New Production Patterns in the World Economy*, Sven W. Arndt and Henryk Kierzkowski, eds. Oxford: Oxford University Press, pp. 35–51.

Dedrick, Jason, Kenneth L. Kraemer, and Greg Linden. 2010. "Who Profits from Innovation in Global Value Chains? A Study of the iPod and Notebook PCs." *Industrial and Corporate Change* 19(1): 81–116.

Dietzenbacher, Erik, Bart Los, Robert Stehrer, Marcel P. Timmer, and Gaaitzen J. de Vries. 2013. "The Construction of World Input-Output Tables in the WIOD Project." *Economic Systems Research* 25(1): 71–98.

Feenstra, Robert C., and J. Bradford Jensen. 2012. "Evaluating Estimates of Materials Offshoring from U.S. Manufacturing." NBER Working Paper No. 17916. Cambridge, MA: National Bureau of Economic Research.

Feenstra, Robert C., Robert E. Lipsey, Lee G. Branstetter, C. Fritz Foley, James Harrigan, J. Bradford Jensen, Lori Kletzer, Catherine Mann, Peter K. Schott, and Greg C. Wright. 2010. "Report on the State of Available Data for the Study of International Trade and Foreign Direct Investment." NBER Working Paper No. 16254. Cambridge, MA: National Bureau of Economic Research.

Fukao, Kyoji, Hikari Ishido, and Keiko Ito. 2003. "Vertical Intra-Industry Trade and Foreign Direct Investment in East Asia." *Journal of the Japanese and International Economies* 17(4): 468–506.

Gereffi, Gary. 1999. "International Trade and Industrial Upgrading in the Apparel Commodity Chain." *Journal of International Economics* 48(1): 37–70.

Goos, Maarten, Alan Manning, and Anna Salomons. 2011. "Explaining Job Polarization: The Roles of Technology, Offshoring, and Institutions." Discussion Paper No. 11.34. Leuven, Belgium: Catholic University of Leuven.

Grossman, Gene M., and Esteban Rossi-Hansberg. 2006. "The Rise of Offshoring: It's Not Wine for Cloth Anymore." In *The New Economic Geography: Effects and Policy Implications*. A Symposium Sponsored by the Federal Reserve Bank of Kansas City. Kansas City, MO: Federal Reserve Bank of Kansas City, pp. 59–102.

Houseman, Susan N., and Kenneth F. Ryder Jr. 2010. *Measurement Issues Arising from the Growth of Globalization: Conference Summary*. Kalamazoo, MI: W.E. Upjohn Institute for Employment Research; and Washington, DC: National Academy of Public Administration.

Institute of Developing Economies, Japan External Trade Organization (IDE-JETRO). 2006. *Asian International Input-Output Table 2000*. Chiba City, Japan: Institute of Developing Economies, Japan External Trade Organization.

Johnson, Robert C., and Guillermo Noguera. 2012. "Accounting for Intermediates: Production Sharing and Trade in Value Added." *Journal of International Economics* 86(2): 224–236.

Koopman, Robert, Zhi Wang, and Shang-Jin Wei. 2014. "Tracing Value-Added and Double Counting in Gross Exports." *American Economic Review* 104(2): 459–494.

Krueger, Alan B. 1999. "Measuring Labor's Share." *American Economic Review* 89(2): 45–51.

Leontief, Wassily. 1949. "Structural Matrices of National Economies." *Econometrica* 17(Suppl.): 273–282.

Lipsey, Robert E. 2010. "Measuring the Location of Production in a World of Intangible Productive Assets, FDI, and Intrafirm Trade." *Review of Income and Wealth* 56(S1): S99–S110.

Los, Bart, Marcel P. Timmer, and Gaaitzen J. de Vries. 2014. "How Global Are Global Value Chains? A New Approach to Measure International Fragmentation." *Journal of Regional Science.*

Miller, Ronald E., and Peter D. Blair. 2009. *Input-Output Analysis: Foundations and Extensions*. 2nd ed. Cambridge: Cambridge University Press.

Narayanan, Badri, and Terrie L. Walmsley, eds. 2008. *Global Trade, Assistance, and Production: The GTAP 7 Data Base*. West Lafayette, IN: Purdue University, Center for Global Trade Analysis.

O'Mahony, Mary, and Marcel P. Timmer. 2009. "Output, Input, and Productivity Measures at the Industry Level: The EU KLEMS Database." *Economic Journal* 119(538): F374–F403.

Pisano, Gary P., and Willy C. Shih. 2012. *Producing Prosperity: Why America Needs a Manufacturing Renaissance*. Boston: Harvard Business Review Press.

Porter, Michael E. 1990. *The Competitive Advantage of Nations*. New York: Free Press.

Strassner, Erich H., Robert E. Yuskavage, and Jennifer Lee. 2009. "Imported Inputs and Industry Contributions to Economic Growth: An Assessment of Alternative Approaches." Paper presented at the Upjohn/NAPA conference "Measurement Issues Arising from the Growth of Globalization," held in Washington, DC, November 6–7.

Timmer, Marcel P., ed. 2012. *The World Input-Output Database (WIOD): Contents, Sources, and Methods*. Brussels: European Commission. http://www.wiod.org/publications/source_docs/WIOD_sources.pdf (accessed February 25, 2014).

Timmer, Marcel P., Abdul Azeez Erumban, Bart Los, Robert Stehrer, and Gaaitzen J. de Vries. 2014. "Slicing Up Global Value Chains." *Journal of Economic Perspectives* 28(2): 99–118.

Timmer, Marcel P., Bart Los, Robert Stehrer, and Gaaitzen J. de Vries. 2013. "Fragmentation, Incomes, and Jobs: An Analysis of European Competitiveness." *Economic Policy* 28(76): 613–661.

Yamano, Norihiko, and Nadim Ahmad. 2006. "The OECD Input-Output Database: 2006 Edition." OECD Science, Technology, and Industry Working Paper No. 2006/8. Paris: Organisation for Economic Co-operation and Development.

6
Measuring Trade in Value-Added and Beyond

Nadim Ahmad
Organisation for Economic Co-operation and Development

Global value chains (GVCs) have become a dominant feature of today's global economy. This growing process of international fragmentation of production, driven by technological progress, cost, trade policy reforms, and access to resources and markets, has challenged the conventional wisdom on how we look at and interpret trade and, in particular, the policies that we develop around it. Indeed, taken by themselves, traditional measures of trade, which record gross flows of goods and services each and every time they cross borders, may lead policymakers to make misguided decisions.

In practice, two main approaches (micro and macro) have been used to shed light on this issue. The former is perhaps best characterized by the well-known Apple iPod example (Dedrick, Kraemer, and Linden 2010), which showed that of the $144 factory-gate price of an iPod dispatched from China, less than 10 percent represented Chinese value-added, with the bulk of the components (costing about $100) being imported from Japan and much of the rest coming from the United States and Korea.

But this stylized approach can generally only be conducted for specific products and, even then, only reveals part of the story related to who benefits from trade and how GVCs work, as it is typically unable to reveal how the intermediate parts are created. For example, the message would be significantly different if, for sake of argument, the imported parts from Japan used to make the iPod required significant Chinese content. To deal with the bigger picture and also to capture all of the upstream effects, a number of studies have adopted a macro approach based on the construction of intercountry or world input-output tables (Daudin, Rifflart, and Schweisguth 2009; Hummels, Ishii, and Yi 2001;

Johnson and Noguera 2012; Koopman et al. 2011). And a number of pioneering initiatives, such as those of the Global Trade Analysis Project (GTAP), collaborative efforts between the World Trade Organization (WTO) and the Institute of Developing Economies–Japan External Trade Organization (IDE-JETRO), and the World Input-Output Database (WIOD), have helped accelerate improvements in the underlying statistics used to construct the results.

But these studies and initiatives have generally been one-off in nature and often require the use of nonofficial statistical data. What has been lacking thus far has been a systematic attempt to mainstream the development of statistics in this area. In response to this need, on March 15, 2012, the Organisation for Economic Co-operation and Development (OECD) and WTO joined forces to develop a database of Trade in Value-Added (TiVA) indicators and to mainstream their production within the international statistics system. The first preliminary results from this intiative were released on January 16, 2013, and some highlights from this first release are presented in the following sections of this chapter. But, as described below, further work is needed (and can be done) in order to improve the quality of the estimates produced under the "trade in value-added" umbrella.

Ultimately this chapter acts, in some ways, as a clarion call to statistical agencies to alert them that the world is increasingly interconnected and that conventional approaches used to understand how economies work can no longer rely solely on national statistics. Increasingly, it is necessary to see the whole in order to understand how economies work and, for example, how to target and create industrial policies focusing on competitiveness (notwithstanding trade policies and the implications and importance of trade). National statistics build pictures based on interrelationships between producers and consumers and the rest of the world. But these relationships, particularly those with the rest of the world, have become increasingly more complex, and, as such, there is an increasing need to consider global production within a global accounting framework. This implies a departure from the traditional role of international organizations as compilers of internationally comparable national statistics, such as national input-output or supply-use tables. Instead, it requires that they bring together these national tables to create a global table.

The remainder of this chapter describes the policy drivers and needs for such a framework, as well as the underlying methodology and assumptions used to estimate trade in value-added, before assessing the implications for statistics offices, data collection, and national input-output tables in particular. It ends by describing longer-term future avenues of research.

WHAT IS TRADE IN VALUE-ADDED?

The "trade in value-added" initiative addresses the double counting implicit in current gross flows of trade. Instead of using that method, it measures flows related to the value that is added (labor compensation, other taxes on production, and operating surplus, or profits) by a country in the production of any good or service that is exported.

The simple example shown in Figure 6.1, below, illustrates this. Country A exports $100 of goods, produced entirely within A, to Country B, which further processes them before exporting them to Country C, where they are consumed. Country B adds value of $10 to the goods and so exports $110 to C. Conventional measures of trade show total global exports and imports of $210, but only $110 of value-added has been generated in their production. Conventional measures also show that C has a trade deficit of $110 with B, and no trade at all with A, despite the fact that A is the chief beneficiary of C's consumption.

Figure 6.1 Exports: Gross and Value-Added Flows, in US$

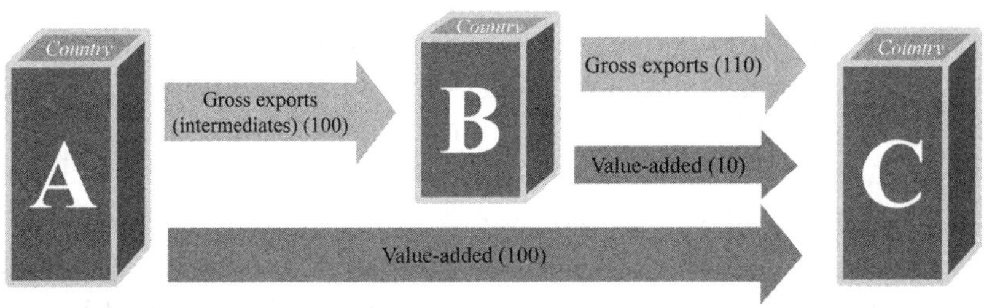

SOURCE: Author's composition.

If instead we track flows in value-added, one can recalculate C's trade deficit with B on the basis of the value-added it "purchases" from B as final demand, which reduces its deficit on this basis to $10, and apply the same approach to A's value-added to show C running a deficit of $100 with A. Note that C's overall trade deficit with the world remains at $110. All that has changed is its bilateral positions. This simple illustration reveals how output in one country can be affected by consumers in another, and by how much. (An example of this is C's consumers driving A's output.) However, it can also reveal many other important insights into global value chains. For example, it shows that B's exports depend significantly on intermediate imports from A, and so reveals that protectionist measures on imports from A could harm its own exporters and hence competitiveness. Indeed, by providing information at the level of specific industries, it is possible to provide insights in other areas, too, such as the contribution of the service sector to international trade.

HOW CAN MEASURES OF TRADE IN VALUE-ADDED INFORM POLICYMAKING?

Even though the literature on trade in value-added is quite technical, it has attracted a lot of attention from policymakers. What initially seemed a concern for trade statisticians is now understood as a key issue for the policy debate. For example, Pascal Lamy, the director-general of the World Trade Organization (WTO), noted that "the statistical bias created by attributing commercial value to the last country of origin perverts the true economic dimension of the bilateral trade imbalances. This affects the political debate, and leads to misguided perceptions" (Lamy 2011). Recently, the French Senate devoted a special seminar to the related statistical and policy issues (WTO and Sénat 2011). There are a number of areas where measuring trade in value-added terms brings a new perspective and is likely to have an impact on policies. Seven key areas are described below:

1) **Trade, growth, and competitiveness.** A better understanding of how much domestic value-added is generated by the export of a good or service in a country is crucial for devel-

opment strategies and industrial policies. Some countries have capitalized on GVCs by developing comparative advantages in specific parts of the value chain. For example, in China, many of its exports involve assembly work, where the foreign content is high. Access to efficient imports therefore matters as much in a world of international fragmentation as access to markets. Conventional gross trade statistics, however, are not able to reveal the foreign content of exports, and so there is a risk that policies to protect industries where gross statistics reveal a comparative advantage may decrease the competitiveness of those very same domestic industries. Because of this, mercantilist-style "beggar thy neighbor" strategies can turn out to be "beggar thyself" miscalculations.

2) **Domestic value-added in imports**. Domestic value-added is found not only in exports but also in imports: Goods and services produced in one domestic industry are intermediates shipped abroad whose value comes back to the domestic economy embodied in the imports of other, and often the same, industries. As a consequence, tariffs, nontariff barriers, and trade measures—such as antidumping rights—can also affect the competitiveness of domestic upstream producers (as well as the competitiveness of downstream producers, as mentioned above), in addition to foreign producers. For example, a study on the European shoe industry undertaken by the Swedish National Board of Trade highlights that shoes "manufactured in Asia" incorporate between 50 and 80 percent of European Union (EU) value-added. In 2006, antidumping rights were introduced by the European Commission on shoes imported from China and Vietnam. An analysis in value-added terms would have revealed that EU value-added was in fact subject to the antidumping rights (Isakson and Verrips 2012).

3) **Improving competitiveness in upstream domestic industries can boost exports**. Looking at trade from a value-added perspective is also a way to better reveal how upstream domestic industries contribute to exports, even if those same industries have little direct international exposure. Gross trade statistics, for example, reveal that less than one-quarter of total global

trade is in services. But in value-added terms the share is significantly higher. Goods industries require significant intermediate inputs of services, both from foreign and also from domestic suppliers. Looking at trade in value-added terms therefore can reveal that policies to encourage services trade liberalization and more foreign direct investment (and so policies designed to improve access to more efficient services) can improve the export competitiveness of goods industries.

4) **Global imbalances**. Accounting for trade in value-added (specifically accounting for trade in intermediate parts and components), and taking into account "trade in tasks," does not change the overall trade balance of a country with the rest of the world—rather, it redistributes the surpluses and deficits across partner countries. When bilateral trade balances are measured in gross terms, the deficit with final goods producers (or the surplus of exporters of final products) is exaggerated because it incorporates the value of foreign inputs. The underlying imbalance is in fact with the countries who supplied inputs to the final producer. As pressure for rebalancing increases in the context of persistent deficits, there is a risk of protectionist responses that target countries at the end of global value chains on the basis of an inaccurate perception of the origin of trade imbalances. As shown in the section starting on p. 172, the preliminary results from the OECD-WTO database point to significant changes.

5) **The impact of macroeconomic shocks**. The 2008–2009 financial crisis was characterized by a synchronized trade collapse in all economies. Authors have discussed the role of global supply chains in the transmission of what was initially a shock on demand in markets affected by a credit shortage. In particular, the literature has emphasized the "bullwhip effect" of GVCs (Escaith, Lindenberg, and Miroudot 2010; Lee, Padmanabhan, and Whang 1997). When there is a sudden drop in demand, firms delay orders and run down inventories, with the consequence that the fall in demand is amplified along the supply chain and can translate into a standstill for companies located upstream. A better understanding of value-added trade flows would provide tools for policymakers to anticipate the impact

of macroeconomic shocks and adopt the right policy responses. Any analysis of the impact of trade on short-term demand is likely to be biased when looking only at gross trade flows. This was recently demonstrated in the aftermath of the natural disaster that hit Japan in March 2011.[1]

6) **Trade and employment**. Several studies on the impact of trade liberalization on labor markets try to estimate the "job content" of trade. Such analysis is only relevant if one looks at the value-added of trade. What the value-added figures can tell us is where exactly jobs are created. Decomposing the value of imports into the contribution of each economy (including the domestic one) can give an idea of who benefits from trade. The EU shoe industry example given above can be interpreted in terms of jobs. Traditional thinking in gross terms would regard imports of shoes manufactured in China and Vietnam by EU shoe retailers as EU jobs lost and transferred to these countries. But in value-added terms, one would have to account for the EU value-added, and while workers may have indeed lost their jobs in the EU at the assembly stage, value-added-based measures would have highlighted the important contribution made by those working in the research, development, design, and marketing activities that exist because of trade (and the fact that this fragmented production process keeps costs low and EU companies competitive). When comparative advantages apply to "tasks" rather than to "final products," the skill composition of labor embedded in the domestic content of exports reflects the relative development level of participating countries. Industrialized countries tend to specialize in high-skilled tasks, which are better paid and capture a larger share of the total value added. A WTO and IDE-JETRO study on global value chains in East Asia shows that China specializes in low-skilled types of jobs. Japan, on the other hand, has been focusing on export activities intensive in medium- and high-skilled labor while importing goods produced by low-skilled workers. The study also shows that in 2006 the Republic of Korea was adopt-

ing a middle-ground position but was also moving closer to the pattern found in Japan (WTO and IDE-JETRO 2011).

7) **Trade and the environment.** Another area where the measurement of trade flows in value-added terms would support policymaking is in the assessment of the environmental impact of trade. For example, concerns over greenhouse gas emissions and their potential role in climate change have triggered research on how trade openness affects CO_2 emissions. The unbundling of production and consumption and the international fragmentation of production require a value-added view of trade to understand where imported goods are produced (and hence where CO_2 is produced as a consequence of trade). Various OECD studies note that the relocation of industrial activities can have a significant impact on differences in consumption-based and production-based measures of CO_2 emissions (Ahmad and Wyckoff 2003; Nakano et al. 2009).

EARLY EVIDENCE FROM THE OECD-WTO DATABASE

Currently, the database is based on a global input-output table that brings together national input-output tables for 57 economies, combined with bilateral trade data on goods and services broken down into 37 industries aggregated from a 48-industry list (see Table 6.1). The following provides an overview of the key messages provided by the data.[2]

Exports Require Imports

The data reveal that the import content of exports—the share of value added by the export of a given product that originates abroad—is significant in all countries for which data are presented (40 at the time of this writing: all 34 OECD countries, Brazil, China, India, Indonesia, the Russian Federation, and South Africa—see Figure 6.2).

Typically, the larger a country, the lower the overall foreign content; this reflects, in part, scale and cost. But a number of smaller economies also have relatively low foreign content in their exports, such as Aus-

Table 6.1 OECD Input-Output Industry Classification and Concordance with ISIC

ISIC Rev. 3 code		Description
1 + 2 + 5	1	Agriculture, hunting, forestry, and fishing
10 + 11 + 12	2	Mining and quarrying (energy)
13 + 14	3	Mining and quarrying (nonenergy)
15 + 16	4	Food products, beverages, and tobacco
17 + 18 + 19	5	Textiles, textile products, leather, and footwear
20	6	Wood and products of wood and cork
21 + 22	7	Pulp, paper, paper products, printing, and publishing
23	8	Coke, refined petroleum products, and nuclear fuel
24ex2423	9	Chemicals, excluding pharmaceuticals
2423	10	Pharmaceuticals
25	11	Rubber and plastics products
26	12	Other nonmetallic mineral products
271 + 2731	13	Iron and steel
272 + 2732	14	Nonferrous metals
28	15	Fabricated metal products, except machinery and equip.
29	16	Machinery and equipment, n.e.c.
30	17	Office, accounting and computing machinery
31	18	Electrical machinery and apparatus, n.e.c.
32	19	Radio, television, and communication equipment
33	20	Medical, precision, and optical instruments
34	21	Motor vehicles, trailers, and semitrailers
351	22	Building and repairing of ships and boats
353	23	Aircraft and spacecraft
352 + 359	24	Railroad equipment and transport equipment, n.e.c.
36 + 37	25	Manufacturing, n.e.c.; recycling (including furniture)
401	26	Production, collection, and distribution of electricity
402	27	Manufacture of gas; distribution of gaseous fuels through mains
403	28	Steam and hot water supply
41	29	Collection, purification, and distribution of water
45	30	Construction
50 + 51 + 52	31	Wholesale and retail trade; repairs
55	32	Hotels and restaurants
60	33	Land transport; transport via pipelines
61	34	Water transport

(continued)

Table 6.1 (continued)

ISIC Rev. 3 code		Description
62	35	Air transport
63	36	Supporting and auxiliary transport activities; activities of travel agencies
64	37	Post and telecommunications
65 + 66 + 67	38	Finance and insurance
70	39	Real estate activities
71	40	Renting of machinery and equipment
72	41	Computer and related activities
73	42	Research and development
74	43	Other business activities
75	44	Public administration and defense; compulsory social security
80	45	Education
85	46	Health and social work
90–93	47	Other community, social, and personal services
95 + 99	48	Private households and extraterritorial organizations

NOTE: "n.e.c." stands for "not elsewhere classified."
SOURCE: Author's compilation.

tralia, Chile, and Norway. This can be explained by their high share of exports of natural resource goods, such as ores, oil, and copper, which have, not surprisingly, a low foreign content. Geography also plays a role; this helps to explain New Zealand's relatively low ratio, as well as its relatively high dependency on agricultural exports, which also have a low foreign content. For midsize economies, however, particularly those in Eastern Europe, the norm is that around one-third of the value of exports reflects foreign content.

Notwithstanding some of the interpretative caveats above, the ratio is perhaps the single most digestible indicator of the propensity of a country to engage in global value chains. It reveals the existence of European, Asian, and North American production hubs and also the significant dependency many countries have on imports to generate exports. In Mexico, with its maquiladoras, and in China, with its processors/assemblers, about one-third of overall exports reflect foreign content (and, as described below, these are considered to be conservative estimates).

Figure 6.2 Domestic Content of Exports: Percentage of Total Gross Exports Represented by Domestic Value-Added Exports, 2009

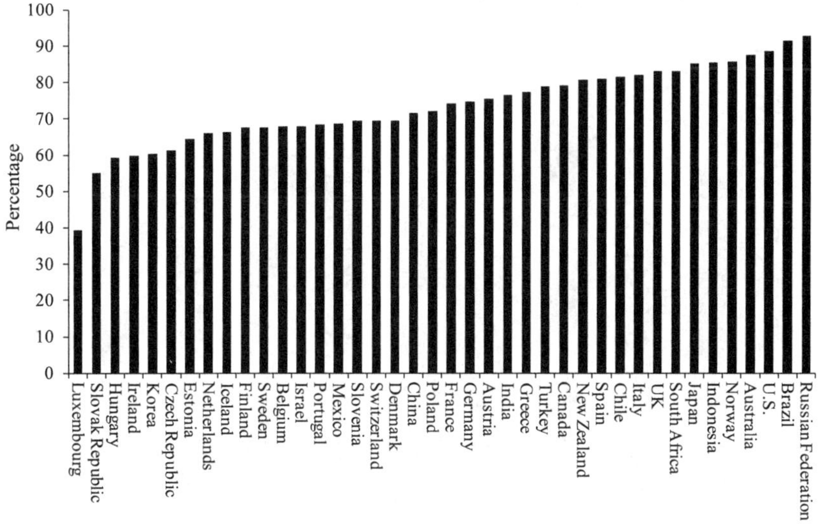

SOURCE: OECD-WTO Trade in Value-Added (TiVA) indicators, preliminary results from OECD, January 2013, http://stats.oecd.org.

Some care is needed in interpreting the results, however: 2009 was an exceptional year, the year that signified perhaps the nadir of the recent financial crisis. As such, it was partly characterized by an unprecedented slowdown in global trade. Although the database only provides data as far back as 2005, illustrative data going back to 1995 suggest that international fragmentation of production (in other words, the import content of exports) had been steadily rising in most countries over recent decades, which continued over the period 2005–2008 (Figure 6.3), despite the slowdown that began in many countries in 2008. But 2009 saw drops in the import content of exports, an indication that the greater the fragmentation of a good or service, the more likely it was to be affected by the synchronized slowdown in trade. In most countries, therefore, the import content of overall exports in 2009 returned to around the ratios seen in 2005, but in China the data point to a steady rise over the period, suggesting developments that saw China begin to move up the value-added chain.

Figure 6.3 Domestic Content of Exports: Percentage of Total Gross Exports Represented by Domestic Value-Added Exports, 2005, 2008, and 2009

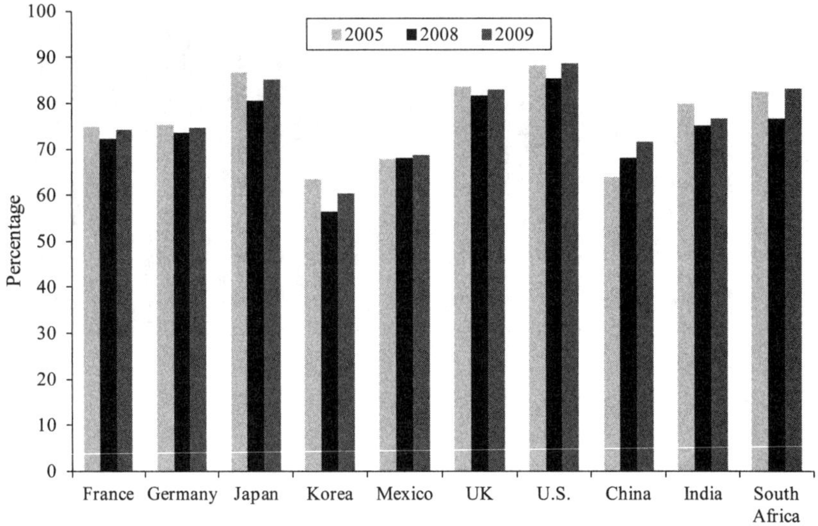

SOURCE: OECD-WTO Trade in Value-Added (TiVA) indicators, preliminary results, OECD, January 2013.

Tangible evidence of the scale of global value chains emerges more clearly when considering specific sectors. For example, between one-third and one-half of the total value of exports of transport parts and equipment by most major producers originated abroad in 2009 (Figure 6.4), driven by regional production hubs. In the United States and Japan, the shares were only about one-fifth, reflecting the larger scope in those countries of source inputs from domestic providers. However, this was also the case for Italy, and there it may have reflected efficient upstream domestic networks of small and medium enterprises. Interestingly, in 2009, Germany exported 25 percent more transport parts and equipment output than the United States in gross terms but only 5 percent more in value-added terms.

Similar patterns emerge in other sectors with a high degree of international fragmentation. For example, in China and Korea, in 2009, the

Figure 6.4 Transport Equipment, Gross Exports Decomposed by Source, 2009 (billions of US$)

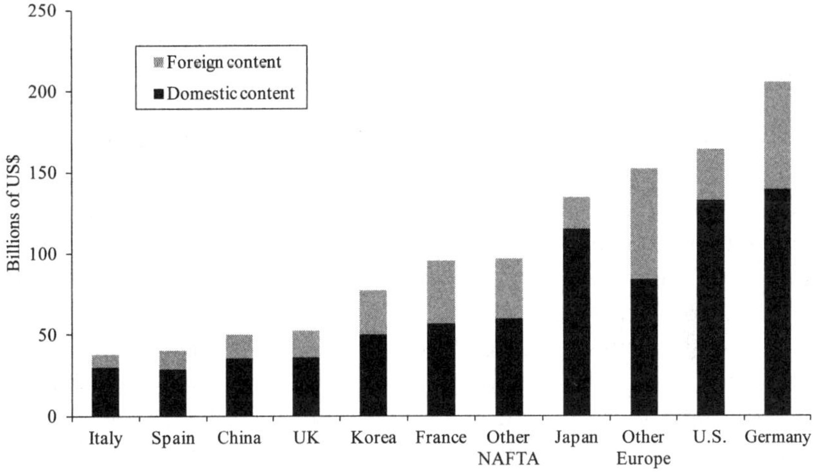

SOURCE: OECD-WTO TiVA indicators, preliminary results, OECD, January 2013.

Figure 6.5 Electronic Equipment, Gross Exports Decomposed by Source, 2009 (billions of US$)

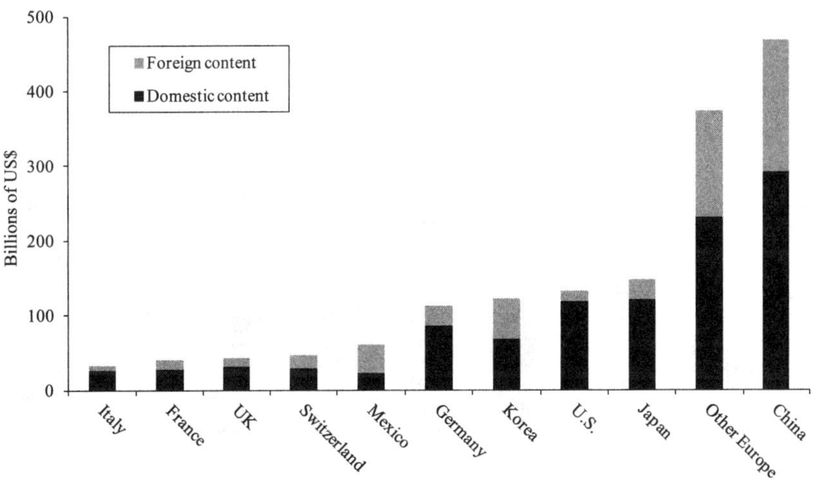

SOURCE: OECD-WTO TiVA indicators, preliminary results, OECD, January 2013.

foreign content of exports of electronic products was about 40 percent, and in Mexico, the share was over 60 percent (Figure 6.5).

High Shares of Intermediate Imports Are Used to Serve Export Markets

The figures above reveal that exporting firms require access to efficient imports in order to be competitive, and so highlight the potential counterproductive effects of protectionist measures. But an alternative way of indicating the adverse effects of such policies can be seen when looking at the overall share of intermediate imports that are used to serve export markets.

In most economies, around one-third of intermediate imports are destined for the export market. Not surprisingly, typically, the smaller the economy the higher the share, but even in the United States and Japan these shares are 15 and 20 percent, respectively, at the total economy level, with a higher incidence of intermediate imports in some

Figure 6.6 Intermediate Imports Embodied in Exports: Percentage of Total Intermediate Imports, 2009

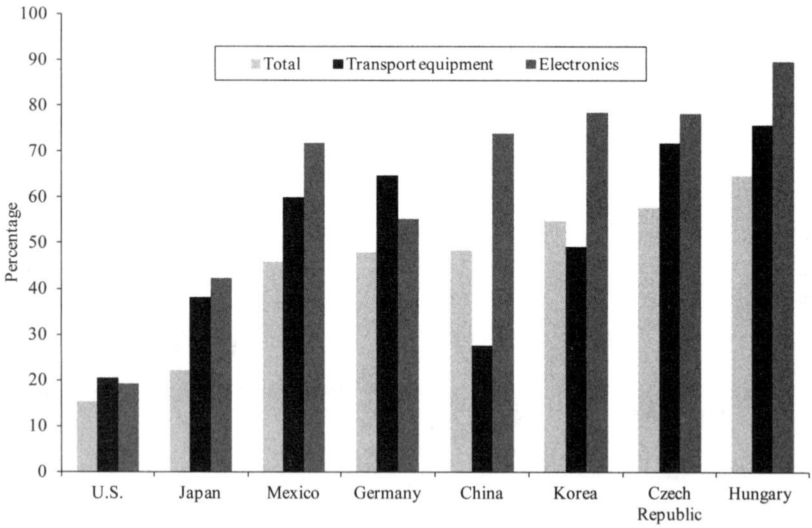

SOURCE: OECD-WTO TiVA indicators, preliminary results, OECD, January 2013.

highly integrated industries (Figure 6.6). In Japan, for example, nearly 40 percent of all intermediate imports of transport equipment end up in exports.

In many other countries, the share of intermediate imports embodied in exports is significantly higher. In Hungary, two-thirds of all intermediate imports are destined for the export market after further processing, and the share reaches 90 percent for electronic intermediate imports. In China, Korea, and Mexico, around three-quarters of all intermediate imports of electronics are embodied in exports. The database also shows that close to 85 percent of China's intermediate imports of textile products end up in exports.

Open and Efficient Service Markets Matter

Services make up about two-thirds of gross domestic product (GDP) in most developed economies, but in gross terms, trade in services typically accounts for less than one-quarter of their exports This partly reflects the fact that significant shares of services output are generally not tradable—e.g., government services, many personal services, and imputations such as those made in GDP calculations to reflect the rent homeowners are assumed to pay themselves (between 6 and 10 percent of GDP in most developed economies). But it also reflects the fact that the service sector provides significant intermediate inputs to domestic goods manufacturers.

Accounting for the value-added produced by the service sector in the production of goods shows that the service content of total gross exports is over 50 percent in many OECD economies, and it approaches two-thirds of the total in the United Kingdom (Figure 6.7). Canada, because of its significant exports of natural resources, which typically have low service content, has the lowest service content of its exports in the G7—but even here the share is close to 40 percent.

Typically, emerging economies and other large exporters of natural assets, such as Norway, Chile, and Australia, have the lowest shares of services. But in India, over half of the value of its gross exports originates in the service sector. Indonesia has the lowest share of the 40 countries in the database at around 20 percent.

Part of the explanation for the difference between OECD countries and emerging economies can be found in the relatively higher degree of

Figure 6.7 Services Value-Added: Percentage of Total Exports, 2009

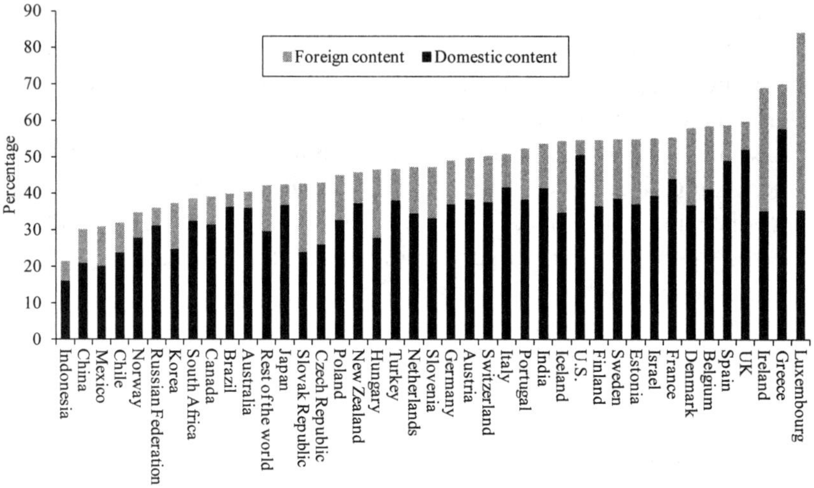

SOURCE: OECD-WTO Trade in Value-Added (TiVA) indicators, preliminary results, OECD, January 2013.

(largely domestic) outsourcing of services by manufacturers in OECD countries in recent decades, suggesting that a similar process could lead to improvements in the competitiveness of emerging economy manufacturers. Figure 6.7 also reveals a not insignificant contribution to exports coming from foreign service providers.

Another, perhaps clearer way of illustrating the importance of services to exports is to consider the services content of specific exports in goods-producing sectors. Figure 6.8 takes an average of all 40 countries in the database and shows that services make a significant contribution (typically one-third) across all manufacturing sectors, with significant shares provided by both foreign and domestic service providers. For individual sectors in specific countries the importance of the service sector is often starker. In France, for example, the data reveal that over half of the domestic value-added generated in producing transport equipment originates in the French service sector.

Figure 6.8 Services Value-Added: Percentage of Total Exports of Goods, 2009

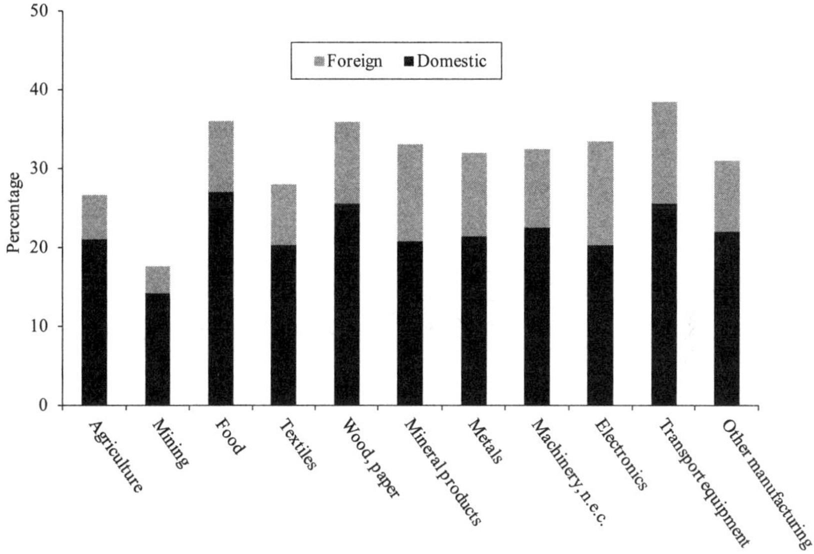

NOTE: "n.e.c." stands for "not elsewhere classified."
SOURCE: OECD-WTO Trade in Value-Added (TiVA) indicators, preliminary results, OECD, January 2013.

Intermediate Imports Often Embody a Country's Own (Returned) Domestic Value-Added

Imports can also contain "returned" value-added, which is value-added that originated in the importing country. The preliminary—and, one should stress, conservative—estimates in the OECD-WTO database show that in the United States, for example, nearly 5 percent of the total value of imported intermediate goods reflects U.S. value-added, and in China the equivalent shares are close to 7 percent. For electronic goods, Chinese intermediate imports contain over 12 percent of returned Chinese domestic value-added, and Korean intermediate imports contain close to 5 percent of returned Korean domestic value-added.

Figure 6.9 Difference between China's Value-Added and Gross Trade Balances, 2009 (billions of US$)

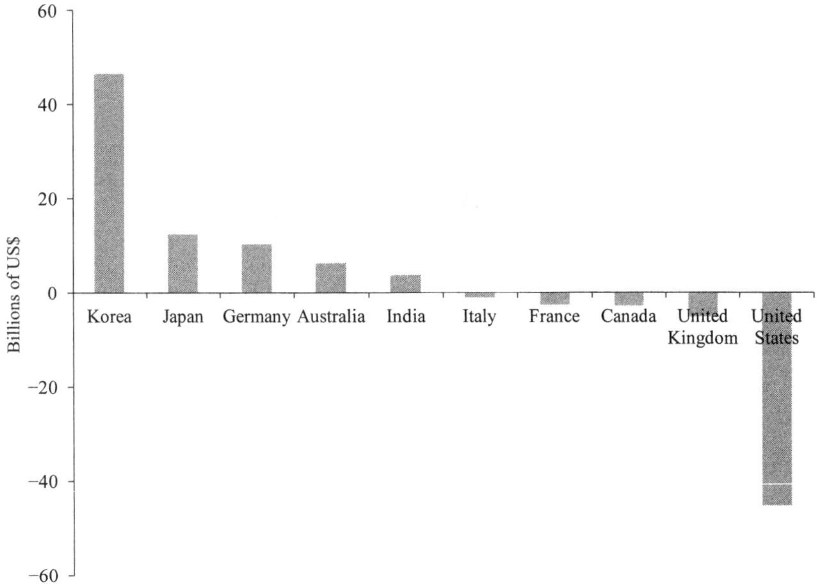

SOURCE: OECD-WTO TiVA indicators, preliminary results, OECD, January 2013.

What You See Is Not What You Get: Trade Patterns Change

Bilateral trade balance positions can change significantly when measured in value-added terms, even though the total trade balance is unaffected. Figure 6.9 shows that China's bilateral trade surplus with the United States was over US$40 billion (25 percent) smaller in value-added terms in 2009. (It was 30 percent smaller in 2005.) This partly reflects the higher share of U.S. value-added imports in Chinese final demand but also the fact that a significant share (one-third) of China's exports reflects foreign content—the "Factory Asia" phenomenon. The data illustrate that significant exports of value-added from Korea and Japan pass through China on their way to final consumers, resulting in significantly smaller Chinese trade deficits with these countries but also typically higher Japanese and Korean trade surpluses with other countries. Similarly, the database shows that Korea's significant trade deficit with Japan in gross terms almost disappears when measured in value-added terms.

ESTIMATING TRADE IN VALUE-ADDED

Creating a Multiregional Input-Output Table

As mentioned above, several initiatives have tried to address the issue of the measurement of trade flows in the context of the fragmentation of world production.[3] The most commonly used approach to develop a macro picture is based on global input-output tables, using simple standard Leontief inverses. More detail can be found in a joint report by the OECD and WTO (2012) and in an online appendix to this chapter, "Appendix 6A: Indicator Descriptions and Definitions," which can be found at http://www.upjohn.org/MEG/ahmad-appendix.pdf.

Constructing a global table is a data-intensive process and presents numerous challenges. The key challenge is to identify and create links between exports in one country and the purchasing industries (as intermediate consumers) or final-demand consumers in the importing country. In this respect, it is important to note that the data issues faced by the OECD are similar to those confronted by other initiatives, such as IDE-JETRO (which has produced intercountry input-output tables for Asia) or the World Input-Output Database project, with whom (along with the U.S. International Trade Commission) the OECD and WTO have been actively coordinating in order to share experiences and derive a set of best practices.

The data sources at OECD are harmonized input-output tables and bilateral trade coefficients in goods and services, derived from official sources.[4] The model specification and estimation procedures can be summarized as follows:

- Preparation of input-output (I-O) tables for reference years, using the latest published data sources—e.g., supply-and-use tables, national accounts, and trade statistics.
- Preparation of bilateral merchandise data by end-use categories for reference years. The published trade statistics are adjusted

for analytical purposes (such as confidential flows, reexports, waste and scrap products, and valuables). Trade coefficients of utility services are estimated based on cross-border energy transfers. Other trade coefficients of service sectors are based on the OECD Statistics on International Trade in Services and the United Nations (UN) Service Trade statistics. However, many missing flows are currently estimated using econometric model estimates.

- Conversion of "cost, insurance, and freight" (CIF) price-based import figures to "free on board" (FOB) price-based imports to reduce the inconsistency issues of mirror trade. (Because of asymmetry in reporting exports and imports in national trade statistics, imports of Country A from Country B often differ significantly from the exports reported from Country B to Country A). In an international I-O system, trade flows need to be perfectly symmetrical (i.e., the bilateral trade flows should be consistent at the highest relevant level of disaggregation) and consistent with the supply-utilization tables' trade data.
- Creation of import matrices.
- Total adjustment (missing sectors, trade with rest of the world, and other factors) and minimization of discrepancy columns using biproportional methods.

The OECD has been updating and maintaining harmonized I-O tables—that is, splitting intermediate flows into tables of domestic origin and imports—since the mid-1990s. Usually this process follows the rhythm of national releases of benchmark I-O tables. The first edition of the OECD Input-Output Database came out in 1995. It covered 10 OECD countries, and its I-O tables spanned the period from the early 1970s to the early 1990s. The first updated edition of this database, released in 2002, increased the country coverage to 18 OECD countries, China, and Brazil, and introduced harmonized tables for the mid-1990s. The database now includes national I-O tables for 34 OECD member countries and 18 non-OECD countries.[5]

The I-O tables show transactions between domestic industries but, as a complement, also include supplementary tables, which break down total imports by user (industry and category of final demand). Some countries provide these import tables in conjunction with their I-O tables, but in other cases they are derived from calculations by the OECD.

The OECD's input-output tables are based on an industry-by-industry basis, reflecting the fact that the underlying source data measure both the activities and production of industries. This means that the relationships between value-added and industrial output are unaffected by the statistical manipulations that will be required to build product-by-product-based input-output tables. The industry classification used in the current version of OECD's I-O database is based on the International Standard Industrial Classification of All Economic Activities, Revision 3 (ISIC Rev. 3) (Table 6.1), meaning that it is compatible with other industry-based analytical data sets, and in particular with the OECD bilateral trade in goods by industry data set (derived from merchandise trade statistics through the standard Harmonized System to ISIC conversion keys). The system, by necessity (in other words, to maximize cross-country comparability), is relatively aggregated. Differentiating between types of companies within a given sector is essential, however, to improve the quality of trade in value-added results (particularly in the context of exporting and nonexporting companies), and so part of future work will be to explore ways to do this, using microdata that could improve the quality of results (which is discussed in more detail in the following section).

In essence, a global I-O table is little different from a national I-O table except that while the matrix of flows of intermediate goods and services in a national table can be industry × industry, in a global I-O table, the rows and columns are country-industry combinations. In addition, in a global I-O table there are separate columns for each country's final demand. For illustration, Table 6.2 shows a two-country, two-sector representation.

Most of the components intuitively follow from the row and column headings, but by way of explanation, $Z_{12}{}^{AB}$ = intermediate purchase by Sector 2 of Country B from Sector 1 of Country A; $F_1{}^{AB}$ = final demand of consumers in Country B of output of Sector 1 in Country A.

Typically in the above matrix, statistics offices are able to provide most of the blocks required (recalling that supply-use tables can be readily converted to the above format and, moreover, that the above format can be initially constructed as a global supply-use table, which

Table 6.2 A Simplified ICIO System

	Country A		Country B		Final demand	
	Sector 1	Sector 2	Sector 1	Sector 2	Country A	Country B
Country A						
Sector 1: Goods	Z_{11}^{AA}	Z_{12}^{AA}	Z_{11}^{AB}	Z_{12}^{AB}	F_{1}^{AA}	F_{1}^{AB}
Sector 2: Services	Z_{21}^{AA}	Z_{22}^{AA}	Z_{21}^{AB}	Z_{22}^{AB}	F_{2}^{AA}	F_{2AB}
Country B						
Sector 1: Goods	Z_{11}^{BA}	Z_{12}^{BA}	Z_{11}^{BB}	Z_{12}^{BB}	F_{1}^{BA}	F_{1}^{BB}
Sector 2: Services	Z_{21}^{BA}	Z_{22}^{BA}	Z_{21}^{BB}	Z_{22}^{BB}	F_{2BA}	F_{2}^{BB}
Tax less subsidy on products	NTZ_{1}^{A}	NTZ_{2}^{A}	NTZ^{1B}	NTZ_{2}^{B}	NTF^{A}	NTF^{B}
International trade margin and insurance	TIZ_{1}^{A}	TIZ_{2}^{A}	TIZ_{1}^{B}	TIZ_{2}^{B}	TIF^{A}	TIF^{B}
Value-added						
Labor compensation	VL_{1}^{A}	VL_{2}^{A}	VL_{1}^{B}	VL_{2}^{B}		
Operating surplus	VO_{1}^{A}	VO_{2}^{A}	VO_{1}^{B}	VO_{2}^{B}		
Tax less subsidy on production	VT_{1}^{A}	VT_{2}^{A}	VT_{1}^{B}	VT_{2}^{B}		
Output	X_{1}^{A}	X_{2}^{A}	X_{1}^{B}	X_{2}^{B}		

SOURCE: Author's compilation.

will form the long-term approach to be used by the OECD). But even though some countries are able to estimate the overall import of a given product used by a particular industry, many are not, and none are able to show, systematically, the source of that import (by originating country and industry) by the using industry (or "final demand" category).

Central to the construction of a global input-output table, therefore, is the estimation of trade flows between industries and consumers across countries. Indeed, these trade flows in intermediate goods and services are the glue that binds together the national individual input-output tables. A positive spin-off of the work is worth mentioning in this context. National estimates of trade (exports and imports) are not coherent across countries, even after adjusting for price differences, CIF, and FOB. The process of constructing a global I-O table confronts this issue head-on. The spin-off to the work is therefore a mechanism to reveal where global imbalances lie. The results and policy implications of the work highlight the importance that should be attached to reconciling these flows at the national level. Over the coming years, this will form an important part of the OECD's work program, through its Working Party on Trade in Goods and Services.

Bilateral trade in goods and services and I-O balancing

Given the fact that many imports enter countries through intermediaries (wholesalers), it is highly unlikely that countries will ever be able to collect statistics that systematically show the country source of all imports consumed by all industries, nor does it seem likely that countries will be able to show which foreign industries consume their products. But, as shown below, it is possible, at least in the medium term, for countries to do more in this field by capitalizing on microdata and links between trade and business registers.

In the short term, however, more can be—and is being—done to improve how imports are allocated to using industries. Most countries are able to produce estimates of bilateral trade in goods and services showing the export of a given good or service to a given partner country. And indeed, most countries are able to further reveal whether any particular import or export of a good (at least, for most imports and exports) was intermediate, an investment, or a consumer good.

In constructing the import (and export) flows of its global I-O table, the OECD necessarily uses a number of assumptions. The main assumption used in creating these import matrices is the "proportionality" assumption, which assumes that the country-of-origin share of a given import consumed by a given industry in a given country is the same for all industries in that country. For countries that are not able to provide any "import-flow" matrices at all—i.e., the intermediate consumption of imports by origin and destination industries—the OECD necessarily assumes that the share of intermediate imports in total intermediate consumption for a given imported product is the same for all using industries. Furthermore, the OECD assumes that this share is equivalent to the overall share of intermediate imports to total intermediates supplied for that product. In all cases, the OECD has been able to significantly improve the quality of the assumptions it necessarily uses by creating a new database of bilateral trade (for goods) that breaks down imports (and exports) on the basis of the nature of the traded product (intermediate, household, investment, other). This database is called the Bilateral Trade Database by Industry and End-Use category (BTDIxE), and is derived from the United Nations Statistics Division (UNSD) UN Comtrade database, where values and quantities of imports and exports are compiled according to product classifications and by partner.[6]

UN Comtrade data are classified by declaring country (the country supplying the information), by partner country (the origin of imports or destination of exports), and by product (according to Harmonized System, or HS). Trade flows are stored according to the product classification used by the declaring country at the time of data collection. In general, source data are held according to Standard International Trade Classification (SITC) Revision 2 (Rev. 2) for the time period 1978–1987, the Harmonized System (1988) for 1988–1995, HS Rev. 1 (1996) for 1996–2001, HS Rev. 2 (2002) for 2002–2006, and HS Rev. 3 (2007) from 2007 onwards.

To generate estimates of trade in goods by industry and by end-use category, six-digit product codes from each version of HS from UN Comtrade are assigned to a unique ISIC Rev. 3 industry and a unique end-use category—and hence, assigned to a basic class of goods as specified in the System of National Accounts (SNA) (European Commission et al. 2009; see Table 6.3).

Notwithstanding the known problems relating to the asymmetries that exist within bilateral trade statistics (i.e., global exports do not equal global imports), these bilateral statistics form the basis for populating the international flows in goods used in the OECD's global input-output tables, before balancing.

The approach used for bilateral trade in services statistics is in essence similar: Estimates based on official bilateral statistics form the basis for the original estimates of exports and imports by country. However, the quality of bilateral trade in services statistics is notoriously poor, and so the original partner-share coefficients used to populate I-O cells of international trade in services are based on gravity model techniques (see Miroudot, Lanz, and Ragoussis 2009), which are subsequently balanced within the overall system.

Only very few countries have a consistency between bilateral trade flows (imports and exports) by partner country and the corresponding flows shown in their supply-use tables (the basis for the creation of national I-O tables), reflecting the fact that, for goods at least, bilateral trade flows follow merchandise trade accounting standards. As such, there are a number of recommendations that follow for official statisticians:

Coherent bilateral trade and national accounts data. Producing bilateral trade flows that are consistent with underlying supply-use tables should form a high priority of national statistics offices.

Confidential trade. In some countries, disclosure rules suppress six-digit HS components in UN Comtrade and also higher two-digit HS chapter levels. This should be avoided where possible by adopting other forms of preserving confidentiality, such as suppressing another six-digit category.

Reexports. Adjustments are required for reexports—and, for major continental trading hubs, these adjustments can be significant. Sufficient data are available to adjust for reported trade between China and the rest of the world via Hong Kong, but not currently for other major hubs such as Belgium, the Netherlands, and Singapore.

Identifying used capital goods. HS codes, and thus reported trade in UN Comtrade, cannot differentiate between new and old capital goods (such as secondhand aircraft and ships). Estimating international

Table 6.3 Current BEC and SNA Classes of Goods

	End-use			
		Final-demand goods		
Product characteristics	Intermediate	Household consumption	Industrial capital goods	Other
Primary products	Food and beverages (111)	Food and beverages (112)		
	Industrial supplies (21)			
	Fuels and lubricants (31)			
Processed unfinished	Fuels and lubricants (32)	Fuels and lubricants (32)		
	Industrial supplies (22)	Food and beverages (122)		
	Parts and components of transport equipment (53)			
	Parts and components of capital goods (42)			
Processed finished	Packed medicaments (part of 63)	Packed medicaments (part of 63)	Capital goods (41)	
		Nonindustrial transport equipment (522)	Industrial transport equipment (521)	
		Nondurable consumer goods (63)		
		Semidurable consumer goods (62)		
		Durable consumer goods for households (61)		
		Durable personal consumer goods, e.g., personal computers (part of 61)	Durable personal consumer goods, e.g., personal computers (part of 61)	
		Mobile phones (part of 41)	Mobile phones (part of 41)	

	Passenger motor cars (51)	Passenger motor cars (51)	
	Fixed-line phones (part of 62)	Fixed-line phones (part of 62)	
Other			Goods n.e.c. (7)

NOTE: Numbers are in Broad Economic Categories (BEC) codes. “SNA” stands for “System of National Accounts.” “n.e.c.” stands for “not elsewhere classified.”

SOURCE: United Nations Statistics Division (2013).

trade in these flows in a value-added context requires an elaboration on the input-output framework that allows these flows to be recorded in a way that aligns with total global value-added produced in a given period.

Unidentified scrap and waste. Certain types of waste and scrap do not have separate six-digit HS codes—e.g., PCs and other electrical equipment exported (often to developing countries) for recycling.

Better services data. Moreover, for services, countries are encouraged to provide more detail on partner countries and also on the type of products (following EBOPS 2010).[7]

Coherent international trade data. Greater efforts are needed to reconcile asymmetries in international trade flows.

Without the issues outlined above being resolved, the OECD's global input-output table must necessarily balance global discrepancies in trade using a quasi automatic (RAS) balancing procedure. This process constrains each country's exports and imports to published national accounts totals, while also constraining estimates of national GDP. Resolving these asymmetries in bilateral trade statistics is a work in progress, and efforts to improve the nature of the balancing process are ongoing (Ahmad, Wang, and Yamano 2013).

Given the assumptions and balancing adjustments necessarily used, it is important to stress that the indicators shown in the database are *estimates*. Official gross statistics on international trade produced by national statistics institutions result in inconsistent figures for total global exports and total global imports, inconsistencies that are magnified when bilateral partner country positions are considered. The global input-output tables from which trade in value-added indicators are derived necessarily eliminate these inconsistencies, such as those that reflect different national treatments of reexports and transit trade (e.g., going through hubs such as the Netherlands), to achieve a coherent picture of global trade. For the countries for which data are presented, total exports and imports are consistent with official national accounts estimates.

Level of detail in national supply-use and input-output (I-O) tables—future improvements

Indicators created by input-output techniques are limited by the degree of industry disaggregation that the tables provide. The national input-output tables used by the OECD are based on a harmonized set of 37 industries. In simple terms, therefore, any given indicator for a particular industry assumes that all consumers of that industry's output purchase exactly the same shares of products produced by all of the firms allocated to that industry.

In practice, this boils down to (but is not the same thing as) assuming that there exists only one single production technique for all of the firms (and all of the products) in the industry grouping. We know that this is not true and that different firms, even those producing the same products, will have different production techniques (and so technical I-O coefficients), and we also know that different firms produce different products and that these products will be destined for different types of consumers and markets.

Of chief concern in this respect is the evidence that points to exports having very different coefficients from the coefficients of goods and services produced for domestic markets, particularly when the exports (typically intermediate) are produced by foreign-owned affiliates in a global value chain. Because exporting firms are generally more integrated into value-added chains, they will typically have higher foreign content ratios, particularly when they are foreign-owned. Generally, therefore, an ability to account for this heterogeneity in producing trade in value-added estimates will result in lower shares of foreign content than might be recorded if more detailed input-output tables were available.

It is important to note, however, that more detail does not necessarily translate into more disaggregated industries. What matters for developing indicators on GVCs is more detail on firms trading internationally. In this sense, given a choice between doubling the number of industries available within current national I-O or supply-and-use tables or providing a split of existing industries into one group of exporting firms and another of nonexporting firms, the latter may, arguably, be preferable.

Ideally, therefore, countries should attempt to construct supply-use or input-output tables that better respond to the challenges presented by GVCs. In a project coordinated by the OECD and the Chinese Ministry of Commerce (the latter in collaboration with the Chinese National Bureau of Statistics), an input-output table for China was created that split all of its industrial sectors into three categories: 1) processing firms, 2) other exporting firms, and 3) all other firms (Cuihong et al 2013).

Ideally, countries could adopt similar approaches in constructing their I-O or supply-and-use tables, using splits based on national circumstances. Processing firms form a significant part of China's exporters, so such a classification made sense in the case of China, but this may not be optimal for all countries. For most countries, achieving changes to national I-O or supply-and-use tables may take some time.

Other, potentially simpler, approaches, however, could be used to significantly improve the quality of the information I-O tables are able to produce for analyzing GVCs.

In October 2012, the OECD and Eurostat launched one such approach by building on the OECD-Eurostat Trade by Enterprise Characteristics (TEC) data collection. The TEC exercise collects information on the turnover generated through exports broken down by size class, industry, and partner country. For imports, similar information is provided but with a more limited breakdown on the importing industry. But these indicators only begin to scratch the surface of the potential, if researchers can make links to structural business statistics (Ahmad et al. 2011). With these further links, they can create information on the direct value-added of exporting firms, as well as information on employment. In addition, they can create indicators broken down by whether the firms are foreign or domestically owned, an important additional breakdown required for analyses of "trade in income." (This topic of trade in income is further addressed under the subsection heading of that name, below.) Moreover, information that links the data on importing firms with those on exporting firms can provide vital insights into the nature of global production chains. Importantly, for those countries that already produce TEC statistics, researchers could develop this information without necessarily using links to structural business statistics, although they would have to do so on the basis of turnover flows. This information could form the basis for disaggregating I-O or supply-and-use industries into characteristics required to better measure GVCs.

The questionnaire that was circulated to test the feasible and practical level of detail that could be collected, bearing in mind disclosure rules, focused only on export intensities (rather than on import intensities, where it was recognized that other steps would need to precede development of a questionnaire on that aspect). The primary purpose of the questionnaire was to categorize firms on the basis of their share of output generated by exports (i.e., export intensities). The form provided for three different levels of breakdown; it asked countries to use the level of breakdown that best suited their disclosure rules and resources:

1) Firms that export (i.e., more than 0 percent of output is made up by exports) and firms that don't (0 percent of output is exported).
2) A breakdown of firms by export-intensity quartiles, with a separate category for nonexporting firms: 0 percent, between >0 and 25 percent, between >25 and 50 percent, between >50 and 75 percent, and greater than 75 percent.
3) A more aggregated breakdown of export intensity into three categories: a) nonexporting firms, b) firms with exports between >0 and 50 percent, and c) firms with exports greater than 50 percent.

Seven variables, described below, were requested in the exercise, and each was broken down by industry, size class, and ownership. However, recognizing that disclosure rules would restrict what could realistically be produced for public consumption, the distributors of the survey asked countries to prioritize their information along the following lines:

- Priority 1: Industries (preferably, ISIC Rev. 4) for two-digit groupings
- Priority 2: Export intensities (exports as a percentage of output)
- Priority 3: Ownership (a breakdown into foreign/domestic ownership)
- Priority 4: Size class (a breakdown preferably done by number of employees)

The seven variables requested were as follows:

1) The number of statistical units, participating or otherwise, in exports, ideally using a concept consistent with that used in preparing supply-use and input-output tables.

2) The value-added generated by firms in national currency units, ideally at basic prices.
3) The value of exports generated by firms in national currency units, ideally at FOB (free on board) prices.
4) The output generated by firms in national currency units, ideally at basic prices.
5) The total employment of firms, ideally on a full-time equivalent basis.
6) The total compensation of employees of firms.
7) Direct imports of firms in national currency units, ideally at CIF (cost, insurance, and freight) prices.

Going beyond Trade in Value-Added

Looking at trade in value-added terms provides a valuable insight into broader notions of competitiveness (in addition to providing insights into trade policies) by illustrating interlinkages between countries and also by illustrating those activities (or tasks) that generate the most value. But additional indicators and insights can be gained by considering extensions to the accounting framework.

Trade in jobs

One immediate area relates to jobs. This requires consistent estimates of employment measures (employment, employees, actual hours worked) using the underlying value-added estimates produced by national statistics offices in their supply-use tables.

Countries have already begun to make improvements in this area, driven by a need to produce coherent productivity estimates by industry, and it is hoped that highlighting the important insights that can be gained by looking at trade in jobs will reinforce and support these national initiatives aimed at improving coherence. Going a step further, we can state that, particularly because international fragmentation has meant industries across countries are less comparable than they used to be (as countries specialize in those stages of the underlying activity where they have a comparative advantage), it is increasingly becoming necessary to link jobs statistics to skills statistics.

The OECD's ANSKILL database (in the process of being updated) provides information on employment and skill composition at the industry level. The database matches industry data at the two-digit level (classified according to the ISIC Rev. 3) to occupations at the two-digit level (classified according to International Standard Classification of Occupations [ISCO]-88). It also includes an additional proxy for skills, in the form of data on the educational attainment of employees (classified on the basis of International Standard Classification of Education [ISCED]-97). The database covers 26 countries, mostly for 1997–2005, although coverage of seven of the countries is much more limited.

For ANSKILL, the ISCO-88 occupation classification corresponds to high-, medium-, and low-skilled levels, as follows:

- Categories 1 (legislators, senior officials, managers), 2 (professionals), and 3 (technicians and associate professionals) are regarded as high-skilled.
- Categories 4 (clerks), 5 (service workers and shop and market sale workers), 6 (skilled agricultural and fishery workers), and 7 (craft and related trade workers) are regarded as medium-skilled.
- Categories 8 (plant and machine operators and assemblers) and 9 (elementary occupations) are regarded as low-skilled.

The ISCED-97 educational classification maps to high, medium, and low skill levels in ANSKILL as follows:

- Categories 1 (primary education) and 2 (lower secondary/second stage of basic education) are regarded as low-skilled.
- Categories 3 (upper secondary education) and 4 (postsecondary nontertiary education) are regarded as medium-skilled.
- Categories 5 (first stage of tertiary education) and 6 (second stage of tertiary education) are regarded as high-skilled.

Trade in income

Conventional trade statistics do not always record transactions between affiliates as sales or purchases of goods and services. This is especially true of intellectual property products (IPPs).

Consider, for example, an affiliate enterprise, recognized in the national accounts of its resident economy as the economic owner of an

IPP that it uses to produce goods, which it sells. The affiliate's value-added would reflect in part the return on this underlying asset, realized as profits (operating surplus). These profits would subsequently be recorded as reinvested earnings, whether or not any actual flows occur between the parent and its affiliate. Ultimately, therefore, it is the parent (often the entity that finances the underlying IPP) that benefits from the use of the IPP. (Indeed, this in itself raises questions about how economic ownership of IPPs should be considered with respect to multinationals—an issue that is currently being tackled by the international statistics community.)

However, the difficulties raised by the current recording of IPPs in the balance of payments and national accounts of countries extend beyond this simple example (which correctly records flows in line with current standards and guidelines). Often, for example, the national accounts in the economy of the parent company will record the asset, but there will not be any flows related to the use the owner makes of its affiliates, which use is frequently driven by tax minimization purposes. Often, as well, the owner may transfer the asset to an affiliate (such as a special purpose enterprise, or SPE), with the parent and other affiliates making explicit payments to the SPE, again driven to do so by tax minimization purposes.

What is clear from the above, therefore, is that flows related to IPPs require an extension of accounting systems beyond looking merely at value-added flows in order to fully understand who benefits from trade and indeed trade liberalization (and investment). Sometimes these flows will increase value-added, sometimes they will not. But in both cases the beneficiary is arguably the same (the parent company).

But the flows merely illustrate a wider issue, notwithstanding the obvious implications they raise for multifactor productivity calculations. First, they illustrate the potential distortions that may arise when one factors in the scope for transfer pricing manipulations. Second, such interpretations extend beyond looking only at the conventional set of assets recognized as such in the 2008 SNA. Other knowledge-based assets, such as brands and organizational capital, can also increase an affiliate's value-added, and even though these assets are not recognized in the SNA, the profits recorded by the affiliate compensate for their use, and these still flow back to the parent, eventually, as reinvested earnings flows in the accounts. But these flows are typically not available on a bilateral partner country basis, let alone a partner country–industry basis, which is what is needed to analyze trade in income analogously with trade in value-added.

Recording these flows, therefore, is crucial. Part of the solution lies in producing supply-use tables (or indicators) that capture foreign ownership. Clearly, it is unlikely that it will be feasible to produce supply-use tables that capture foreign ownership by country for all of the owners of the affiliates. But a separate breakdown of activities in a supply-use table that differentiates between foreign- and domestic-owned firms should be feasible, as it relates to confidentiality rules and burdens.

By supplementing this with bilateral trade in primary income statistics (a from-whom-to-whom framework) broken down by type of income (in particular, reinvested earnings and interest), it should be possible to create extensions to the trade-in-value-added accounting framework by treating the primary income flows (and components) as if they were services produced by artificial industries in the host country of the parent company.

Some of the tools to do this already exist. Foreign affiliate trade statistics (FATS) can be combined, for example, with information in supply-use tables that shows breakdowns based on ownership. And there is also scope to link this further to balance-of-payment (BoP) data flows. The OECD is looking at developing a more detailed accounting framework and set of recommendations in this area, which could form the basis for estimating flows of trade in income.

Figure 6.10 provides an illustration of the potential impact this may have on our understanding of trade relationships. For illustrative purposes only, the operating surplus generated by U.S.-owned affiliates in the "Chemicals and electronics" sector in Ireland (available from FATS) is considered to be equivalent to value-added generated by U.S. firms. These flows can then be treated as exports from the United States to those countries consuming the U.S. affiliate exports from Ireland, revealing not insignificant changes in bilateral trade positions. For example, for France the trade deficit in value-added terms becomes a trade surplus again, which is what gross flows show.

To further illustrate the potential impact of accounting for these flows between multinationals, about 70 percent of China's gross high-tech exports were made by foreign affiliates in 2009, according to data

Figure 6.10 U.S. Trade Balance, Adjusted for U.S. Affiliates' Exports from Ireland, $US Billions, 2009

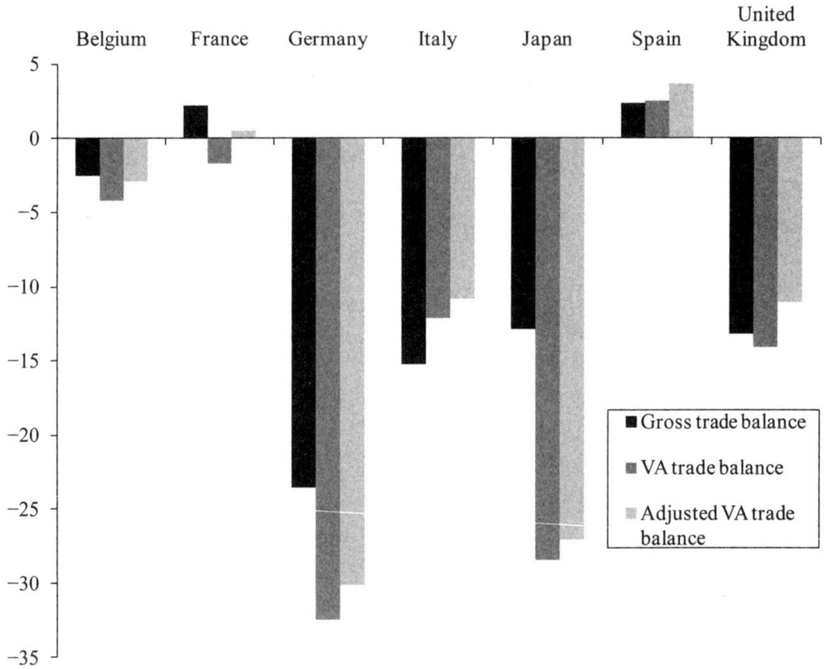

NOTE: "VA" stands for "value-added."
SOURCE: OECD calculations, based on the OECD-WTO Trade in Value-Added (TiVA) database and the OECD Activity of Multinational Enterprises (AMNE) database.

supplied by the Chinese Ministry of Commerce. Furthermore, between 1995 and 2007, Japanese foreign affiliates increased their employment in China eightfold, from just over one hundred thousand employees to more than one million, and in Thailand fourfold, from over one hundred thousand to over four hundred thousand; the pattern was similar in other Association of Southeast Asian Nations (ASEAN) countries, such as the Philippines, Malaysia, and Indonesia. And from 1995 to 2009, Japan's primary income trade surplus increased by around $100 billion, more than offsetting the $50 billion reduction in its gross trade surplus over the same period.

Trade in CO_2 (and other emissions)

One additional extension that follows from the accounting framework for trade in value-added (and trade in jobs) is carbon footprints. Carbon footprint calculations are typically estimated using I-O tables (Ahmad and Wyckoff 2003).

Incorporating capital flows

Other areas where extensions to the accounting framework would be desirable include the contribution made by capital more generally. Because of the way capital (gross fixed capital formation) is recorded in the accounting system, analyses that look at trade in value-added do not fully capture how production across countries is linked and how capital goods (and services) produced in one country contribute to the value-added in another. For example, all the value-added exported by Japan in producing machinery for manufacturers in China will be recorded as Chinese imports from Japan. But, arguably, the capital service values embodied in the goods produced and exported by China should show Japan as the beneficiary. This requires high-quality capital flow (and capital stock) matrices.

Distribution sectors and trade

One final area of work that merits attention concerns the value added by distributors through sales of final imported goods. The estimates of trade in value-added do not reveal how cheap imports are also important to retailers, who are able to generate domestic value-added through sales to consumers. Tariff measures will necessarily impose additional costs on these goods which, all other things being equal, could suppress demand and so in turn lead to lower value-added in the distribution sectors. The OECD is also considering how these estimates could be incorporated within its accounting framework, using margin rates for all products in national supply-use tables, and through this usage motivating the further development of such data.

Notes

1. See an application of international I-O in Escaith et al. (2011).
2. For more information on the database, see OECD (2013).
3. An OECD–World Bank workshop on "New Metrics for Global Value Chains" was held on September 21, 2010. WTO hosted a "Global Forum on Trade Statistics" on February 2–4, 2011, in collaboration with Eurostat, the United Nations Statistics Division (UNSD), and the United Nations Conference on Trade and Development (UNCTAD).
4. Some research-oriented initiatives have been using the GTAP database for international input-output data. This database is not, however, based on official sources of statistics.
5. For more details, see OECD (2012b). The list of countries includes Australia, Austria, Belgium, Canada, Chile, the Czech Republic, Denmark, Estonia, Finland, France, Germany, Greece, Hungary, Iceland, Ireland, Israel, Italy, Japan, Korea, Luxembourg, Mexico, the Netherlands, New Zealand, Norway, Poland, Portugal, the Slovak Republic, Slovenia, Spain, Sweden, Switzerland, Turkey, the United Kingdom, the United States, Argentina, Brazil, China, Chinese Taipei, Cyprus, India, Indonesia, Latvia, Lithuania, Malaysia, Malta, Romania, the Russian Federation, Singapore, South Africa, Thailand, and Vietnam.
6. For more details, see OECD (2012a).
7. EBOPS stands for Extended Balance of Payments Services Classification; see the service list of EBOPS items at http://unstats.un.org/unsd/servicetrade/mr/rfCommoditiesList.aspx.

References

Ahmad, Nadim, Sónia Araújo, Alessia Lo Turco, and Daniela Maggioni. 2011. "Using Trade Microdata to Improve Trade in Value-Added Measures: Proof of Concept Using Turkish Data." OECD Statistics Directorate Working Paper No. 2011/16. Paris: Organisation for Economic Co-operation and Development. http://search.oecd.org/officialdocuments/displaydocumentpdf/?cote=STD/TBS/WPTGS%282011%2916&doclanguage=en (accessed October 18, 2013).

Ahmad, Nadim, Zhi Wang, and Norihiko Yamano. 2013. "A Three-Stage Reconciliation Method to Construct a Time Series International Input-Output Database." In *Trade in Value Added: Developing New Measures of Cross-Border Trade*, Aaditya Mattoo, Zhi Wang, and Shang-Jin Wei, eds. London: Centre for Economic Policy Research; and Washington, DC: World Bank, pp. 253–288.

Ahmad, Nadim, and Andrew Wyckoff. 2003. "Carbon Dioxide Emissions Embodied in International Trade of Goods." OECD Science, Technology, and

Industry Working Paper No. 2003/15. Paris: Organisation for Economic Co-operation and Development. http://www.oecd-ilibrary.org/science-and-technology/carbon-dioxide-emissions-embodied-in-international-trade-of-goods_421482436815 (accessed October 18, 2013).

Cuihong, Yang, Chen Xikang, Duan Yuwan, Jiang Xuemei, Pei Jiansuo, Xu Jian, Yang Lianling, and Zhu Kunful. 2013. "Measurement of Trade in Value-Added: Using Chinese Input-Output Tables Capturing Processing Trade." Paper presented at the Fifty-Ninth ISI World Statistics Congress, held in Hong Kong, August 25–30.

Daudin, Guillaume, Christine Rifflart, and Danielle Schweisguth. 2009. "Who Produces for Whom in the World Economy?" Document de Travail de l'OFCE No. 2009-18. Paris: Observatoire Français des Conjonctures Économiques.

Dedrick, Jason, Kenneth L. Kraemer, and Greg Linden. 2010. "Who Profits from Innovation in Global Value Chains? A Study of the iPod and Notebook PCs." *Industrial and Corporate Change* 19(1): 81–116.

Escaith, Hubert, Nannette Lindenberg, and Sébastien Miroudot. 2010. "International Supply Chains and Trade Elasticity in Time of Global Crisis." WTO Staff Working Paper ERSD-2010-08. Geneva: World Trade Organization.

Escaith, Hubert, Robert Teh, Alexander Keck, and Coleman Nee. 2011. "Japan's Earthquake and Tsunami: International Trade and Global Supply Chain Impacts." London: VoxEU.org. http://www.voxeu.org/article/japans-earthquake-and-tsunami-global-supply-chain-impacts (accessed October 21, 2013).

European Commission, International Monetary Fund, Organisation for Economic Co-operation and Development, United Nations, and World Bank. 2009. *System of National Accounts 2008*. New York: United Nations.

Hummels, David, Jun Ishii, and Kei-Mu Yi. 2001. "The Nature and Growth of Vertical Specialization in World Trade." *Journal of International Economics* 54(1): 75–96.

Isakson, Henrik, and Paul Verrips. 2012. *Adding Value to the European Economy: How Anti-Dumping Can Damage the Supply Chains of Globalised European Companies. Five Case Studies from the Shoe Industry*. Stockholm: Kommerskollegium, National Board of Trade.

Johnson, Robert C., and Guillermo Noguera. 2012. "Accounting for Intermediates: Production Sharing and Trade in Value Added." *Journal of International Economics* 86(2): 224–236.

Koopman, Robert, William Powers, Zhi Wang, and Shang-Jin Wei. 2011. "Give Credit Where Credit Is Due: Tracing Value Added in Global Production Chains." NBER Working Paper No. 16426. Cambridge, MA: National Bureau of Economic Research.

Lamy, Pascal. 2011. "'Made in China' Tells Us Little about Global Trade." *Financial Times*, January 24.

Lee, Hau L., V. Padmanabhan, and Seungjin Whang. 1997. "The Bullwhip Effect in Supply Chains." *Sloan Management Review* 38(3): 93–102.

Miroudot, Sébastien, Rainer Lanz, and Alexandros Ragoussis. 2009. "Trade in Intermediate Goods and Services." OECD Trade Policy Paper No. 93. Paris: Organisation for Economic Co-operation and Development.

Nakano, Satoshi, Asako Okamura, Norihisa Sakurai, Masayuki Suzuki, Yoshiaki Tojo, and Norihiko Yamano. 2009. "The Measurement of CO2 Embodiments in International Trade: Evidence from the Harmonised Input-Output and Bilateral Trade Database." OECD Science, Technology, and Industry Working Paper No. 2009/03. Paris: Organisation for Economic Co-operation and Development.

Organisation for Economic Co-operation and Development (OECD). 2012a. *Bilateral Trade in Goods by Industry and End-Use Category*. Paris: OECD.

———. 2012b. *Input-Output Tables*. Paris: Organisation for Economic Co-operation and Development. http://www.oecd.org/trade/input-outputtables.htm (accessed October 24, 2013).

———. 2013. *Industry and Globalisation—Measuring Trade in Value Added: An OECD-WTO Joint Initiative*. Paris: Organisation for Economic Co-operation and Development. http://www.oecd.org/industry/ind/measuringtradeinvalue-addedanoecd-wtojointinitiative.htm (accessed October 22, 2013).

Organisation for Economic Co-operation and Development and World Trade Organization (OECD and WTO). 2012. *Trade in Value-Added: Concepts, Methodologies, and Challenges*. Paris: Organisation for Economic Co-operation and Development; and Geneva: World Trade Organization.

United Nations Statistics Division (UNSD). 2013. *Detailed Structure and Explanatory Notes: BEC (Classification by Broad Economic Categories)*. New York: United Nations Statistics Division.

World Trade Organization and Commission des Finances du Sénat (WTO and Sénat). 2011. "Globalization of Industrial Production Chains and Measurement of Trade in Value Added: Measuring International Trade in Value Added for a Clearer View of Globalization." Proceedings of a joint conference by the Senate Finance Commission and the Secretariat of the World Trade Organization (WTO), held in Paris on October 15, 2010. Geneva: World Trade Organization; and Paris: Commission des Finances du Sénat.

World Trade Organization and Institute of Developing Economies–Japan External Trade Organization (WTO and IDE-JETRO). 2011. *Trade Patterns and Global Value Chains in East Asia: From Trade in Goods to Trade in Tasks*. Geneva: World Trade Organization; and Chiba, Japan: Institute of Developing Economies–Japan External Trade Organization.

7
Import Uses and Domestic Value-Added in Chinese Exports

What Can We Learn from Chinese Microdata?

Shunli Yao
Institute for Applied International Trade

Hong Ma
Tsinghua University

Jiansuo Pei
University of International Business and Economics

Estimating the economy-wide and sectoral domestic value-added in exports requires an input-output (I-O) table with good information on import uses. Normally, statistical agencies do not compile this information at the sectoral level. The I-O experts either break down the data on total import uses or make an inference from available but limited microdata. In so doing, they often explicitly rely on the proportionality assumption to assign imported inputs to different sectors, or else they implicitly resort to the proportionality assumption when making generalizations about the import use patterns by a sample of firms. However, this assumption is hardly valid in reality, because individual sectors normally do not have the same patterns of import use as the overall economy, and also because firms are heterogeneous and they often behave differently in international trade (Bernard et al. 2007). As a result, these approaches tend to lead to biased estimates, as shown by the microdata work at the U.S. Census Bureau (Feenstra and Jensen 2012) and the microdata work for Germany (Winkler and Milberg 2009). Meanwhile, I-O-based trade-related estimates are sensitive to the structure of the import matrix, such as for emission estimation, as shown in Dietzenbacher, Pei, and Yang (2012), and for vertical specialization (VS) estimation, as in Yang et al. (2013).[1]

Therefore, when the World Trade Organization (WTO) and the Organisation for Economic Co-operation and Development (OECD) launched the "Made in the World Initiative" in 2011 to promote worldwide research on domestic value-added share (DVS) estimation and to enhance understanding of the global value chain, they pointed out that "the key challenges in the immediate future concern the quality of trade statistics and the assumptions made to allocate imports to users" and that linking traders to the manufacturers would form an important part of the work (Ahmad et al. 2011). In addition to the Trade by Enterprise Characteristics (TEC) joint project with Eurostat, the OECD's exercise with Turkish microdata is another attempt to reveal the patterns of firm heterogeneity in trade and production and, based on that, to improve trade in value-added measures (Ahmad and Araujo 2011).

There are two threads of methodologies with which to estimate China's DVS in exports under an I-O framework: one relies on assumptions or optimization programming to derive key coefficients, and the other employs real data to obtain these coefficients. The former approach includes the work of Dean, Fung, and Wang (2011) and of Koopman, Wang, and Wei (2012). Koopman, Wang, and Wei split the officially published Chinese 2007 I-O tables into two parts—1) processing and 2) normal trade—in their modified Chinese I-O tables. Ma, Wang, and Zhu (2013) take the modified I-O table that Koopman, Wang, and Wei developed and further split it by producers' ownership. In doing so, Ma, Wang, and Zhu also incorporate micro firm-level data and other real data. Even though their approach contains real data, it falls into the former category, given the complexity of the I-O tables' structure after two rounds of splitting and the lack of import-use information in the microdata, as will be shown in this chapter.

On the other hand, the Chinese National Bureau of Statistics (NBS) follows the latter approach. When compiling China's 2007 input-output table, NBS researchers for the first time used a survey of firms to prepare the import-use coefficients. Recently, in updating the I-O tables and also as China's response to the WTO/OECD Made in the World Initiative, the NBS decided to employ import-use matrices from two sources. While the NBS will keep the previous 2007 matrix, the Chinese General Administration of Customs has started its own independent firm survey on import uses. The approaches by the two agencies are quite different. The NBS has jurisdiction over enterprise production data collection, and its survey is an added module to its existing annual survey on above-scale industrial production enterprises, called the Annual Survey of Industrial Production (ASIP). On the other hand, Customs is responsible for managing the customs clearance documents provided by firms doing international trade. These firm-level trade data form the basis on which Customs conducts the survey.

The two agencies are trying to reach the same goal from different starting points and by taking different routes. The two microdata sets have rich information on firms' production, financial positions, and trade. Combined, they would be able to provide much-needed information on firms' import uses. However, the two threads of similar work are independent of each other. Therefore, among various sampling problems, the biggest problem with the two approaches is that neither of them is based on prior knowledge of both production and trade distribution patterns in the population.[2] Although this chapter does not include them, surveys on import uses by the two agencies serve as background for our analysis of the combined production and trade microdata sets on import uses.

Surveys are costly. Unless existing microdata are exhausted, surveys would not be efficient and, even worse, could lead to aggregation bias if they were not based on samples representative of Chinese firms' trade and production patterns, as the proportionality assumption would be implicitly applied.

Needless to say, the ideal approach is to make the best use of existing microdata on trade and production. Upward, Wang, and Zheng (2013) made the first attempt to do so in estimating China's DVS in exports. However, their work suffers from several flaws. These include

- proportionality assumption on import uses between domestic and export production,
- no differentiation regarding the proprietary rights between the two submodes of processing trade—1) processing with imported materials (PWIM) and 2) processing and assembly with provided imported materials (P&A),
- ignoring trading agency issues,
- treating the import and export data in the firm-level trade data set as having been used or produced by the same firms, and

- giving no consideration of the imported inputs embodied in domestic inputs.

Despite the above problems, Upward, Wang, and Zheng (2013) represent the right direction in which to move to pursue the microdata work in order to estimate the Chinese DVS in exports. This chapter follows this direction. Specifically, like Upward, Wang, and Zheng, we combine the two microdata sets used respectively and independently by the NBS and Customs. We identify the production enterprises that also do international trade by linking the two data sets. This enables us to reveal the patterns of Chinese firm heterogeneity in trade and production, which justify further exploration of the microdata in import uses and DVS estimation. After appropriately treating the problems in Upward, Wang, and Zheng, identified above, this chapter provides various estimates of DVS boundaries.

The chapter has five sections, counting this one. The next section, "Chinese I-O Table Development: Backgrounding the Microdata Work," introduces the recent development of Chinese I-O tables as background for our microdata work. Section Three, "Chinese Microdata and Firm Heterogeneity," explores the merged microdata and reports various measures of firm exposure to international trade to illustrate not only the within-sample but also the between-sample firm heterogeneity. Section Four, "Estimating DVS: Boundaries and Confidence," estimates Chinese DVS in exports based not only on various samples pulled from the microdata population but also on the aggregate commodity-level trade data. It provides lower and upper boundaries for DVS and the associated confidence levels. Section Five concludes with our speculation on how a firm survey project might improve the VS/DVS estimation.

CHINESE I-O TABLE DEVELOPMENT: BACKGROUNDING THE MICRODATA WORK

Recent Chinese I-O Table Development

As a tool of central planning, Chinese I-O tables traditionally had a domestic focus when the country was closed to the outside world, before 1978. The treatment of international trade in the I-O tables was minimal, assuming as it did that domestic and imported goods were identical. But with China increasingly opening up to foreign trade and investment, this assumption was later relaxed so that domestic and imported goods were treated as differentiated products. Pioneered by Chen et al. (2001) and continued in Chen et al. (2012), the structure of Chinese I-O tables has undergone dramatic change in the past decade to reflect the unique feature of Chinese foreign trade: About half of the country's foreign trade is administered under the processing trade regime. The separation of processing trade, normal trade, and domestic production in the Chinese I-O tables is justified by the theory of firm heterogeneity (Melitz 2003). The new I-O table has a rich trade structure and requires more information to fill in the coefficients, including the import-use matrices, which are crucial to estimating DVS in exports.

DVS Estimation without Import-Use Information

What can we know about the Chinese DVS in exports if we do not know the information on import uses? Table 7.1 shows several estimates based on public data. When talking about DVS in exports, one may be quick to think of it as a country's net exports in goods and services, or its current account balances. This is true only if imports used for final domestic consumption replace the same amount of domestic resources, which would otherwise be used for the same domestic production but instead are allocated to export production. This is a strong assumption. More often than not, imports for final domestic use are not perfect substitutes for goods or services in the export sector. This proxy overestimates the foreign content in exports or underestimates the DVS in exports. The proxy could be treated as the lower bound of the real DVS in exports. As shown in Table 7.1, this measure of lower-bound DVS (Total DVS1_lower) ranges between 8.2 and 25.3 percent over the period 2001–2010, reaching its high of 25.3 percent in 2007.

Furthermore, by breaking down Chinese foreign trade into normal and processing trade, the numbers for which are readily available from major Chinese government Web sites, we could treat processing imports as the only imported intermediates used for exports. This allows us to obtain an estimate of lower-bound vertical specialization, or VS, ranging from 26.4 to 37.5 percent over 2001–2010 and measuring 30.3 percent for 2007, which translates into an upper bound of DVS in exports of 69.7 percent for that year (Total DVS2_upper in Table 7.1).

Table 7.1 Estimates of Domestic Value-Added Shares in Exports without Import-Use Information (%)

	CA balances/ total exports	Total			L&M firms		
Year	Total DVS1_lower	Processing imports/ processing exports	Processing imports/ total exports	Total DVS2_upper	Processing imports/ processing exports	Processing imports/ total exports	Total DVS3_upper
2001	10.6	63.7	35.3	64.7	64.9	49.2	50.8
2002	11.5	67.9	37.5	62.5	67.9	51.0	49.0
2003	8.2	67.4	37.2	62.8	67.3	51.1	48.9
2004	8.3	67.6	37.4	62.6	69.9	50.6	49.4
2005	16.4	65.8	36.0	64.0	67.9	49.6	50.4
2006	21.6	63.0	33.2	66.8	62.4	44.8	55.2
2007	25.3	59.6	30.3	69.7	57.6	40.5	59.5
2008	24.4	56.0	26.4	73.6	—	—	—
2009	18.3	54.9	26.8	73.2	—	—	—
2010	14.7	56.4	26.5	73.5	—	—	—

NOTE: "CA" stands for "current account." "L&M" stands for "large and medium-sized firms." "DVS" stand for "domestic value-added share." — = data not available.

SOURCE: Authors' calculations based on data from National Bureau of Statistics of China Web site and China Customs Statistics (CCS).

In short, with the data on current account balances and the Chinese trade statistics alone, we can at best estimate only a range of Chinese DVS in exports, which for 2007 is 25.3 to 69.7 percent. To narrow down the lower and upper boundaries, we need to explore other data sources, which is the focus of the remaining part of the chapter.

Microdata Approach: What Can We Do, and What Can't We Do?

At the firm level, the Customs statistics have the same variables as those in the commodity-level trade statistics. Together with the firm production data, they raise the hope of estimating firm-level I-O tables. However, the following three problems hamper our efforts to do so:

1) The production enterprise data contain only total input use, but not its breakdown into domestic or foreign sources, or into different sectors.
2) The production enterprise data, normally without an import-use module, do not have import information and only have total exports. There is detailed import and export information in the firm trade data set, but the trading companies may resell the imports to other production firms and may also help export products made by other firms.
3) Neither of the two data sets has interfirm transaction information in either inputs or final products.

As a result, with the current Chinese firm-level data, it is difficult to give a precise DVS estimate. However, with rich information, it could be used to reveal the stylized patterns of firms' trade and production and serve as the basis for sensible assumptions and for efficient and unbiased survey design.

CHINESE MICRODATA AND FIRM HETEROGENEITY

Chinese Microdata Sets and Their Matching

We use two sets of 2007 Chinese firm-level data. First, the Customs data has product-level transaction information for 236,505 trading companies, which is the entire population of firm-level trade statistics. Second, ASIP data has 336,768 enterprises—all state-owned enterprises and other enterprises with annual sales of more than 5 million yuan—and covers 95 percent of industrial output and 98 percent of industrial exports, approximately the whole population of the Chinese industrial enterprises.

To merge the two data sets by firm name and other identifying information produces the linked data set, which is a subset of each of the two data sets. This is a standard exercise for researchers working on Chinese microdata. They may differ in specific matching criteria, but they use a similar strategy and therefore produce similar overall results. In this chapter, the matching exercise includes only trade data with nonzero exports and excludes those with zero exports but nonzero imports. This is a shortcoming for research on import uses. In terms of firm size, firms in the matched data set do both production and direct trade and tend to be large and medium (L&M), while firms in the nonmatched data set are generally small. Key summary statistics of the matching exercise for this chapter are presented in Table 7.2.

Among the 336,768 firms in the ASIP data set and the 236,505 firms in the trade data set, only 65,545 firms are successfully matched, accounting for 19.5 and 27.7 percent of the two data sets, respectively. The shares are small, but they account for 82.9 percent of the total of 79,103 exporting ASIP firms. In terms of trade volume, the matched firms handle 35.1 and 27.8 percent of the total exports for the two data sets, respectively. The ASIP data set does not have the import variable, and this data set accounts for only 16.9 percent of the total imports for the trade data set, lower than the same export share. The output and sales variables only appear in the ASIP data set, and they are almost the same in value, roughly 40–41 trillion yuan in total and 21–22 trillion yuan for exporting ASIP. Therefore, the L&M firms produce and sell about 18.5 percent of all ASIP firms' sales/output and 34.5 percent of exporting ASIP firms' sales/output.

There are several reasons that a large number of firms in the two data sets are not matched, in addition to the lack of accurate identification information. For the 80.5 percent of the total ASIP firms and the 17.1 percent of the exporting ASIP firms that are not matched, they either do not export at all or do not export directly, and therefore their names do not show up in the Customs registry. As for the 72.3 percent

Table 7.2 Summary Statistics of the 2007 Enterprise and Trade Data

Data Set	Firm numbers	Exports	Imports	Output	Sales
ASIP	336,768	7.34		40.50	40.00
Exporting ASIP	79,103	7.34		21.90	21.30
Trade data	236,505	9.27	7.27		
L&M (matched)	65,545	2.58	1.23	7.54	7.34
L&M ASIP exp > 0	50,277	2.31	1.05	5.95	5.81
L&M imp > 0	37,536	2.17	1.23	5.48	5.38

NOTE: Values for "Exports," "Imports," "Output," and "Sales" columns are in trillions of yuan. "ASIP" stands for "Annual Survey of Industrial Production." "L&M" stands for "large and medium-sized firms." Blank cell = data not applicable.

SOURCE: Authors' calculations based on data from National Bureau of Statistics of China Web site and China Customs Statistics (CCS).

of the firms in the trade data set that are not matched, they could be pure trading companies with no production at all, or they could be production firms that are not included in the ASIP data set.

In the L&M data set, there are two subsets that are used in this chapter. The subset "L&M ASIP exp > 0" represents the firms whose exports in the production data are also positive. The last row in Table 7.2 shows a subset of the matched data with positive imports (L&M imp > 0). This is the data set that Upward, Wang, and Zheng (2013) use in estimating China's DVS in exports. Because it is the smallest sample in terms of number of firms, its representativeness of the whole population is in doubt, and both firm heterogeneity within the data set and firm heterogeneity across samples deserve careful scrutiny if the aggregate DVS is to be derived from it.

Firm Heterogeneity in Trade and Production Patterns

The intermediates include two parts: 1) processing imports are treated as intermediates, and 2) intermediates under normal imports are identified with the "broad economic categories" (BEC) classification developed by the United Nations Statistics Division. Because of the existence of two submodes of processing imports, two different definitions are adopted for imported intermediates under processing imports in estimating DVS. One defines all processing imports as intermediates, and the other includes only processing with imported materials, or PWIM. To be consistent, the second definition is adopted when firms' input and output are used in estimating DVS together with import data, as the P&A (processing and assembly with provided imported materials) imports are not counted as input and not part of the output, either.

Trade intensity by ownership is shown in Table 7.3. The shares of intermediate imports in processing exports are listed in the first two columns. In comparing the shares in the L&M samples with those in the total population of trade statistics, we see that collective enterprises, wholly foreign-funded enterprises, and joint ventures behave similarly, whereas state-owned enterprises and private firms show significant differences. These differences possibly stem from the high concentration of pure trading companies among state-owned trading enterprises and the prevalence of small private firms in China's processing trade sector, since neither of these concentrations is included in the L&M samples. In both the total population and the L&M samples, only wholly foreign-funded enterprises have higher-than-average shares.

In the third and fourth columns in Table 7.3, normal imports of intermediates (defined in the BEC classification as a share of normal exports) are listed, showing large differences between the L&M samples and the population for all types of firms. Therefore, L&M samples are not representative of the population for this indicator either. Foreign firms (wholly foreign-funded firms and joint ventures) and state-owned enterprises have higher-than-average shares in both the total population and the L&M samples.[3]

In terms of the share of processing exports in total exports, shown in the fifth and sixth columns in Table 7.3, foreign firms (wholly foreign-funded firms and joint ventures) have the highest shares, and they are even higher in the L&M samples (85.9 and 65.5 percent, respectively), far ahead of the closest state-owned enterprises (34.2 percent). But the opposite is true for normal export share in total exports, as foreign firms have the lowest shares, shown in the seventh and eighth columns.

Across and within sample variations

Firm heterogeneity can be revealed in many ways. As we report in an earlier version of this chapter, which is available on the Web (Yao, Ma, and Pei 2013), when constructing export intensity (export/output)

Table 7.3 Use of Imported Intermediates and Exports Breakdown by Firm Type, 2007 (%)

	Imported intermediates as share of export value				Share of exports by customs category			
Formula	Processing imports/ processing exports		Normal BEC input imports/normal exports		Processing exports/ total exports		Normal exports/ total exports	
Firm type	Total	L&M firms	Total	L&M firms	Total	L&M firms	Total	L&M firms
Collective enterprises	41.6	41.0	37.8	14.9	24.1	15.4	75.9	84.6
Wholly foreign-funded enterprises	63.1	61.9	78.7	52.4	81.8	85.9	18.2	14.1
Joint ventures	48.3	46.7	73.7	59.2	59.7	65.5	40.3	34.5
Private firms	58.7	47.2	25.6	6.4	9.8	14.9	90.2	85.1
State-owned enterprises	63.4	38.0	104.4	64.3	26.6	34.2	73.4	65.8
All	59.7	57.6	62.7	40.7	50.6	70.4	49.4	29.6

NOTE: "L&M" stands for "large and medium-sized firms." "BEC" stands for the "broad economic categories" classification.
SOURCE: Authors' calculations based on data from National Bureau of Statistics of China Web site and China Customs Statistics (CCS).

and intermediates import intensity (imports input/output and imports input/input) indicators, we see considerable firm heterogeneity across and within sectors or samples, as well as evidence of importing agency problems, shown as larger-than-one intermediate import ratios over total output or input. To put things in perspective, Table 7.4 assembles some aggregate measures together with shares of value-added in output, with breakdown by firm ownership (domestic or foreign) and size.

For import intensity, large discrepancies exist between domestic and foreign firms, as foreign firms' import shares are much higher. There are some differences across firm size but more differences within the same size group for the share of imported input in total input, as shown by the difference between the weighted and simple averages, where total input value is used as the weight.

For export intensity, too, domestic and foreign firms behave differently: Again, foreign firms' export shares are higher. Compared to the "L&M ASIP exp > 0" sample, firm size matters more for the "Other exporting ASIP" sample, in which larger firms tend to export a smaller share of total output.

Value-added share in total output (Value-added/output) is a new indicator. While the aggregate measures in the two samples are quite similar, they can differ by as much as 6.3 and 58.6 percent, respectively, for the sectors "Artcrafts and other manufacturing" (China Industrial Classification [CIC] 42) and "Tobacco" (CIC 16), as shown in the tables of an earlier version of this chapter (Yao, Ma, and Pei 2013).

In summary, the existence of firm heterogeneity is extensive, and the issues of proprietary rights in processing imports and trading agency are real. These will complicate the efforts to estimate the DVS in Chinese exports.

ESTIMATING DVS: BOUNDARIES AND CONFIDENCE

Proportionality Assumption on Domestic and Export Production

Proportionality assumption regarding import uses means two things: 1) imports are proportionally allocated among different sectors, and 2) within each sector, they are further proportionally allocated between

Table 7.4 Summary Indicators by Type of Ownership and Firm Size, 2007 (%)

				Type of ownership		Firm size (no. of employees)			
Indicator	Data set	Average	All	Domestic	Foreign	<50	50–200	200–1,000	>1,000
Import input/	L&M	Weighted	22.8	6.3	29.4	28.7	24.6	21.3	23.9
input		across firms	59.0	22.0	71.0	38.0	57.4	69.5	29.7
Import input/	L&M	Weighted	17.3	4.8	22.2	21.6	18.6	16.2	18.2
output		across firms	16.1	5.3	19.6	18.9	15.8	15.4	18.5
Export/output	L&M	Weighted	45.6	37.0	59.5	55.0	50.1	50.8	52.5
	ASIP exp > 0	across firms	62.1	51.1	68.9	58.9	60.9	63.8	62.6
	Other exporting	Weighted	41.5	37.5	55.3	62.3	55.6	43.1	32.9
	ASIP firms	across firms	66.7	64.3	71.4	70.5	69.4	62.8	46.2
Value-added/	L&M	Weighted	25.9	25.8	26.0	25.7	25.4	26.1	26.0
output		across firms	26.7	25.6	27.4	24.4	26.1	27.6	28.4
	Other exporting	Weighted	27.1	26.9	27.6	24.1	26.6	27.1	27.8
	ASIP firms	across firms	28.3	27.5	30.0	23.8	27.5	31.1	31.8

NOTE: For the first indicator, total input value is used as the weight, and for the remaining three indicators, output value is used as the weight. "L&M" stands for "large and medium-sized firms." "ASIP" stands for "Annual Survey of Industrial Production."

SOURCE: Authors' calculations based on data from National Bureau of Statistics of China Web site and China Customs Statistics (CCS).

domestic and export production. If the importing agency problem could be solved so that the import data truly reflected the amount of intermediate imports used in a firm's production, then the L&M data set would be able to remedy the first problem. Thus, the importing agency issue is a focus of this chapter. As for the second problem, unfortunately, firm-level data alone are of little help, as they do not contain information on how firms split intermediate imports between domestic and export production.

When Hummels, Ishii, and Yi (2001) first employ I-O tables to estimate VS, they assume an equal percentage of foreign input in domestic output and exports. Upward, Wang, and Zheng (2013) retain this assumption in estimating China's vertical specialization (VS). Working from a data set similar to L&M, Upward, Wang, and Zheng distinguish between processing and normal trade and apply this assumption to normal trade only. That is, within normal trade, imports are allocated to domestic and export production proportionally to domestic output and normal exports. This assumption is oversimplified but still acceptable. However, when Upward, Wang, and Zheng actually do the calculation, they use the following formula to determine the ratio of intermediate import in domestic output and normal exports:

$$(7.1) \qquad r^{uwz} = \frac{M^{bec}}{Y - X^{p}} .$$

This is problematic, because imports for processing and assembly ($M^{p\&a}$) in the trade data set are included only in X^p but not in Y. Therefore, the denominator in the above formula gives a lower value for domestic output and normal exports, or a higher share of foreign content in domestic output and normal exports. $M^{p\&a}$ accounts for 17.0 and 24.2 percent of L&M processing imports and total processing imports, respectively, and these are not trivial amounts. As such, the problem associated with $M^{p\&a}$ in the above formula cannot be ignored.

Imports for Processing and Assembly and a Lower VS Boundary

This chapter corrects this problem and modifies the above formula by deducting $M^{p\&a}$ from processing exports when calculating the ratio of normal intermediate imports defined by BEC (M^{bec}):

(7.2) $$r = \frac{M^{bec}}{Y - (X^p - M^{p\&a})} = \frac{M^{bec}}{DN},$$

where *DN* represents domestic output and normal exports.

Export production often uses more foreign inputs than domestic production. This can be seen from trade intensity measures by ownership breakdown in Tables 7.3 and 7.4, where foreign-funded enterprises (FFEs) have higher shares of intermediate imports in normal exports, total input, and total output. Because FFEs dominate Chinese foreign trade in both imports and exports, a link can be established showing that export production has higher shares of foreign intermediates than domestic production. Also, considering that a domestic content requirement is normally imposed on FFEs for domestic production, a lower bound of *VS* exists as a result of this policy. In fact, the proportionality assumption regarding the import uses among domestic and export production, as reflected in Equation (7.2), can be regarded as the lower bound:

(7.3) $$VS^{lower} = M^p + \frac{M^{bec}}{Y - (X^p - M^{p\&a})} X^n = M^p + r \times X^n .$$

Trading Agency Problem

Imports and exports in the above equations mean the actual imports used as inputs by the firms and the actual exports produced by the firms. Because of the trading agency problem, trade volume from the trade data set does not meet this requirement at the firm level. However, since the L&M data already screened out the pure trading companies, production firms doing trading agency business are more likely to deal with firms in the same sector. Based on this assumption, we first sum up the variables across firms within a sector and then proceed to estimate sectoral *VS* using that formula. By so doing, we neutralize the trading agency problem among firms within a sector, but we also risk introducing aggregation bias. This can be illustrated by the following equations:

(7.4) $$VS_i^{lower} = M_i^p + \frac{M_i^{bec}}{DN_i} \times X_i^n ,$$

(7.5) $$VS^{lower} = \sum M_i^p + \frac{\sum M_i^{bec}}{\sum DN_i} \times \sum X_i^n , \text{ and}$$

$$(7.6)\quad VS^{lower} - \sum VS_i^{lower} = \sum \left(\frac{X_i^n}{DN_i} - \frac{\sum X_i^n}{\sum DN_i^n} \right) \times M_i^{bec}.$$

Because both within and between sectors variations could be large, as suggested in the section titled "Chinese Microdata and Firm Heterogeneity," the two approaches may generate different sectoral *VS*, as the right-hand side of Equation (7.6) is not always zero. This potential bias can also occur when estimation is done at the whole manufacturing level. The lower bound of VS thus should be treated with less confidence.[4]

Upper VS Boundary

After determining that the estimation of the lower bound of *VS* should be treated with less confidence, we now turn to the upper-bound *VS* estimation. As exports use more intermediate imports than domestic production, the upper limit of *VS* can be achieved by assuming all intermediate imports are used for export production:

$$(7.7)\quad VS^{upper} = M^p + M^{bec}.$$

In contrast to the lower-bound *VS*, the upper-bound *VS* estimate is invariant of the level of analysis, commodity, or sectoral level. It is not subject to the constraint of the domestic content requirement, either. As a result, the confidence level is high for it, as long as we are confident in the BEC definition of intermediates.[5]

Results and Discussions

Sectoral and whole manufacturing shares of *VS* (*VSS*) over two samples, "L&M imp > 0" and "L&M," are reported in Table 7.5.[6] The lower bound of VSS is converted into the upper bound of DVS through the following formula:

$$(7.8)\quad DVS = 1 - \frac{VS}{X} = 1 - VSS.$$

Across all sectors, DVS upper bounds are 61.0 and 67.2 percent for the respective two samples. Among all sectors, DVS's in the CIC sectors "Food manufacturing" and "Beverages" (CIC 14 and 15), "Furni-

Table 7.5 VS Share (VSS) and DVS by Sector, Estimated with Microdata (%)

		L&M imp > 0		L&M	
CIC[a]	Sector description	VSS_ lower	Total DVS4_ upper	VSS_ lower	Total DVS5_ upper
13	Agriculture and food processing	32.2	67.8	20.5	79.5
14	Food manufacturing	11.5	88.5	8.3	91.7
15	Beverages	8.2	91.8	5.5	94.5
16	Tobacco	56.7	43.3	56.7	43.3
17	Textile	23.1	76.9	16.2	83.8
18	Clothing, footwear, and caps	27.9	72.1	22.7	77.3
19	Leather, fur, feather, and products	35.7	64.3	28.1	71.9
20	Timber and wood products	24.6	75.4	16.2	83.8
21	Furniture	12.5	87.5	10.2	89.8
22	Paper and products	56.9	43.1	50.3	49.7
23	Printing and recording	26.9	73.1	24.0	76.0
24	Culture, educ., and sports products	23.7	76.3	20.2	79.8
25	Energy resource processing	16.6	83.4	6.1	93.9
26	Raw chem. materials and products	49.0	51.0	39.2	60.8
27	Medicines	19.7	80.3	14.3	85.7
28	Chemical fibers	51.8	48.2	48.8	51.2
29	Rubber	39.2	60.8	35.2	64.8
30	Plastics	55.1	44.9	47.2	52.8
31	Nonmetallic mineral products	17.8	82.2	11.7	88.3
32	Ferrous metals processing	72.8	27.2	37.9	62.1
33	Nonferrous metals processing	50.9	49.1	36.8	63.2
34	Metal products	23.6	76.4	18.9	81.1
35	General purpose machinery	22.7	77.3	18.3	81.7
36	Special purpose machinery	29.0	71.0	25.7	74.3
37	Transport equipment	30.0	70.0	26.2	73.8
39	Electrical machinery & equipment	35.6	64.4	30.8	69.2
40	Electronics	66.6	33.4	64.9	35.1
41	Measuring, cultural, office machine	42.0	58.0	39.2	60.8
42	Artcrafts and other manufacturing	30.9	69.1	21.8	78.2
43	Waste recycling and processing	88.8	11.2	80.7	19.3
All		39.0	61.0	32.8	67.2

NOTE: Gross output (rather than total sales) is adopted in the denominator. "VSS" stands for "vertical specialization share." "DVS" stands for "domestic value-added share." CIC category 38 has been omitted from the table.

[a] "CIC" stands for China Industrial Classification.

SOURCE: Authors' calculations based on data from National Bureau of Statistics of China Web site and China Customs Statistics (CCS).

ture" (CIC 21), "Petroleum and coking processing" (shown as "Energy resource processing," CIC 25), and "Nonmetallic mineral products" (CIC 31) are among the highest, because these domestic sectors are not as much globalized as the sectors with the lowest DVS's, such as "Communication, computer, and other electronic equipment" (shown as "Electronics," CIC 40) and "Waste recycling and disposal" (shown as "Waste recycling and processing," CIC 43). The DVS patterns are consistent with import intensity patterns reported in an earlier version of this chapter (Yao, Ma, and Pei 2013), where sectors with higher DVS's tend to have lower intensity of intermediate imports, and vice versa.

Comparing the two data samples, DVS's in the "L&M" sample are consistently higher than those in the "L&M imp > 0" sample, simply because the former data set has records with zero imports. Firms that do not import intermediates may buy from other production firms that are also in the importing agency business. This is another example of the fact that sampling matters in DVS estimation and the view that the trading agency problem deserves careful treatment.

Table 7.6 reports the aggregate DVS's, both lower and upper bounds, for overall and normal trade estimated with different data sets and intermediate definitions. Some of the numbers are drawn from previous tables. The numbers with superscript "a" are the estimates with

Table 7.6 Estimated DVS Boundaries (%)

	Total DVS		Normal DVS		Shares of
Data scope and imports input	Lower	Upper	Lower	Upper	P&A in PI
CA balances (DVS1)	25.3				
Total PI (DVS2)		69.7			
L&M PI (DVS3)		59.5			
L&M imp > 0 PI BEC (DVS4)	50.7	61.0[a]	66.9	94.5[a]	17.0
L&M PI BEC (DVS5)	58.5	67.2[a]	77.8	96.4[a]	17.0
Total PI BEC	38.9	68.0[a]	37.3	96.3[a]	24.2

NOTE: "DVS" stands for "domestic value-added share." "P&A" stands for "processing and assembly." "PI" stands for "processing imports." "L&M" stands for "large and medium-sized firms." "BEC" stands for the "broad economic categories" classification. Blank cell = data not applicable.

[a] Signifies a number that is an estimate with less confidence.

SOURCE: Authors' calculations based on data from National Bureau of Statistics of China Web site and China Customs Statistics (CCS).

less confidence, in part because of the firm heterogeneity issue, as discussed earlier in regard to Equation (7.6).[7] As a reminder, Table 7.6 also lists the shares of processing and assembly imports in total processing imports for the three data sets affected by the proprietary rights issue. Taking this issue into consideration helps improve the confidence level in the GVC upper bounds for the three data sets.

Clearly, the range of DVS estimates varies, depending on the scope of the data and the associated definitions of intermediates. For overall DVS, both lower and upper bounds are estimated with confidence, and the true value could be anywhere in the range of 38.9 to 69.7 percent. For normal trade, the DVS could be anywhere in a much wider range, from 37.3 to 96.3 percent.

What have we learned from our DVS estimation results? First of all, DVS estimates are sensitive to data samples. Cross-sample variations for lower and upper DVS bounds as well as the ranges of possible DVS are significant, especially when compared to the overall DVS estimates. This suggests that none of the samples appear to be representative of the population.

Second, as reflected by the wide range of possible GVC values, DVS estimates are sensitive to assumptions on import uses. This is intuitive, as the import uses across sectors and across domestic and export production directly allocate the flow of foreign intermediates within a country, and they ultimately determine the sectoral and overall DVS's. It is also in line with previous findings in I-O table literature—e.g., Dietzenbacher, Pei, and Yang (2012) and Yang et al. (2013).

Given the uncertainties surrounding the true DVS numbers, it is natural and logical to speculate about a firm survey project on import uses that aims to obtain additional information for better DVS estimation.

CONCLUSION

This chapter does not estimate the exact true DVS value because we do not make arbitrary assumptions. Instead, we take stock of the possible estimates, and in so doing we clarify several conceptual issues, which helps to improve the methodology in the literature. We leave a wide range for possible DVS estimates and only expect them to be narrowed down by future firm survey work.

Firm-level data have rich information that could be used to correct the bias in the import-use matrix caused by proportionality assumption in I-O table development. To realize the potential of such data, surveys need to overcome the nonrepresentative sampling and trading agency problems. They can do so, among other ways, by taking the following steps:

- First, identify the small production firms from firm-level trade data. This could be done by first screening the nonmatched small trading firms and then tracking them through firms' contact information to verify their production status. By incorporating these small trade and production firms, the L&M data set could be expanded to include large, medium, and small firms (LMS).
- Second, select a sample of firms from LMS to be covered by the survey. The questionnaire should include questions on the amount of imports that are for a firm's own use, the exports produced by customs regime, and the amount split between domestic production and export production, among others.

Of course, various other aspects of the firm distribution should also be considered, such as ownership, sector, location, and trading partners.

Firms are able to answer questions regarding direct import uses, but it is difficult for firms to know the uses of imports embodied in domestic inputs. Probably this is the only area that would require an assumption.

Notes

The authors thank Bradford Jensen for his encouragement, and Jie Chen, Kunfu Zhu, and Hongman Jin for their insights on the firm survey projects at the National Bureau of Statistics of China and the China Customs Statistics (CCS). Financial support from the Sloan Foundation is gratefully acknowledged. Jiansuo Pei also acknowledges financial support from the National Natural Science Foundation of China [No. 41205105] and Program for Young Excellent Talents, UIBE [No. 2013YQ01]. The authors are responsible for all errors.

1. The term "vertical specialization" is borrowed from Hummels, Ishii, and Yi (2001) and is defined as the value of imported intermediates in exports.

2. Details on the NBS and Customs import use surveys are documented in an earlier version of this chapter (Yao, Ma, and Pei 2013), which is available on the Web.
3. The higher shares for the state-owned companies are either because some of the traditional state trading companies have diversified their operations into production business and therefore are kept in the L&M data set, or because import of primary resources is often conducted by state-owned production enterprises with overseas investment.
4. Less confidence in the lower bound of VS is also due to lack of an exact minimum for domestic content requirement.
5. According to Timmer (2012), 14 percent of BEC codes can be both final goods and intermediates.
6. We do not attempt to compare the numerical results with those from other studies because our methodology is based on a different set of concepts, which makes it uncomparable.
7. VS is first estimated at sector level and then summed up across sectors. For VS estimation with the entirety of commodity trade data, in the last row of Table 7.6, there is no link between production output and trade data, and estimation can only be done with data summed over the whole database.

References

Ahmad, Nadim, and Sonia Araujo. 2011. *Using Trade Microdata to Improve Trade In Value Added Measures: Proof of Concept Using Turkish Data.* Paris: Organisation for Economic Co-operation and Development. http://search.oecd.org/officialdocuments/displaydocumentpdf/?cote=STD/TBS/WPTGS%282011%2916&doclanguage=en (accessed November 19, 2013).

Ahmad, Nadim, Hubert Escaith, Sébastien Miroudot, Colin Webb, and Norihiko Yamano. 2011. "Trade in Value-Added: Concepts, Methodologies, and Challenges (Joint OECD-WTO Note)." Paris: Organisation for Economic Co-operation and Development; and Geneva: World Trade Organization.

Bernard, Andrew B., J. Bradford Jensen, Stephen J. Redding, and Peter K. Schott. 2007. "Firms in International Trade." *Journal of Economic Perspectives* 21(3): 105–130.

Chen, Xikang, Leonard K. Cheng, Kwok-Chiu Fung, and Lawrence J. Lau. 2001. "The Estimation of Domestic Value-Added and Employment Induced by Exports: An Application to Chinese Exports to the United States." Working paper. Palo Alto, CA: Stanford University, Department of Economics. http://www.stanford.edu/~ljlau/Presentations/Presentations/010618.pdf (accessed November 19, 2013).

Chen, Xikang, Leonard K. Cheng, Kwok-Chiu Fung, Lawrence J. Lau, Yun-Wing Sung, Kunfu Zhu, Cuihong Yang, Jiansuo Pei, and Yuwan Duan. 2012.

"Domestic Value Added and Employment Generated by Chinese Exports: A Quantitative Estimation." *China Economic Review* 23(4): 850–864.
Dean, Judith M., Kwok-Chiu Fung, and Zhi Wang. 2011. "Measuring Vertical Specialization: The Case of China." *Review of International Economics* 19(4): 609–625.
Dietzenbacher, Erik, Jiansuo Pei, and Cuihong Yang. 2012. "Trade, Production Fragmentation, and China's Carbon Dioxide Emissions." *Journal of Environmental Economics and Management* 64(1): 88–101.
Feenstra, Robert C., and J. Bradford Jensen. 2012. "Evaluating Estimates of Materials Offshoring from U.S. Manufacturing." NBER Working Paper No. 17916. Cambridge, MA: National Bureau of Economic Research.
Hummels, David, Jun Ishii, and Kei-Mu Yi. 2001. "The Nature and Growth of Vertical Specialization in World Trade." *Journal of International Economics* 54(1): 75–96.
Koopman, Robert, Zhi Wang, and Shang-Jin Wei. 2012. "Estimating Domestic Content in Exports When Processing Trade Is Pervasive." *Journal of Development Economics* 99(1): 178–189.
Ma, Hong, Zhi Wang, and Kunfu Zhu. 2013. "Domestic Value-Added in China's Exports and Its Distribution by Firm Ownership." Paper presented at the American Economic Association annual meetings, held in San Diego, CA, January 4–6.
Melitz, Marc J. 2003. "The Impact of Trade on Intra-Industry Reallocations and Aggregate Industry Productivity." *Econometrica* 71(6): 1695–1725.
Timmer, Marcel P., ed. 2012. "The World Input-Output Database (WIOD): Contents, Sources, and Methods." WIOD Working Paper No. 10. Brussels: European Commission.
Upward, Richard, Zheng Wang, and Jinghai Zheng. 2013. "Weighing China's Export Basket: The Domestic Content and Technology Intensity of Chinese Exports." *Journal of Comparative Economics* 41(2): 527–543.
Winkler, Deborah, and William Milberg. 2009. "Errors from the 'Proportionality Assumption' in the Measurement of Offshoring: Application to German Labor Demand." SCEPA Working Paper No. 2009-12. New York: Schwartz Center for Economic Policy Analysis and Department of Economics, New School for Social Research.
Yang, Cuihong, Erik Dietzenbacher, Jiansuo Pei, Xikang Chen, Kunfu Zhu, and Zhipeng Tang. 2013. "The Bias in Measuring Vertical Specialization: The Effects of Processing Trade in China." Unpublished paper, Chinese Academy of Sciences, Beijing; and University of Groningen, Netherlands.
Yao, Shunli, Hong Ma, and Jiansuo Pei. 2013. "Import Uses and Domestic Value Added in Chinese Exports: What Can We Learn from Chinese Micro Data?" Paper presented at the conference "Measuring the Effects of Globalization," held in Washington, DC, February 28–March 1.

Part 3

Trade in Intangibles and Data

8
A Formulary Approach for Attributing Measured Production to Foreign Affiliates of U.S. Parents

Dylan G. Rassier
U.S. Bureau of Economic Analysis

Jennifer Koncz-Bruner
formerly of the U.S. Bureau of Economic Analysis

The *Balance of Payments and International Investment Position Manual, Sixth Edition* (BPM), and the *System of National Accounts 2008* (SNA) both recommend attributing production to countries based on the residence of productive entities. The residence of an entity is generally determined to be the country in which a significant amount of production takes place. In cases where an entity has little or no physical presence, residence is determined as the country in which the entity is legally incorporated or registered. In the case of a multinational enterprise (MNE), the residency-based framework of the BPM and the SNA requires that the activities of affiliated entities resident in different countries be measured separately in order to accurately attribute the economic activity of each entity to the country in which it is resident.[1] Likewise, the residency-based framework requires that cross-border transactions between affiliated entities resident in different countries be included in balance of payments statistics.

For practical reasons, statisticians generally measure production and other attributes of MNEs based on accounting data. While the BPM (International Monetary Fund 2009) and the SNA (European Commission et al. 2009) recommend the residency-based framework for attributing measured production, attribution under the framework is not limited to a specific accounting treatment. In this chapter, we focus on formulary apportionment as an alternative treatment to separate accounting, which is the basis for current measures of production. Under separate accounting, accounting records are maintained separately for each entity within an MNE. As a result, accounting measures such as costs and profits are attributed to affiliated entities based on each entity's purpose within the structure of the MNE and not necessarily on the economic activity of the entity. In other words, accounting measures recorded under separate accounting may not accurately reflect the economic activity of the entity. Formulary apportionment is commonly required by U.S. state corporate income tax regulations to determine the income attributable to the state for a corporation that operates in multiple states. Rather than keeping separate accounting records for operations in each state, the corporation keeps consolidated records and attributes income to a state based on prescribed apportionment factors—such as employment, property, and sales—that reflect where income is actually earned.

Residency-based separate accounting may be particularly problematic for statisticians in cases where production is accomplished with inputs that are shared by multiple entities within the same MNE. Shared inputs may include intangible property such as patents, trademarks, formulas, processes, and so forth, or they may include headquarter services such as accounting, finance, and marketing, which do not need to be physically located at an entity in order to provide service (Helpman 1984; Markusen 1984, 1997). If a statistician is able to directly observe the economic activity of the entity in order to determine actual production, residency-based separate accounting may pose no particular problem. However, if the statistician only has accounting data for the entity, then identifying the location of production, which is the essence of the residency-based framework, is particularly difficult when the entity employs relatively few or no local inputs such as labor or property, plant, and equipment (PPE) but reports relatively significant accounting measures related to shared inputs. As shared inputs become more common and as MNE activities increase, challenges encountered under the residency-based framework become more important in the U.S. international transactions accounts (ITAs) and the U.S. National Income and Product Accounts (NIPAs) (Lipsey 2009, 2010; United Nations Economic Commission for Europe 2011).

As is consistent with the residency-based framework, the U.S. Bureau of Economic Analysis (BEA) attributes production to a foreign affiliate of a U.S. parent according to the country in which the affiliate is resident. If the affiliate has little or no physical presence in the country, the BEA follows the BPM and SNA recommendations to attribute production to the affiliate as long as the affiliate is legally incorporated or registered in the country. In addition, the BEA measures production based on accounting measures reported for the affiliate, and the accounting measures are determined under separate accounting according to generally accepted U.S. accounting principles. Thus, if an MNE is structured in a way that attributes accounting measures to an affiliate based on economic activity resulting from shared inputs that are not actually employed by the affiliate, production may be attributed to an affiliate with no economic activity.

In this chapter, we use formulary apportionment, which is also consistent with the residency-based framework, as an alternative for separate accounting to measure value-added at foreign affiliates of U.S. parents. We find that overall reattributions from foreign affiliates to U.S. parents are relatively small—less than 5 percent of total value-added attributed to all majority-owned foreign affiliates and U.S. parents under separate accounting. In contrast, reattributions across global regions including Africa, Asia, Europe, Latin America, and the Middle East are greater than 10 percent of value-added under separate accounting. Moreover, reattributions for foreign affiliates are greater than 10 percent of value-added under separate accounting for all industry sectors except administration, information, and transportation.

In addition to applying formulary apportionment to reattribute value-added, we report preliminary results to reattribute service imports and exports between U.S. parents and their foreign affiliates. We find a relatively large decrease in imports but no meaningful change in exports. The overall effect on gross domestic product (GDP) is only a small increase—approximately 0.1 percent. Based on our preliminary results, we expect to be able to provide a complete picture of the U.S. current account under formulary apportionment in a future paper.

Using factor shares to evaluate the results, we conclude that value-added attributed to foreign affiliates and U.S. parents under formulary apportionment yields a picture of measured production by industry sector and country that is more congruent with economic activity than related measures generated under separate accounting. Thus, formulary apportionment appears to be a viable alternative to separate accounting under the residency-based framework of the BPM and the SNA.

Following this introductory section, the chapter is organized into the five sections that follow. The next section provides an overview of related literature. The third section outlines the BEA's current framework for measuring production based on residency-based separate accounting and outlines the proposed framework for attributing production based on residency-based formulary apportionment. The fourth section describes the BEA's survey data on the operations of MNEs. The fifth section presents the results of the formulary apportionment. The last section offers a conclusion.

RELATED LITERATURE

To provide context for our work, we draw upon four distinct but related lines of literature. First, we borrow features from the industrial-organization (IO) literature on foreign direct investment (FDI) and trade to outline a simple production model for foreign affiliates that underlies our choice of formulary apportionment. Second, we describe the international guidelines that provide a framework for organizing official statistics on FDI and trade. Third, we review the literature that identifies challenges encountered under the residency-based framework and proposes alternative frameworks for organizing official statistics on FDI and trade. Fourth and finally, we discuss the literature on formulary apportionment as it is applied in international taxation and identify features of formulary apportionment as a tool for attributing measured production to entities within an MNE.

Industrial-Organization Literature

The IO literature on FDI and trade focuses on adapting general equilibrium trade models to include endogenous MNEs. Early work explains the origination of MNEs based on the organization of production into one of two types (Caves 1971): 1) vertical integration (Brainard 1993; Helpman 1984) and 2) horizontal integration (Brainard 1997; Markusen 1984). However, Markusen (1997) argues that the outcomes identified by vertical and horizontal models face limitations based on underlying assumptions; he constructs an alternative knowledge-capital model.

Regardless of how production is organized, a useful feature of each of the IO models of FDI and trade is the inclusion of a local input and a firm-specific shared input, which can be used jointly by multiple affiliates. Firm-specific inputs do not need to be physically present for production to take place, but firm-specific inputs cannot generate production without the local input. General equilibrium in each model results under assumptions that include foreign affiliates that produce with constant returns to scale and operate in perfectly competitive markets. The models also assume that production is separable across affiliates and that markets are segmented.

International Guidelines

The international guidelines explain how official FDI and trade statistics should be constructed. In paragraph 4.11 of the BPM, an economy is defined as comprising "all the institutional units that are resident in a particular economic territory."[2] One of the attributes of an institutional unit is the existence of a complete set of accounting records (BPM para. 4.13[d]; SNA para. 4.2[d]), which implies that the possibility of separate accounting is required under the residency-based framework. In addition, the international guidelines consider the possibility that production may be located somewhere other than the economic territory where an entity is legally incorporated or registered. In particular, paragraph 4.134 of the BPM states, "A legal entity is resident in the economic territory under whose laws the entity is incorporated or registered. . . . It must not be combined with entities resident in other economies. If [the entity] has substantial operations in another economy, a branch may be identified there." In this case, the branch is treated as an institutional unit subject to the criterion for accounting records (BPM para. 4.27[a]), and the operations of the branch are to be attributed to the corresponding economic territory (BPM para. 4.26). Thus, as is consistent with the IO literature on FDI and trade, the international guidelines consider the possibility that factors of production may be located somewhere within an MNE other than with an affiliate to which production would be attributed based merely on legal incorporation or registration of the affiliate. Furthermore, the criterion for accounting records does not rule out formulary apportionment as an alternative to separate accounting for either the measurement or the attribution of production at the affiliate. The intent of the guidelines is that production is attributed where it is actually taking place.

Alternative Measurement Frameworks

Challenges in implementing the residency-based framework are widely addressed in international discourse and academic literature. The United Nations recently published a collection of papers that address the impact of globalization on national accounts (United Nations Economic Commission for Europe 2011). An entire chapter is dedicated to identifying and explaining challenges associated with allocating production to national economies under a residency-based framework. Among the challenges are the transfers of intangible property and the attribution of associated income. However, the chapter does not offer any analysis to identify the extent to which allocation of production may be incongruent with actual economic activity. Lipsey (2009, 2010) offers evidence of possible distortions in U.S. outbound FDI and trade flows present in aggregate data published by the BEA for service industries. Lipsey suggests the distortions are a result of global structuring of MNEs and the mobility of productive resources in the service industries. As a result, he suggests but does not develop an alternative location-based framework to accompany the residency-based framework for measuring trade in services.

Early work also suggests supplemental frameworks for organizing FDI and trade statistics based on ownership. Baldwin and Kimura (1998) find that net sales activities of U.S. affiliates of foreign-based MNEs to Americans and of foreign affiliates of U.S.-based MNEs to foreigners are almost as high as measured U.S. imports and exports, respectively. Kimura and Baldwin (1998) find that FDI has an even larger role in the Japanese economy. In each case, the authors use their results to highlight the usefulness of an ownership-based framework. Landefeld, Whichard, and Lowe (1993) explain and evaluate ownership-based trade measures and propose an alternative residency-based trade measure that includes an adjustment for the net effect on the U.S. economy of the operations of U.S.-owned companies abroad and of foreign-owned companies in the United States. As a result of the early work on alternative organizing frameworks, the BEA publishes annual ownership-based measures of the current account of the

ITAs as a supplement to the residency-based framework (Whichard and Lowe 1995). The ownership-based framework is fully consistent with the international standards of the BPM and the SNA and combines with the residency-based measures of U.S. imports and exports the transactions of affiliates that are not captured in the residency-based framework. While the ownership-based framework may address some of the challenges encountered under the residency-based framework, the ownership-based framework is not intended to identify the location of production, which is the centerpiece for national economic accounting purposes.

Formulary Apportionment Literature

While formulary apportionment is historically used in U.S. multistate taxation practice, the treatment of global income under formulary apportionment is also explored in research. In particular, some researchers suggest formulary apportionment as an alternative to the complexities of determining transfer prices and applying the arm's length standard in the determination of international tax obligations of MNEs. Martens-Weiner (2006) discusses the problems related to replacing separate accounting for companies operating in Europe with a system of formulary apportionment for the European Union. The issues span a spectrum including business attitudes toward formulary apportionment, designing an apportionment formula, and tax administration and compliance.

In related work, Fuest, Hemmelgarn, and Ramb (2007) find that smaller European countries that currently attract a relatively large tax base under separate accounting would have a much smaller tax base under formulary apportionment. Avi-Yonah and Clausing (2007) propose a system of formulary apportionment that would include sales as a single apportionment factor. Avi-Yonah and Clausing argue that their proposed method would protect the U.S. tax base by preventing the practice of income-shifting to low-tax countries. Avi-Yonah (2010) proposes a hybrid system in which separate accounting is used to the extent that income can be attributed based on observed determinants and the residual profit is attributed under formulary apportionment. Altshuler and Grubert (2010) simulate firm behavior and U.S. revenue collection and find that different responses to tax incentives yield similar revenue under separate accounting and formulary apportionment. In contrast, Hines (2010) presents evidence that the determination of international tax obligations under formulary apportionment may distort actual income attributable to a given country because of income that is unexplained by apportionment factors; this may lead to inefficient allocation of productive resources because of differences in tax rates across countries.

We are not aware of any previous study that applies formulary apportionment to attribute measured production to entities within an MNE, but the attribution of measured production under formulary apportionment does not invoke the policy concerns described above for international taxation, because MNEs presumably do not make operating decisions based on surveys intended solely for statistical purposes. However, formulary apportionment could affect the picture of global production, which could have policy implications. Given the definitions and concepts underlying the international guidelines for measuring official FDI and trade statistics and the challenges encountered under the resulting residency-based framework when applied to MNEs, we next draw upon the related IO literature to outline a simple production model for foreign affiliates and construct a formulary framework for attributing measured production to foreign affiliates of U.S. parents.

MEASURING PRODUCTION

Before we outline the formulary framework to attribute production to foreign affiliates of U.S. parents, we discuss a production model based in part on Bartelsman and Beetsma (2003), Helpman (1984), and Markusen (1984, 1997). Consider an MNE with one U.S. parent and one or more foreign affiliates. An affiliate engages in actual production, denoted as Q^*, with locally purchased inputs such as labor and PPE, denoted as L, and shared inputs such as intangible property and headquarter services, denoted as H, as follows:[3]

(8.1) $Q^* = f(L,H)$.

While we do not assume a particular functional form, we do assume that shared inputs cannot be utilized without local inputs (i.e., $L > 0$). In contrast, we assume that local inputs do not necessarily require shared inputs (i.e., $H \geq 0$).

In practice, a statistician does not observe actual production for the affiliate. However, value-added, denoted as Q^{ε}, can be measured for the affiliate with one of two approaches. As one approach, value-added can be measured as the difference between gross sales and intermediate inputs. In this case, a discrepancy exists between actual production and measured production to the extent that gross sales and intermediate inputs include related party transactions that do not reflect market prices. Alternatively, value-added can be measured as the sum of costs incurred (other than costs of intermediate inputs) and profits earned in production. In this case, costs and profits reflect returns to local inputs and shared inputs, and a discrepancy exists between actual production and measured production to the extent that returns accruing to local and shared inputs are over- or underattributed to the affiliate. While we can assume returns accruing to local inputs are properly attributed because they are generally determined from market transactions, we cannot be sure that returns to shared inputs are properly attributed, given the mobility of shared inputs and their related returns as well as the possible lack of associated market transactions. In either case, the discrepancy, denoted as ε, between actual production, Q^{*}, and measured production, Q^{ε}, can be written as follows:

(8.2) $\varepsilon = Q^{*} - Q^{\varepsilon}$.

The objective is to choose a measurement approach to minimize ε. Determining the magnitude of ε is difficult, but Lipsey (2009, 2010) provides some evidence of possible distortions in statistics measured for foreign affiliates of U.S. parents.

Residency-Based Separate Accounting

As is consistent with the residency-based framework of the BPM and the SNA, the BEA attributes value-added to a foreign affiliate according to the country in which the affiliate is resident. If the affiliate has little or no physical presence in the country, the BEA follows the BPM and SNA recommendations to attribute value-added to the affiliate, as long as the affiliate is legally incorporated or registered in the country. The BEA measures value-added as the sum of costs incurred and profits earned in production. Both costs and profits are determined under separate accounting, according to generally accepted U.S. accounting principles. Under separate accounting, accounting records are maintained separately for each entity within an MNE. As a result, if the MNE is structured in a way that attributes costs and profits to an affiliate based partially or solely on economic activity related to shared inputs, measured value-added may be attributed to an affiliate with relatively few or no local inputs and relatively little or no economic activity. In other words, value-added attributed to the affiliate may be distorted to the extent that costs and profits reflect economic activity related to shared inputs that are not actually employed by the affiliate.[4]

Figure 8.1 depicts each of the components and subcomponents of value-added that are published as part of the BEA's multinational statistics. Costs incurred include four components: 1) compensation, 2) capital consumption allowance (CCA), 3) indirect business taxes (IBT), and 4) net interest paid (IP). Compensation includes payroll taxes. CCA is an accounting rather than an economic measure of depreciation.[5] IBT includes taxes related to business registry and operations other than income taxes and payroll taxes.[6] IBT is adjusted for government subsidies received and production royalty payments to foreign governments for natural resources. Net IP includes interest expensed or capitalized less interest income. The profits component is referred to as profit-type return (PTR) in the BEA's multinational statistics and includes net income adjusted for foreign income taxes paid, depletion, income from equity investments in foreign affiliates, and realized and unrealized gains and losses.

Using the context of our production model, we identify the components of value-added that reflect returns to local inputs and to shared inputs. In particular, we consider compensation and CCA to only reflect returns to local inputs. Compensation and CCA are returns for services provided by labor and PPE, respectively, which need to be physically located at an affiliate in order to provide service. In contrast, IBT reflects payments to the host government for the privilege of existing in a location, such as fees for licenses and registration, in addition to payments for conducting operations in the location, such as sales taxes and property taxes. Licenses and registration do not require a physical location, but we do consider sales taxes for unaffiliated sales and prop-

Figure 8.1 Measurement Framework for Value-Added Attributable to Foreign Affiliates and U.S. Parents

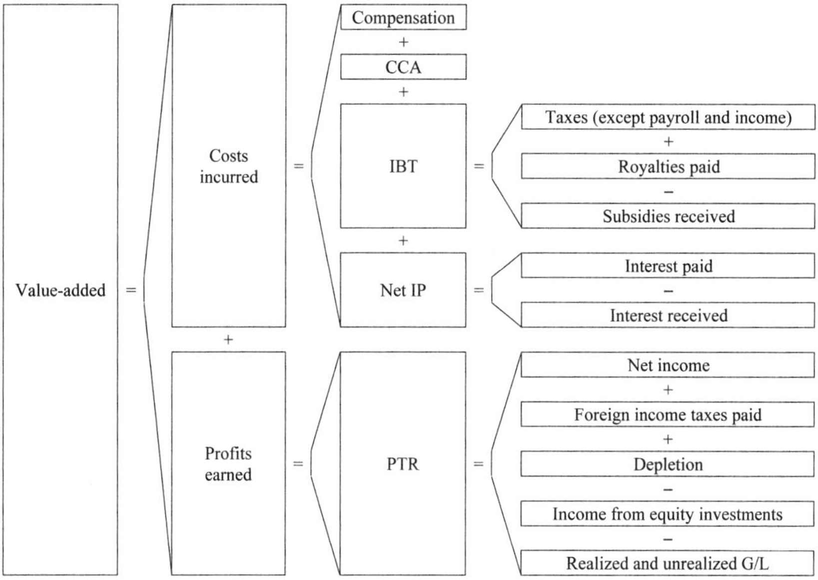

NOTE: "CCA" stands for capital consumption allowance; "IBT" stands for indirect business taxes; "IP" stands for interest paid; "PTR" stands for profit-type return; and "G/L" stands for gain/loss.
SOURCE: Authors' summary based on Table 10 of Mataloni and Goldberg (1994).

erty taxes to require a physical location. Likewise, net IP and PTR can reflect returns to local inputs, shared inputs, or both. However, absent any compensation and CCA (and IBT related to operations), measured value-added that includes only net IP and PTR (and IBT related to registration) under separate accounting cannot be correct, according to our model. According to our assumption for L in Equation (8.1), production is impossible without local inputs. In other words, separate accounting may not minimize ε in Equation (8.2). We refer to IBT, net IP, and PTR collectively as the shared input components of value-added. We turn now to formulary apportionment as an alternative to separate accounting for attributing value-added to foreign affiliates.

Residency-Based Formulary Apportionment

While the BPM and the SNA recommend the residency-based framework for attributing measured production to entities within an MNE, attribution under the framework is not limited to separate accounting and may presumably include formulary apportionment. In contrast to separate accounting, formulary apportionment is based on consolidated accounting measures. Formulary apportionment is commonly required by U.S. state corporate income tax regulations to determine the income attributable to the state for a corporation that operates in multiple states. Rather than keeping separate accounting records for operations in each state, the corporation keeps consolidated records and attributes income to states based on prescribed apportionment factors that ideally reflect where income is actually earned based on economic activity. Apportionment factors generally include factors related to employment, property, and sales, which reflect the presence of local inputs and economic activity specific to the entity.

As is consistent with our production model, consider an MNE m with one U.S. parent and one or more foreign affiliates. Let q_n denote measured production under separate accounting for each entity n (i.e., the U.S. parent and its foreign affiliates) belonging to the MNE m. For flexibility, q may include total value-added or simply include the shared-input components of value-added. Likewise, let $x_{j,n}$ denote apportionment factor j for each entity n, and let α_j denote the weight associated with apportionment factor j, where $\sum_j \alpha_j = 1$. Apportionment factor j should reflect economic activity. Under formulary apportionment, measured production (denoted as $\bar{q}_n$) attributable to entity n within MNE m is calculated as follows:

$$(8.3) \quad \bar{q}_n = \underbrace{\left(\sum_j \alpha_j \frac{x_{j,n}}{\sum_n x_{j,n}} \right)}_{\substack{\text{Apportionment}\\ \text{Weight}}} \underbrace{\left(\sum_n q_n \right)}_{\substack{\text{MNE}\\ \text{Production}}} \quad \forall\, n \in m.$$

As noted under the horizontal brackets in Equation (8.3), measured production attributable to an entity under formulary apportionment, $\bar{q}_n$, is a weighted average of the consolidated measured production determined for the MNE (i.e., the U.S. parent and its foreign affiliates) under separate accounting. Each apportionment weight is a combination of each apportionment factor and its associated weight.

We apply data to q in Equation (8.3) for the shared-input components of value-added (i.e., IBT, net IP, and PTR) for foreign affiliates and their U.S. parents. We then add the shared input components attributed to each entity under formulary apportionment to the local input components of value-added (i.e., compensation and CCA) attributed to each entity under separate accounting in order to obtain a new measure of value-added for each entity under formulary apportionment.[7]

DATA

We use survey data for 2009 that are collected by the BEA from MNEs on direct investment operations and that are used to compile the BEA's published statistics on the activities of MNEs. The data include apportionment factors related to employment, property, and sales. We focus attention on results obtained for foreign affiliates classified in select service-industry sectors because services are a growing component of MNE activities and because of the role shared inputs potentially play in the production attributed to foreign affiliates classified in the select service industry sectors (Lipsey 2010). The select service industry sectors include administration; finance; information; insurance; management of companies; miscellaneous; professional, scientific, and technical (PST); and real estate and leasing.

Data on Operations

We use operations data collected for U.S. parents and their majority-owned foreign affiliates (MOFAs) in the 2009 Benchmark Survey of U.S. Direct Investment Abroad. A foreign affiliate is an enterprise that has more than 10 percent of its voting stock owned by a U.S. parent. A MOFA is a foreign affiliate in which the combined direct and indirect ownership interest of all U.S. interests is more than 50 percent. A U.S. parent is defined as a U.S. person with an investment interest, either directly or indirectly, of 10 percent or more in a foreign business enterprise.

Benchmark-operations survey forms are required to be completed for all U.S. parents (Form BE-10A). In addition, benchmark-operations survey forms are required for each MOFA with more than $80 million in assets, sales, or net income (net loss) (Form BE-10B).[8] Data used in this study for a given U.S. parent pertain only to the activities of the parent. Data for a given foreign affiliate pertain only to the activities of the affiliate. Data collected on the operations survey forms include income statement information and balance sheet information. Income statement information includes sales by type (i.e., goods, services, and investment income), location, and affiliation. In addition, income statement information includes detailed expenses such as compensation, depreciation, interest, and taxes. The BEA uses information from the income statement to measure value-added for each affiliate. Balance sheet information includes details regarding assets, liabilities, and owner's equity. Asset details include PPE.

Apportionment Factors

The choice of apportionment factors and their associated weights influences the results obtained from formulary apportionment. We consider three apportionment factors that are available in the operations data: 1) compensation, 2) net PPE, and 3) unaffiliated sales. Compensation and net PPE reflect local inputs employed in production. Unaffiliated sales may also reflect local inputs that may not be reflected in compensation and net PPE. If an affiliate has no compensation or net PPE, production is still attributed to the affiliate under formulary apportionment if unaffiliated sales are greater than zero. Likewise, if an affiliate has no unaffiliated sales, production is still attributed to the affiliate under formulary apportionment if compensation or net PPE is greater than zero. In other words, production attributed to the affiliate by Equation (8.3) is assumed to be proportional to the economic activity reported for the affiliate.[9]

We report the results from weighting compensation by 60 percent, net PPE by 25 percent, and unaffiliated sales by 15 percent.[10] We determine the factor weights based on each factor's share of the mean value-added, as calculated by using coefficients from a regression of value-added on the apportionment factors. We initially determine factor weights separately for two subsamples of the data: 1) MOFAs and U.S. parents classified in select service industry sectors and 2) MOFAs and U.S. parents classified in all other industry sectors. However, even though the coefficient estimates are statistically different for the two subsamples, the resulting factor weights from each subsample are nearly identical because of differences in the subsample means.[11] Thus, we apply the factor weights obtained from the combined sample of MOFAs and U.S. parents classified in any industry sector. In addition to obtaining reasonable factor weights, the explanatory power of the apportionment factors is high (i.e., adjusted r-squared = 0.84).

RESULTS

Our goal is to use formulary apportionment as a substitute for separate accounting to reattribute measured value-added to foreign affiliates of U.S. parents. Our primary approach is to consolidate the shared-input components of value-added (i.e., IBT, net IP, and PTR) measured under separate accounting for a given MNE (i.e., the U.S. parent and its MOFAs) and reattribute to all entities within the MNE (i.e., the U.S. parent and its MOFAs) based on each entity's apportionment weight. In this case, value-added for an entity within the MNE includes compensation and CCA under separate accounting plus the shared-input components reattributed under formulary apportionment.

We divide the discussion of the results into four subsections: 1) reporting value-added and the related reattributions under formulary apportionment, 2) evaluating value-added under formulary apportionment relative to value-added under separate accounting, 3) interpreting the results in the context of our production model, and 4) discussing implications for the U.S. current account.

Value-Added and Reattributions under Formulary Apportionment

Table 8.1 summarizes value-added by industry sector and by global region for MOFAs and U.S. parents. For reference, the first three columns report published value-added determined under separate account-

Table 8.1 Value-Added by Industry Sector and by Global Region (billions of US$)

		Separate accounting			Formulary apportionment		
		MOFAs	U.S. parents	Total	MOFAs	U.S. parents	Total
	Select service industry sectors						
1	Administration	25.1	59.1	84.2	27.2	60.6	87.8
2	Finance	66.9	192.7	259.6	48.7	206.7	255.4
3	Information	51.0	287.6	338.7	50.7	294.6	345.2
4	Insurance	13.8	67.4	81.2	9.9	74.7	84.6
5	Management of companies	−14.5	−1.3	−15.7	3.2	−0.6	2.7
6	Miscellaneous services	10.3	28.1	38.4	8.4	28.9	37.3
7	Professional, scientific, technical	78.5	177.5	256.1	88.3	176.2	264.5
8	Real estate and rental and leasing	22.7	34.5	57.2	14.1	35.7	49.9
9	Subtotals	254.0	845.6	1,099.6	250.6	876.8	1,127.4
	Other industry sectors						
10	Accommodation and food services	14.3	52.7	67.0	18.2	49.1	67.3
11	Construction	4.9	22.1	27.0	(D)	(D)	(D)
12	Farming, fishing, forestry	0.9	2.2	3.1	(D)	(D)	(D)
13	Health care and social assistance	1.5	31.8	33.3	(D)	(D)	(D)
14	Manufacturing	478.2	1,034.1	1,512.3	411.1	1,147.7	1,558.8
15	Mining	153.7	76.1	229.8	104.4	81.4	185.7
16	Retail trade	57.1	238.6	295.7	50.8	241.0	291.7
17	Transportation and warehousing	18.1	106.1	124.3	17.0	106.9	123.9
18	Utilities	9.5	62.0	71.5	(D)	(D)	(D)

19	Wholesale trade	152.7	124.4	277.1	122.4	128.6	251.1
20	Subtotals	891.0	1,750.1	2,641.1	741.1	1,872.2	2,613.3
21	Totals for industry sectors	1,145.0	2,595.8	3,740.7	991.7	2,749.0	3,740.7
	Global regions						
22	Africa	44.9		44.9	29.7		29.7
23	Asia	241.1		241.1	210.7		210.7
24	Canada	113.7		113.7	111.3		111.3
25	Europe	599.2		599.2	523.7		523.7
26	Latin America	128.4		128.4	102.3		102.3
27	Middle East	17.7		17.7	14.0		14.0
28	United States		2,595.8	2,595.8		2,749.0	2,749.0
29	Totals for global regions	1,145.0	2,595.8	3,740.7	991.7	2,749.0	3,740.7

NOTE: A "(D)" denotes data suppressed to avoid disclosure of data of individual companies. Blank cell = data not applicable. Some totals or subtotals may be slightly off because of rounding.

SOURCE: The first three columns, under the heading "Separate accounting," include statistics published online in the BEA's financial and operating data on direct investment and multinational companies (http://www.bea.gov/iTable/index_MNC.cfm). The second three columns, under the heading "Formulary apportionment," include the authors' calculations after value-added is attributed under Equation (8.3).

ing. The second three columns of Table 8.1 present results determined under formulary apportionment in Equation (8.3). Table 8.2 reports the dollar differences and the percentage differences between value-added under formulary apportionment and value-added under separate accounting from Table 8.1. Table 8.2 shows overall reattributions, reattributions by global region, and reattributions by industry sector.

Overall Reattributions

Line 21 of Table 8.2 shows that the overall reattribution of value-added from MOFAs to U.S. parents is $153.3 billion under formulary apportionment. The percentage decrease in value-added attributable to MOFAs is 13.4 percent (column 4), and the percentage increase in value-added attributable to U.S. parents is 5.9 percent (column 5). Overall, reattributions are small relative to total value-added attributed to all MOFAs and U.S. parents under separate accounting—less than 5 percent.

Reattributions by Global Region

In contrast to overall reattributions from MOFAs to U.S. parents, reattributions across some global regions are relatively large. In particular, the percentage decreases in value-added are greater than 10 percent for Africa, Asia, Europe, Latin America, and the Middle East but less than 10 percent for Canada (Table 8.2, column 4). Under both formulary apportionment and separate accounting, more value-added is attributed to MOFAs in Europe than in any other global region (Table 8.1, line 25). However, Canada and Latin America change places under formulary apportionment in the distribution of value-added by global region (Table 8.1, lines 24 and 26). Under formulary apportionment, more production is attributable to MOFAs in Canada than in Latin America. Thus, in addition to less measured production attributable to MOFAs in each of the six global regions, there are interregional changes in the distribution of measured production attributable to MOFAs of U.S. parents as a result of formulary apportionment.

Reattributions by Industry Sector

Reattributions across some industry sectors are also relatively large. The percentage changes in value-added are greater than 10 percent for MOFAs classified in all industry sectors except administration, information, and transportation (Table 8.2, column 4). Reattributions greater than 10 percent also result for U.S. parents classified in insurance, management, and manufacturing (Table 8.2, column 5).

Under both formulary apportionment and separate accounting, more value-added is attributed to MOFAs classified in PST than for any other select service sector (Table 8.1, line 7), and more value-added is attributed to MOFAs classified in manufacturing than for any of the other industry sectors (Table 8.1, line 14). The distribution of value-added under formulary apportionment is also the same for MOFAs classified in all other select service sectors except finance and information (Table 8.1, lines 2 and 3, respectively). However, the distribution of value-added under formulary apportionment changes for MOFAs classified in accommodation, mining, transportation, and wholesale (Table 8.1, lines 10, 15, 17, and 19, respectively). The industry distribution of value-added under formulary apportionment does not change for U.S. parents. Thus, we observe an interindustry change in the distribution of measured production attributable to MOFAs but not to U.S. parents.

As is consistent both with overall reattributions and with reattributions by global region, value-added reported in Table 8.1 for each industry sector is generally higher under formulary apportionment for U.S. parents and lower for MOFAs. While this is not directly observable in Table 8.2, we look at the underlying data to trace reattributions to U.S. parents from MOFAs. Reattributions to U.S. parents classified in manufacturing are due in large part to reattributions from MOFAs classified in manufacturing and mining. Likewise, increases for U.S. parents classified in information and manufacturing are explained in large part by decreases for MOFAs classified in leasing. There are also reattributions from MOFAs classified in finance to U.S. parents classified in insurance. The remaining reattributions are among MOFAs classified in management and MOFAs and U.S. parents classified in finance, insurance, miscellaneous, PST, retail, and wholesale.

Table 8.2 Value-Added Reattributable under Formulary Apportionment

		Billions of US$			Percentage		
		MOFAs	U.S. parents	Total	MOFAs	U.S. parents	Total
	Select service industry sectors						
1	Administration	2.0	1.5	3.6	8.1	2.6	4.3
2	Finance	−18.2	14.0	−4.2	−27.2	7.3	−1.6
3	Information	−0.4	6.9	6.6	−0.7	2.4	1.9
4	Insurance	−3.9	7.3	3.4	−28.0	10.8	4.2
5	Management of companies	17.7	0.7	18.4	122.5	53.5	116.9
6	Miscellaneous services	−1.9	0.8	−1.0	−18.1	2.9	−2.7
7	Professional, scientific, technical	9.8	−1.3	8.4	12.4	−0.7	3.3
8	Real estate and rental and leasing	−8.6	1.2	−7.3	−37.8	3.6	−12.8
9	Subtotals	−3.4	31.2	27.8	−1.3	3.7	2.5
	Other industry sectors						
10	Accommodation and food services	3.8	−3.5	0.3	26.6	−6.7	0.4
11	Construction	(D)	(D)	(D)	(D)	(D)	(D)
12	Farming, fishing, forestry	(D)	(D)	(D)	(D)	(D)	(D)
13	Health care and social assistance	(D)	(D)	(D)	(D)	(D)	(D)
14	Manufacturing	−67.0	113.5	46.5	−14.0	11.0	3.1
15	Mining	−49.3	5.2	−44.1	−32.1	6.9	−19.2
16	Retail trade	−6.3	2.4	−4.0	−11.1	1.0	−1.3

17	Transportation and warehousing	−1.1	0.8	−0.3	−6.1	0.7	−0.3
18	Utilities	(D)	(D)	(D)	(D)	(D)	(D)
19	Wholesale trade	−30.3	4.2	−26.1	−19.8	3.4	−9.4
20	Subtotals	−149.9	122.1	−27.8	−16.8	7.0	−1.1
21	Totals for industry sectors	−153.3	153.3	0.0	−13.4	5.9	0.0
	Global regions						
22	Africa	−15.2		−15.2	−33.8		−33.8
23	Asia	−30.4		−30.4	−12.6		−12.6
24	Canada	−2.4		−2.4	−2.1		−2.1
25	Europe	−75.5		−75.5	−12.6		−12.6
26	Latin America	−26.2		−26.2	−20.4		−20.4
27	Middle East	−3.6		−3.6	−20.5		−20.5
28	United States		153.3	153.3		5.9	5.9
29	Totals for global regions	−153.3	153.3	0.0	−13.4	5.9	0.0

NOTE: A "(D)" denotes data suppressed to avoid disclosure of data of individual companies. The values for "Billions of US$" (first three columns) are calculated by subtracting value-added under separate accounting from value-added under formulary apportionment. Percentages (second three columns) are calculated by dividing the values for "Billions of US$" by the absolute value of value-added under separate accounting. Some totals or subtotals may be slightly off because of rounding. Blank cell = data not applicable.
SOURCE: Authors' tabulations.

Evaluation of Value-Added under Separate Accounting and Formulary Apportionment

We calculate approximate factor shares of value-added using the local input components and shared input components of value-added. Factor shares are informative because they reveal the relative contributions of local inputs and shared inputs to total measured production. We interpret factor shares using global factor shares as a reference. Published returns to local inputs as a share of published value-added are 52.8 percent for all MOFAs and 75.3 percent for all U.S. parents. Published returns to local inputs for all MOFAs and all U.S. parents combined are 68.4 percent of published value-added for all MOFAs and all U.S. parents combined. Thus, we use 68.4 percent as a reference for factor shares based on local inputs for both separate accounting and formulary apportionment. Likewise, we use 31.6 percent as a reference for factor shares based on shared inputs. In other words, we expect the relative contributions of local inputs and of shared inputs to total measured production to be about 68.4 percent and 31.6 percent, respectively.

Given differences in production functions, we expect some variation in factor shares across MOFAs and U.S. parents, across industry sectors and global regions, and across industries and countries. In addition, the factor shares are affected to the extent that returns to local inputs are included in the shared input components of value-added. However, given our model, in which affiliate production is a function of both local inputs and shared inputs, we consider differences in factor shares between formulary apportionment and separate accounting based on local inputs to be indicative of possible over- or underattributed returns to entities, based on shared inputs under separate accounting.[12]

Table 8.3 reports factor shares based on local input components under separate accounting and under formulary apportionment. Table 8.4 reports factor shares based on shared input components. Overall, the factor shares reflect the net reattribution of value-added from MOFAs to U.S. parents presented in Table 8.2. In particular, the local input shares of value-added increase for MOFAs and decrease for U.S. parents under formulary apportionment (Table 8.3, line 21). In contrast, the shared input shares of value-added decrease for MOFAs and increase for U.S. parents (Table 8.4, line 21). Local input shares are lower for MOFAs than for U.S. parents, and shared input shares are higher for MOFAs than for U.S. parents; however, local input shares and shared input shares for MOFAs and U.S. parents combined are generally closer to the global reference points under formulary apportionment.

Across all industry sectors, local input shares and shared input shares display considerable variation under separate accounting and under formulary apportionment. Local input shares are generally higher for the select service industry sectors than for the other industry sectors. Local input shares for MOFAs classified in finance, information, leasing, management, manufacturing, mining, miscellaneous, transportation, and wholesale increase under formulary apportionment. Conversely, local input shares for MOFAs classified in accommodation, administration, insurance, and PST decrease under formulary apportionment. These results imply that separate accounting may result in over- or underattributed returns to local inputs in some industries.

Across global regions, local input shares increase by more than 10 percentage points for Africa, Latin America, and the Middle East and by less than 10 percentage points for Asia, Canada, and Europe. Increases in Latin America are driven in large part by considerable increases in Barbados, Bermuda, and the UK Caribbean islands. Increases in Asia are explained primarily by increases in Hong Kong, Malaysia, Singapore, and Thailand. Increases in Europe are a result in part of increases in Denmark, Finland, Hungary, Ireland, Luxembourg, and Norway. We do not report numerical results for individual countries, in order to avoid disclosure of individual companies.

Economic Interpretation

According to our production model and the related empirical framework, value-added may be overattributed to a MOFA under separate accounting based on the availability of shared inputs within an MNE. The shared input components of value-added (i.e., IBT, net IP, and PTR) reflect, in part, returns to shared inputs that may not actually be employed by the MOFA to the extent reflected under separate accounting. In contrast, formulary apportionment attributes returns to shared inputs based on the MOFA's proportion of economic activity reflected in the chosen apportionment factors. As is consistent with our produc-

Table 8.3 Factor Shares Based on Local Input Components

		Separate accounting (%)			Formulary apportionment (%)		
		MOFAs	U.S. parents	Total	MOFAs	U.S. parents	Total
	Select service industry sectors						
1	Administration	89.5	86.4	87.3	82.8	84.2	83.8
2	Finance	72.9	91.4	99.3	99.9	97.2	97.7
3	Information	63.8	66.0	65.7	64.3	64.5	64.4
4	Insurance	92.1	81.2	83.9	82.0	87.0	86.4
5	Management of companies	12.5	20.4	13.2	73.8	29.8	94.1
6	Miscellaneous services	61.2	82.3	76.6	74.7	78.8	77.8
7	Professional, scientific, technical	74.5	73.5	73.8	66.2	74.0	71.4
8	Real estate and rental and leasing	51.8	81.2	69.5	83.2	78.4	79.8
9	Subtotals	77.0	85.6	83.6	78.0	82.5	81.5
	Other industry sectors						
10	Accommodation and food services	77.1	71.4	72.6	60.9	76.5	72.2
11	Construction	76.3	89.7	87.3	(D)	(D)	(D)
12	Farming, fishing, forestry	79.8	99.1	93.4	(D)	(D)	(D)
13	Health care and social assistance	73.3	79.1	78.8	(D)	(D)	(D)
14	Manufacturing	51.3	72.8	66.0	59.7	65.6	64.1
15	Mining	28.2	57.5	37.9	41.5	53.8	46.9
16	Retail trade	46.5	60.5	57.8	52.3	59.9	58.6
17	Transportation and warehousing	69.9	76.7	75.7	74.4	76.1	75.9
18	Utilities	39.9	49.7	48.4	(D)	(D)	(D)

19	Wholesale trade	39.5	74.7	55.3	49.3	72.3	61.1
20	Subtotals	45.9	70.3	62.1	55.2	65.8	62.7
21	Totals for industry sectors	52.8	75.3	68.4	60.9	71.1	68.4
	Global regions						
22	Africa	29.1		29.1	44.0		44.0
23	Asia	51.8		51.8	59.3		59.3
24	Canada	63.0		63.0	64.3		64.3
25	Europe	54.6		54.6	62.5		62.5
26	Latin America	46.3		46.3	58.2		58.2
27	Middle East	45.2		45.2	56.9		56.9
28	United States		75.3	75.3		71.1	71.1
29	Totals for global regions	52.8	75.3	68.4	60.9	71.1	68.4

NOTE: A "(D)" denotes data suppressed to avoid disclosure of data of individual companies. We calculate factor shares based on local inputs by dividing the sum of compensation and CCA by the sum of compensation, CCA, and the absolute value of shared inputs [i.e., local input share = (compensation + CCA) ÷ (compensation + CCA + | IBT + net IP + PTR |)]. Blank cell = data not applicable.
SOURCE: Authors' tabulations.

Table 8.4 Factor Shares Based on Shared Input Components

		Separate accounting (%)			Formulary apportionment (%)		
		MOFAs	U.S. parents	Total	MOFAs	U.S. parents	Total
	Select service industry sectors						
1	Administration	10.5	13.6	12.7	17.2	15.8	16.2
2	Finance	27.1	8.6	0.7	0.1	2.8	2.3
3	Information	36.2	34.0	34.3	35.7	35.5	35.6
4	Insurance	7.9	18.8	16.1	18.0	13.0	13.6
5	Management of companies	87.5	79.6	86.8	26.2	70.2	5.9
6	Miscellaneous services	38.8	17.7	23.4	25.3	21.2	22.2
7	Professional, scientific, technical	25.5	26.5	26.2	33.8	26.0	28.6
8	Real estate and rental and leasing	48.2	18.8	30.5	16.8	21.6	20.2
9	Subtotals	23.0	14.4	16.4	22.0	17.5	18.5
	Other industry sectors						
10	Accommodation and food services	22.9	28.6	27.4	39.1	23.5	27.8
11	Construction	23.7	10.3	12.7	(D)	(D)	(D)
12	Farming, fishing, forestry	20.2	0.9	6.6	(D)	(D)	(D)
13	Health care and social assistance	26.7	20.9	21.2	(D)	(D)	(D)
14	Manufacturing	48.7	27.2	34.0	40.3	34.4	35.9
15	Mining	71.8	42.5	62.1	58.5	46.2	53.1
16	Retail trade	53.5	39.5	42.2	47.7	40.1	41.4
17	Transportation and warehousing	30.1	23.3	24.3	25.6	23.9	24.1
18	Utilities	60.1	50.3	51.6	(D)	(D)	(D)

19	Wholesale trade	60.5	25.3	44.7	50.7	27.7	38.9
20	Subtotals	54.1	29.7	37.9	44.8	34.2	37.3
21	Totals for industry sectors	47.2	24.7	31.6	39.1	28.9	31.6
	Global regions						
22	Africa	70.9		70.9	56.0		56.0
23	Asia	48.2		48.2	40.7		40.7
24	Canada	37.0		37.0	35.7		35.7
25	Europe	45.4		45.4	37.5		37.5
26	Latin America	53.7		53.7	41.8		41.8
27	Middle East	54.8		54.8	43.1		43.1
28	United States		24.7	24.7		28.9	28.9
29	Totals for global regions	47.2	24.7	31.6	39.1	28.9	31.6

NOTE: A "(D)" denotes data suppressed to avoid disclosure of data of individual companies. We calculate factor shares based on shared inputs by dividing the absolute value of shared inputs by the sum of compensation, CCA, and the absolute value of shared inputs [i.e., shared input share = (| IBT + net IP + PTR |) ÷ (compensation + CCA + | IBT + net IP + PTR |)]. Blank cell = data not applicable.

SOURCE: Authors' tabulations.

tion model, our results for value-added imply that too much production is attributed to MOFAs and too little production is attributed to U.S. parents under separate accounting.

Given the economic activity embodied in each of the apportionment factors (i.e., compensation, net PPE, and unaffiliated sales), the modest overall reattributions from MOFAs to U.S. parents in Table 8.2 and the relatively large reattributions across some global regions in Table 8.2 imply an overstatement of economic activity for MOFAs under separate accounting. Likewise, the relatively large reattributions across some industry sectors in Table 8.2 and across MOFAs and U.S. parents by industry sector in Table 8.2 reveal considerable differences in economic activity as reflected under formulary apportionment and in economic activity as reflected under separate accounting. Value-added measures constructed under a method of separate accounting generally imply more economic activity than under a method of formulary apportionment for MOFAs classified in finance, information, insurance, leasing, manufacturing, mining, miscellaneous, retail, transportation, and wholesale and for U.S. parents classified in accommodation and PST. In contrast, less economic activity is generally implied under separate accounting than under formulary apportionment for MOFAs classified in accommodation, administration, management, and PST and for U.S. parents classified in industry sectors other than accommodation and PST.

The reattributions reported in Table 8.2 and the factor shares reported in Tables 8.3 and 8.4 generally support formulary apportionment as an alternative to separate accounting. Given the results obtained for value-added, formulary apportionment appears to yield measures of production that are more congruent with economic activity for MOFAs and U.S. parents and more consistent with expectations based on global factor shares. Thus, formulary apportionment appears to be a viable alternative to separate accounting under the residency-based framework of the BPM and the SNA.

Implications for the U.S. Current Account

In addition to applying formulary apportionment to reattribute value-added, we apply formulary apportionment to reattribute service imports and exports between U.S. parents and their foreign affiliates.

Since imports and exports are components of GDP, our results enable us to assess the effect on GDP of formulary apportionment as we apply it here. However, given data limitations and other practical considerations, our work with the current account is very preliminary and does not yet incorporate income payments and receipts. Based on our preliminary results, we expect to be able to provide a complete picture of the U.S. current account under formulary apportionment in a future paper.

We use cross-border transactions data collected from U.S. parents on service imports and exports with their foreign affiliates for 2008 because the cross-border transactions data for 2008 have already been linked with the operations data, which contain the apportionment factors (Barefoot and Koncz-Bruner 2012).[13] Based on our model, in which production is a function of local inputs and shared inputs, we do not expect exports by U.S. parents to their foreign affiliates to be as affected under formulary apportionment as imports by U.S. parents from their foreign affiliates, because the data indicate U.S. parents generally have a meaningful amount of local inputs. As is consistent with our expectations, exports are nearly unchanged under formulary apportionment. However, the overall reattribution of imports from foreign affiliates to U.S. parents is $10.9 billion, which is almost 13 percent of published private-service imports from affiliated parties (an amount totaling $85.2 billion) but only about 3 percent of published total private service imports ($371.2 billion).

Given the role imports and exports play as components of GDP, we also assess the overall effect of reattributing service imports and exports under formulary apportionment. U.S. goods and services imports decrease by approximately 0.4 percent, but exports remain unchanged. Net exports increase by approximately 1.5 percent. The overall effect on GDP is only an approximate 0.1 percent increase. Thus, while reattributions of U.S. service imports and exports under formulary apportionment have a relatively moderate effect on the foreign transactions component of GDP and a bit larger effect on the closely related statistics of the ITAs, the impact on GDP is relatively small.[14]

SUMMARY AND CONCLUSIONS

The BEA currently measures value-added of foreign affiliates and U.S. parents based on separate accounting. Based on a simple production model and a related empirical framework, value-added may be over-attributed to foreign affiliates under separate accounting; this is due to the availability of shared inputs within an MNE. In particular, the shared-input components of value-added (i.e., IBT, net IP, and PTR) reflect, in part, returns to shared inputs that may not actually be employed by foreign affiliates to the extent reflected under separate accounting. In this chapter, we use formulary apportionment as an alternative for separate accounting to reattribute measured value-added to foreign affiliates of U.S. parents.

We find that overall reattributions from foreign affiliates to U.S. parents are relatively small—less than 5 percent of total value-added attributed to all majority-owned foreign affiliates and U.S. parents under separate accounting. In contrast to overall reattributions, reattributions across global regions including Africa, Asia, Europe, Latin America, and the Middle East are greater than 10 percent of value-added under separate accounting. In addition, reattributions for foreign affiliates are greater than 10 percent of value-added under separate accounting for all industry sectors except administration, information, and transportation.

In addition to applying formulary apportionment to reattribute value-added, we report preliminary results to reattribute service imports and exports between U.S. parents and their foreign affiliates. We find a relatively large decrease in imports but no meaningful change in exports. The overall effect on GDP is only a small increase—approximately 0.1 percent. Based on our preliminary results, we expect to be able to provide a complete picture of the U.S. current account under formulary apportionment in a future paper.

Given the economic activity embodied in each of the apportionment factors (i.e., compensation, net PPE, and unaffiliated sales), the reattributions summarized here imply an overstatement of economic activity for MOFAs under separate accounting. Using factor shares to evaluate the results, we conclude that value-added attributed to foreign affiliates and U.S. parents under formulary apportionment yields a picture of measured production by industry sector and country that is more congruent with economic activity than related measures generated under separate accounting. Thus, formulary apportionment appears to be a viable alternative to separate accounting under the residency-based framework of the BPM and the SNA.

Notes

The statistical analysis of firm-level data on U.S. multinational enterprises and companies engaged in international transactions was conducted at the Bureau of Economic Analysis, U.S. Department of Commerce, under arrangements that maintain legal confidentiality requirements. The views expressed in this chapter are solely those of the authors and not necessarily those of the U.S. Department of Commerce or the Bureau of Economic Analysis.

1. Throughout the chapter, we use "MNE" or "enterprise" to refer to a group of affiliated entities that includes both U.S. parents and foreign affiliates. We use "entity" to refer to individual establishments within the MNE; such individual establishments may be either a U.S. parent or a foreign affiliate. We also use "parent" or "affiliate" to refer to a U.S. parent or a foreign affiliate, respectively.
2. Economic territory is discussed in paragraphs 4.3–4.11 of the BPM, institutional units are discussed in paragraphs 4.12–4.56, and residence is discussed in paragraphs 4.113–4.168.
3. We do not distinguish between nominal output and real output. In the absence of data to adjust for price differences, we treat real output as proportional to nominal output.
4. The BEA publishes estimates of value-added for MNEs as part of the annual statistics on direct investment and multinational companies.
5. In the NIPAs, consumption of fixed capital is the measure of economic depreciation. Given that depreciation is a cost in affiliates' accounting records, any difference between CCA and consumption of fixed capital is reflected in profits. Thus, measured value-added is unaffected (Mataloni and Goldberg 1994).
6. IBT includes sales tax, value-added tax, consumption tax, excise tax, taxes on property and other assets, duties, license fees, fines, penalties, and any other taxes other than payroll taxes and income taxes.
7. Equation (8.3) inevitably changes the industry and country composition of value-added from that measured under separate accounting, because there are no restrictions by industry or country. In other words, value-added attributed under separate accounting to an affiliate classified in one industry may be reattributed under formulary apportionment to an affiliate classified in another industry. Likewise, value-added attributed to an affiliate located in one country may be reattributed to an affiliate located in another country. If returns accruing to shared inputs are under- or overattributed to an entity under separate accounting, then statistics by industry and country do not accurately reflect actual output, and reattributing across industries and countries is presumably justified. However, we also restrict

reattributions by industry while assuming the same production function across countries within a given industry, because entities in different countries belong to the same MNE. While restricting reattributions by industry does affect the results under formulary apportionment, the restriction does not affect our conclusions.

8. Less information is collected for each MOFA with assets, sales, or net income (net loss) of less than $80 million (Form BE-10C or Form BE-10D).
9. In addition to compensation, net PPE, and unaffiliated sales, we consider other possible apportionment factors. In particular, we consider research and development expenditures, which are reported for MOFAs. However, R&D expenditures are likely in some cases to be made pursuant to intercompany cost-sharing arrangements. In addition, we are unable to discern the extent to which R&D expenditures reflect intercompany transactions. Thus, we limit the apportionment factors to compensation, net PPE, and unaffiliated sales.
10. We also weight compensation by 100 percent in Equation (8.3), which does not affect our conclusions. In addition to reflecting the number of employees employed by an affiliate, compensation reflects wages. Thus, if workers are paid according to their value marginal product, compensation reflects variation in economic activity across industries and countries. In other words, using compensation as an apportionment factor yields relatively more output attributable to high-margin industries and high-wage countries and relatively less output attributable to low-margin industries and low-wage countries. In addition, compensation is based on market transactions rather than accounting conventions, which may affect both net PPE and unaffiliated sales. Furthermore, unaffiliated sales may reflect local inputs or shared inputs. Thus, compensation may provide the most objective measure of economic activity.
11. The subsample of select service-industry sectors yields factor weights of 0.63, 0.28, and 0.09 for compensation, net PPE, and unaffiliated sales, respectively. The subsample of other industry sectors yields factor weights of 0.64, 0.21, and 0.15 for compensation, net PPE, and unaffiliated sales. The combined sample yields factor weights of 0.61, 0.24, and 0.15 for compensation, net PPE, and unaffiliated sales.
12. Since compensation and CCA are always nonnegative, the local input components are always nonnegative. However, since net IP or PTR may be negative, the shared input components and total value-added may be negative. In order to obtain factor shares between 0 and 100 percent, we calculate local input shares by dividing the sum of compensation and CCA by the sum of compensation, CCA, and the absolute value of shared inputs. Likewise, we calculate shared input shares by dividing the absolute value of shared inputs by the sum of compensation, CCA, and the absolute value of shared inputs.
13. The cross-border transactions include annual amounts reported on the Quarterly Survey of Insurance Transactions by U.S. Insurance Companies with Foreign Persons (Form BE-45), the Quarterly Survey of Transactions in Selected Services and Intangible Assets with Foreign Persons (Form BE-125), and the Quarterly Survey of Financial Services Transactions between U.S. Financial Services Providers and Foreign Persons (Form BE-185).

14. Small differences exist between foreign transactions published in the NIPAs and foreign transactions published in the ITAs because of adjustments for gold, U.S. territories, and other small statistical differences.

References

Altshuler, Rosanne, and Harry Grubert. 2010. "Formula Apportionment: Is It Better Than the Current System and Are There Better Alternatives?" *National Tax Journal* 63(4, Part 2): 1145–1184.

Avi-Yonah, Reuven S. 2010. "Between Formulary Apportionment and the OECD Guidelines: A Proposal for Reconciliation." *World Tax Journal* 2(1): 3–18.

Avi-Yonah, Reuven S., and Kimberly A. Clausing. 2007. "Reforming Corporate Taxation in a Global Economy: A Proposal to Adopt Formulary Apportionment." Hamilton Project Discussion Paper No. 2007-08. Washington, DC: Brookings Institution.

Baldwin, Robert E., and Fukunari Kimura. 1998. "Measuring U.S. International Goods and Services Transactions." In *Geography and Ownership as Bases for Economic Accounting*, Robert E. Baldwin, Robert E. Lipsey, and J. David Richardson, eds. NBER Studies in Income and Wealth 59. Chicago: University of Chicago Press, pp. 9–48.

Barefoot, Kevin, and Jennifer Koncz-Bruner. 2012. "A Profile of U.S. Exporters and Importers of Services." *Survey of Current Business* 92(6): 66–87.

Bartelsman, Eric J., and Roel M. W. J. Beetsma. 2003. "Why Pay More? Corporate Tax Avoidance through Transfer Pricing in OECD Countries." *Journal of Public Economics* 87(9–10): 2225–2252.

Brainard, S. Lael. 1993. "An Empirical Assessment of the Factor Proportions Explanation of Multinational Sales." NBER Working Paper No. 4583. Cambridge, MA: National Bureau of Economic Research.

———. 1997. "An Empirical Assessment of the Proximity-Concentration Trade-Off between Multinational Sales and Trade." *American Economic Review* 87(4): 520–544.

Caves, Richard E. 1971. "International Corporations: The Industrial Economics of Foreign Investment." *Economica* 38(149): 1–27.

European Commission, International Monetary Fund, Organisation for Economic Co-operation and Development, United Nations, and World Bank. 2009. *System of National Accounts 2008*. New York: United Nations.

Fuest, Clemens, Thomas Hemmelgarn, and Fred Ramb. 2007. "How Would the Introduction of an EU-Wide Formula Apportionment Affect the Distribution and Size of the Corporate Tax Base? An Analysis Based on German Multinationals." *International Tax and Public Finance* 14(5): 605–626.

Helpman, Elhanan. 1984. "A Simple Theory of International Trade with Multinational Corporations." *Journal of Political Economy* 92(3): 451–471.

Hines, James R. 2010. "Income Misattribution under Formula Apportionment." *European Economic Review* 54(1): 108–120.

International Monetary Fund. 2009. *Balance of Payments and International Investment Position Manual, Sixth Edition (BPM6)*. Washington, DC: International Monetary Fund.

Kimura, Fukunari, and Robert E. Baldwin. 1998. "Application of a Nationality-Adjusted Net Sales and Value-Added Framework: The Case of Japan." In *Geography and Ownership as Bases for Economic Accounting*, Robert E. Baldwin, Robert E. Lipsey, and J. David Richardson, eds. NBER Studies in Income and Wealth 59. Chicago: University of Chicago Press, pp. 49–82.

Landefeld, J. Steven, Obie G. Whichard, and Jeffrey H. Lowe. 1993. "Alternative Frameworks for U.S. International Transactions." *Survey of Current Business* 73(12): 50–61.

Lipsey, Robert E. 2009. "Measuring International Trade in Services." In *International Trade in Services and Intangibles in the Era of Globalization*, Marshall Reinsdorf and Matthew J. Slaughter, eds. NBER Studies in Income and Wealth 69. Chicago: University of Chicago Press, pp. 27–74.

———. 2010. "Measuring the Location of Production in a World of Intangible Productive Assets, FDI, and Intrafirm Trade." *Review of Income and Wealth* 56(1): S99–S110.

Markusen, James R. 1984. "Multinationals, Multi-Plant Economies, and the Gains from Trade." *Journal of International Economics* 16(3–4): 205–226.

———. 1997. "Trade versus Investment Liberalization." NBER Working Paper No. 6231. Cambridge, MA: National Bureau of Economic Research.

Martens-Weiner, Joann. 2006. *Company Tax Reform in the European Union: Guidance from the United States and Canada on Implementing Formulary Apportionment in the EU*. New York: Springer.

Mataloni, Raymond J. Jr., and Lee Goldberg. 1994. "Gross Product of U.S. Multinational Companies, 1977–91." *Survey of Current Business* 74(2): 42–63.

United Nations Economic Commission for Europe. 2011. *The Impact of Globalization on National Accounts*. Geneva: United Nations.

Whichard, Obie G., and Jeffrey H. Lowe. 1995. "An Ownership-Based Disaggregation of the U.S. Current Account, 1982–93." *Survey of Current Business* 75(10): 52–61.

9
Data, Trade, and Growth

Michael Mandel
Progressive Policy Institute

The architecture of the Internet is designed as a "network of networks." As such, one of its key attributes is making the passage of data from one network to another easy. So when a user sends an e-mail, views a video, or downloads a file from a Web site, the data may pass through a large number of different networks on the way from its origin to its destination, with the routing virtually invisible to the user. This architecture has proven to be extremely flexible and powerful, both nationally and globally. People and businesses with Internet access can easily get data of all sorts from around the world. Similarly, companies can efficiently and cheaply provide services such as e-mail and Web search on a global basis, in many cases without charge.

One sign of the Internet's global success is this: the rapid growth of cross-border data flows. Cross-border data flows are growing far faster than conventionally measured trade in goods and services. According to TeleGeography, a consulting firm that keeps track of international data flows, demand for international bandwidth increased at an annual rate of 49 percent between 2008 and 2012 (TeleGeography 2012). By comparison, the overall volume of global trade in goods and services, adjusted for inflation, rose at an annual rate of 2.4 percent over the same period.

Looking at the data links between the United States and Europe in particular, the data-carrying capacity of transatlantic submarine cables rose at an average annual rate of 19 percent between 2008 and 2012. Meanwhile, the overall volume of trade in goods and services between the United States and Europe, adjusted for inflation, is barely above prerecession peaks.

Indeed, the global economic and financial system, as it stands today, would not function without cross-border data flows. Data flows that cross national borders are essential to almost everything: manufacturing supply chains, global finance, international medical and physics research, entertainment, tourism, education, social media, and community. Indeed, cross-border data is becoming increasingly important as an input to production, and as a crucial element for economic growth. "The cross-border free flow of information enables international trade which can lead to increased innovation, productivity, and economic growth," writes Meltzer (2013, p. 11) in a paper from the Brookings Institution.

Moreover, trade in data creates positive externalities and gives an extra boost to global growth. Unlike exports of goods, data can be shipped from one country to another without depriving the first country of the benefits. All other things being equal, growth in cross-border data flows can be a far more powerful impetus to consumer welfare and economic growth than growth in trade in goods and services.

However, despite the importance of cross-border data flows, current international economic statistics are mostly uninformative and even misleading about their magnitude. First, note that cross-border data flows are not tracked as a separate category in the trade statistics. Instead, cross-border trade that involves data is lumped in with trade in services. For example, international telecommunications are treated as the export/import of a service. The World Trade Organization (WTO) estimates that global exports of telecommunications services totaled $111.5 billion in 2012 (WTO 2013).

But treating cross-border data as a service creates the real problem: By international agreement among statistical agencies, the export or import of services is defined to occur when there is a monetary payment from a resident of one country to a resident of another in exchange for the service. For example, if a U.S. business hires accountants in London, that becomes an export of accounting services from the United Kingdom to the United States.

Virtually all of the existing statistics about cross-border trade in data are based on this monetary definition of service exports and imports. The July 2013 report from the United States International Trade Commission, *Digital Trade in the U.S. and Global Economies, Part 1*, identifies the Bureau of Economic Analysis (BEA), the U.S. Census Bureau, the Organisation for Economic Co-operation and Development (OECD), and Eurostat as the main sources for statistics on "digital trade." Each of these relies on the same basic definition of service exports and imports as being tied to a monetary exchange between residents of two different countries (U.S. Internationl Trade Commission 2013, Table 4.2, p. 4.24). Currently, international agencies such as the International Telecommunications Union (ITU) only collect fragmentary statistics on cross-border data flows, though they are putting more effort into estimating such figures (see, for example, ITU [2012]).

I will show in this chapter that the efficient global architecture of the Internet allows and even encourages data to cross national borders without leaving a significant monetary footprint. As a result, economically important cross-border data flows are simply not being counted by current international economic statistics. I will offer evidence in this chapter that both the level and rate of growth of data trade are being significantly understated.

This understatement has serious policy implications. First, the data sector is a bigger contributor to U.S. and global growth than current economic statistics show. Second, to the degree that trade negotiators prioritize their goals according to the relative magnitude of different trading sectors, trade policy should place more emphasis on maintaining the free flow of data. Similarly, international tax policy should place more emphasis on maintaining the free flow of data.

Third, attempts by various countries to implement barriers to the free flow of data may do considerably more economic damage than the current trade statistics show. This is especially important in the wake of recent revelations about the extent to which the National Security Agency (NSA) has monitored data flows around the world. This news has caused a rising demand within countries such as Brazil for certain data to be kept within national borders—so-called data localization or data protectionism. The European Union is also considering new data privacy regulations that could potentially act as an impediment to flows of data in and out of the EU.

Finally, it's becoming clear that better statistics about cross-border data flows are needed to convince policymakers of how important data is to economic health. That might help avoid trade and tax policies that are detrimental to growth. It is self-evident that good policy rests on a foundation of accurate and comprehensive knowledge about current and emerging trade flows.

HOW CROSS-BORDER DATA FLOWS ARE MEASURED TODAY

The WTO and national statistical agencies such as the BEA regularly produce figures on cross-border trade in data-related services such as telecommunications services, computer and information services, and financial services. Table 9.1, below, shows the reported dollar value of global exports of selected data-related services (WTO 2013).

According to international standards, trade in services is typically measured by monetary transactions between residents of one country and residents of another country. That's the main principle laid out in the *Manual on Statistics of International Trade in Services*, approved in 2010 by the United Nations Statistical Commission:

> The market price is used as the basis for valuation of transactions in international trade in services. Market prices for transactions are defined as amounts of money that willing buyers pay to acquire something from willing sellers. The exchanges are made between independent parties and based on commercial considerations only and are sometimes called 'at arm's length' transactions. (United Nations 2011, p. 34)

Similarly, the BEA—the statistical agency in charge of tracking service trade—measures data-related exports and imports by tracking

Table 9.1 Reported Global Exports of Selected Data-Related Services, 2012, and Annual Growth Rate, 2008–2012

Service	Global exports ($US billions)	Annual growth rate, 2008–2012 (%)
Communications services (both voice and data)	111.5	3.4
Financial services	303.1	0.3
Computer and information services (including Web search)	262.7	7.2
Royalties and license fees	289.6	5.9
Sum of selected data-related services	966.9	4.0
Merchandise exports	18,401.0	3.3

SOURCE: WTO (2013).

the money received from "foreign persons" and the money paid to "foreign persons."

The BEA collects much of its data on service sector exports and imports through surveys: specifically the BEA Benchmark (BE-120) and Quarterly (BE-125) Surveys of Transactions in Selected Services and Intellectual Property with Foreign Persons (BEA 2011). Table 9.2 shows the fairly long list of service and intellectual property export transactions that are covered in the benchmark survey. The list of service and intellectual property import transactions is similar, while the quarterly survey covers a similar but slightly shorter list of traded services. Many of these include cross-border data flows such as telecommunication services, royalties and license fees, database and other information services, and financial services.

These surveys feed into the widely cited monthly report "U.S. International Trade In Goods and Services," including the goods and services trade deficit, which is a key number for economists in government and the private sector. In addition, the BEA produces an annual report on trade in services. Table 9.3 shows statistics on exports for selected data-related services in 2012.

THE ARCHITECTURE OF THE INTERNET AND DATA TRADE

The figures in the previous section raise two disturbing questions. First, when measured as a service, the rate of growth of the cross-border data-related services is barely higher than the growth rate of merchandise trade, both for the globe and for the United States. Second, the aggregate numbers make cross-border data trade look relatively unimportant. For example, reported U.S. telecom exports of $14 billion in 2012 are roughly the same size as U.S. exports of newsprint. (Box 9.1 explains how international phone calls are treated in the trade statistics.)

The global and national statistics on trade in services are based on tracking monetary exchanges between residents of different countries. In theory, this principle can be applied to trade in data as well. If a person in the United States downloads a file from a Web site in a different country, it's theoretically possible that he or she could be charged both

Table 9.2 Selected Service and Intellectual Property Export Transactions Tracked by BEA Survey BE-120

Types of export transactions
Receipts for intellectual property
Rights related to industrial processes and products
Rights related to books, music, etc.
Rights related to trademarks
Rights related to performance and events prerecorded on motion picture film and TV tape (include digital recordings)
Rights related to broadcast and recording of live events and performances
Rights related to general use software
Business format franchising fees
Other intellectual property
Receipts for selected services
Accounting, auditing, and bookkeeping services
Advertising services
Auxiliary insurance services
Computer and data processing services
Data base and other information services
Educational and training services
Industrial engineering services
Industrial-type maintenance, installation, alteration, and training services
Legal services
Management, consulting, and public relations services (including expenses allocated by a U.S. parent to its foreign affiliates)
Merchandising services
Operational leasing services
Trade-related services, other than merchandising services
Performing arts, sports, and other live performances, presentations, and events
Research and development services
Telecommunications services
Agricultural services
Disbursements to fund production costs of motion pictures
Disbsursements to fund news-gathering costs and production costs of program material other than news
Waste treatment and depollution services
Other selected services

SOURCE: BEA Form BE-120: “Benchmark Survey of Transactions in Selected Services and Intellectual Property with Foreign Persons,” p. 6, http://www.bea.gov/surveys/pdf/be120.pdf (accessed December 2013).

Table 9.3 Reported U.S. Exports of Selected Data-Related Services, 2012, and Annual Growth Rate, 2008–2012

Service	Global exports ($US billions)	Annual growth rate, 2008–2012 (%)
Communications services (both voice and data)	14.0	8.8
Financial services	76.4	4.9
Computer and information services (including Web search)	17.3	7.2
Royalties and license fees	124.2	5.0
Sum of selected data-related services	231.9	5.3
Goods exports	1,536.0	4.3

SOURCE: BEA international services statistics, Table 1: "Trade in Services, 1999–2012." http://www.bea.gov/international/xls/tab1a.xls (accessed December 2013).

for the cross-border telecommunications link and for the content in the file.

However, in practice the architecture of the Internet has developed in such a way that many or perhaps most cross-border data flows do not result in an exchange of money between residents of different countries. Let us illustrate this important point with a simple example: an American economist who visits the Web site for the Bank of Russia (www.cbr.ru) and wants to obtain statistics about the latest movement of the Russian monetary supply.

First, imagine that these statistics were in bound volumes that had to be shipped from Moscow. There's little doubt that the cost of the volumes and the shipping would be quite high and would register as imports in the trade statistics.

But when the data is downloaded, there is no charge for content. The Russian central bank is not charging U.S. economists for downloading data. So if this cross-border data transfer is going to create a monetary footprint and show up in the BEA statistics, it will happen because the telecommunications transport across national borders involves an exchange of money between a U.S. resident and a non–U.S. resident.

Obviously, the economist or his or her institution pays a domestic Internet service provider such as Comcast or Verizon for an Internet connection. But unlike an international phone call, no extra money is paid for the foreign Web site. The data request is passed from network

Box 9.1 The International Phone Call and Foreign Trade

Historically the major cross-border data flow was the conventional international phone call. In the United States, the originator of an international phone call picked up a telephone, dialed 011, then the country code and phone number, and paid an international charge to his or her phone company. The provider then paid the carrier in the receiving country according to a government-mandated settlement schedule. Conversely, the recipient of an overseas call did not pay an international charge—instead, the overseas caller paid the local provider in his or her own country, who settled up with the U.S. phone company.

Under this scheme, calls from the United States to overseas points were classified as imports, because the foreign carrier received the payments. Calls from other countries were classified as exports, since the payments came to the U.S. carriers. So if U.S. customers made more overseas calls than they received, the telecom trade balance would be negative. Indeed, that was true for many years. According to an FCC report from 1998, "U.S. carriers owe settlement payments for the services that they bill, and are owed payments for the services that the foreign carriers bill. In addition, U.S. carriers are owed payments for switched traffic that transits U.S. points. Because U.S. customers place far more calls than they receive and because U.S. carriers terminate more collect calls that generate surcharges for the originating carrier, U.S. carriers make net settlement payments to most foreign carriers. The total net payment for all U.S. carriers grew from $0.4 billion in 1980 to $5.6 billion in 1996" (Blake and Lande 1998).

Reading this explanation, however, should make it clear that this definition of telecom imports and exports is an artifact of a regulatory convention that "calling party pays" for wireline calls. Suppose instead that we had a rule that "receiving party pays," as in a collect call or an 800 number. Under that alternative regulatory regime, the toll on an outgoing international call would be collected from the recipient of the call by his or her (foreign) carrier. The foreign carrier would then remit a portion of the charge to the originating domestic carrier. As a result, with "receiving party pays," an outgoing international call would be treated as an export. Similarly, an incoming call would be treated as an import. Thus, a shift in regulatory conventions from "caller pays" to "recipient pays" would immediately turn a telecom trade deficit into a trade surplus, without altering the final allocation of revenues to the respective telecom carriers after the settlement process. In addition, outgoing and incoming international calls are physically indistinguishable, in terms of the equipment used.

to network until it reaches the Russian central bank, which then sends the money supply figures back again. At some point, that data request passes from a U.S.-owned network to a foreign-owned network. For the sake of clarity of the example, let's assume that the U.S.-owned network also owns the submarine cable between New York and the United Kingdom, so that the interchange between the U.S.-owned network and the foreign network physically occurs in the UK.[1]

Is there an exchange of money between the U.S-owned and the foreign-owned network? Now we have to delve into the architecture of the Internet. Networks are connected in two ways, by peering or by the payment of transit fees. *Peering* is an agreement between two networks to exchange traffic without exchanging money. Peering agreements, especially between large networks, are so ubiquitous that they are basically conducted on a handshake, as one authoritative OECD study shows: "A survey of 142,000 peering agreements conducted for this report shows that the terms and conditions of the Internet interconnection model are so generally agreed upon that 99.5 percent of interconnection agreements are concluded without a written contract" (Weller and Woodcock 2013, p. 3).

In fact, the largest global networks—the so-called 'Tier 1' networks—almost by definition peer with every other Tier 1 network. That means if a data packet goes from AT&T's network to British Telecom's on the way from Russia, it is unlikely that money changed hands at the interconnect between the two.

It might seem as if peering is a barter-type agreement that should generate revenue recognition on the financial books, even if no money changes hands. However, peering takes place mostly in situations of balanced traffic, so the revenues and costs would net out. The accounting firm KPMG notes that, "in our experience, peering arrangements between Tier 1 telecoms do not result in the recognition of revenue even though a service is provided and value is transferred between telecoms in much the same way as under traditional interconnect arrangements" (KPMG 2010, p. 30).

It's worth noting that peering is a key reason that you can access Web sites from all over the world without having additional charges added to your Internet bill.

Alternatively, smaller networks can connect to larger ones by paying transit fees—also known as buying Internet transit. In theory, these

Internet transit payments could show up as trade in telecommunications services if the smaller network was paying a provider from a different country for transit. However, the price of Internet transit has been dropping sharply. According to the market research firm TeleGeography, the price of IP transit at major hubs has dropped by roughly 30 percent a year over the past five years (TeleGeography 2013). To my knowledge, no statistical agency currently uses the price of Internet transit to adjust service trade.

ESTIMATING ONE COMPONENT OF DATA TRADE

For the reasons described in the previous section, we would expect that the official statistics on cross-border data trade (trade in data-related services) far understate both the actual economic value and the growth of cross-border data flows. But how big is the understatement?

In this section I will try to answer one small piece of this question. In particular, we will delve deeper into the measurement of U.S. telecom exports and construct an alternative estimate based on directly measuring cross-border data flows. For 2012, the BEA reports that exports of communications services from the United States amounted to $14 billion (payments from nonresidents to residents). Imports of communications services into the United States amounted to $8 billion (payments from residents to nonresidents). These numbers have been rising, but they are still minuscule compared to the importance and amount of international data traffic in and out of the United States.

However, a closer look helps explain why these have to be understatements. Let's start with a simple example. Suppose a major U.S. telecom provider builds its own submarine cable to Great Britain, say, or Singapore. That expenditure will show up in the company's capital spending budget, rather than as a payment for cross-border telecom services. Then, if the U.S. provider peers with foreign providers at the non-U.S. cable landing, no money will change hands at the connection point. The result: The telecom provider has made a major investment in providing cross-border data flows, none of which show up in the trade account. The export benefits of capital investment by the telecom industry are not being counted.

More generally, most submarine cables are being built these days by a consortium of companies, each of whom gets access to a share of the bandwidth. The same principle shows up as in the previous example—the spending on the cable appears as a capital investment, rather than as a payment for cross-border telecom services. From here, we can construct increasingly complicated examples that arrive at the same place—cross-border transport of data without a corresponding monetary transfer between residents and nonresidents.

How can we construct a better estimate of cross-border telecom services? In an earlier paper, I discussed the idea that the production and use of data should be treated as a fundamental component of economic activity, parallel to the production and use of goods and services (Mandel 2012). This approach leads naturally to an increased focus on directly measuring data generation, data flows, and data storage as a way of understanding economic activity.

One pioneer in such efforts has been Martin Hilbert, who has been developing a systematic methodology for comparing the communications capacity of various media, ranging from mobile to television (Hilbert and López 2011). Based on this work, the International Telecommunications Union (ITU) has been gradually moving toward direct measures of data flows, as opposed to indirect measures such as number of cellular subscriptions or broadband connections. A recent publication from the ITU notes,"Using the unifying metric of bits per second, employed for measuring global technological capacity to communicate, it is possible to compare different communication technologies. It is also possible to analyse bits per second per capita, per technology, per country, or per any other relevant socio-economic or demographic parameter" (ITU 2012, p. 167).

This section follows in the same spirit of direct measurement of data flows. For the purposes of this section, data flow is measured in terabits per second (Tbps). The telecommunications market research and consulting firm TeleGeography estimates that the United States had 23 Tbps of international Internet capacity in 2012, with an average utilization of 29 percent and a peak utilization of 49 percent.[2] This suggests that, on average, the U.S. cross-border data flow is roughly 6.7 Tbps.[3]

Is this volume of cross-border data a large number or a small number? I compare the cross-border data flow with a recent Cisco Systems–sponsored projection of data traffic, by country and type (Cisco Systems 2013).[4] For 2012, the Cisco study estimates Internet and IP traffic in the United States at 8 exabytes per month and 13 exabytes per month, respectively.[5] That translates into roughly 26.5 Tbps and 42.2 Tbps.[6]

Table 9.4, below, compares the U.S. cross-border data flows with the overall U.S. Internet and IP traffic. I find that cross-border data flows are roughly 25 percent and 16 percent of U.S. Internet and IP traffic, respectively. To put this in perspective, U.S. exports of goods and services are 14 percent of U.S. gross domestic product (GDP) in 2012, while U.S. imports of goods and services are 18 percent of U.S. GDP in 2012. (Box 9.2 briefly reports similar calculations for Europe.)

This calculation offers us a reasonable way of estimating the size of the international component of the U.S. telecom sector. According to the BEA (2014), the gross output for the telecommunications industry in 2011 was $556 billion. After adjusting for growth, that puts the gross output at roughly $575–$600 billion in 2012.

If we assume that the international component of the telecom industry is proportional to the size of the data flow, the international component of U.S. telecom would be roughly $92–$150 billion. That's compared to the $14 billion in exports and $8 billion in imports that the official statistics report.

Table 9.4 Cross-Border Data Flows, 2012: United States

	Terabits per second (except as noted)
International Internet capacity connected to the U.S.	23.0
Average utilization (%)	29.0
Average cross-border data flow (average international traffic)	6.7
All U.S. Internet traffic	26.5
All U.S. IP traffic	42.2
Average U.S. cross-border data flow as a percentage of:	
All U.S. Internet traffic (%)	25.0
All U.S. IP traffic (%)	16.0

SOURCE: International capacity and utilization estimates from TeleGeography (2014). Traffic estimates from Cisco. IP includes both Internet traffic and managed IP such as consumer video. Figures omit mobile.

Box 9.2 Europe's Data Connections

Using a similar methodology as for the United States, we can calculate interregional cross-border data flows as a share of Internet traffic for Europe. TeleGeography estimates that international bandwidth in Europe was 56.5 Tbps in 2012, but that 78 percent of that bandwidth was between cities in the same region. As a result, "interregional Internet capacity connected to Europe" equaled 12.6 Tbps in 2012. Based on this figure, we calculate that cross-border data flows between Europe and the rest of the world equaled 16 percent of the region's Internet traffic and 13 percent of the region's IP traffic.

These results, which should be viewed as highly imprecise and tentative, suggest that the United States is more interconnected with the rest of the world than Europe. The sources of error enumerated in the caveats above are potentially very significant.

Obviously, this should be viewed as an exploratory effort, with plenty of caveats. However, the revised estimates intuitively make more sense than the official statistics, in terms of measuring the importance of cross-border telecom services. Of course, these numbers are accompanied by substantial and worrisome caveats, as well as the possibility of large errors in both directions. In particular, these include the following:

- **Coverage and methodology may differ.** Cisco's projections include all IP usage. TeleGeography's estimates of international capacity by country do not include private networks such as intracorporate networks, Google and other content providers' networks, and research networks. This factor would tend to underestimate the share of cross-border traffic.
- **Double-counting is inevitable**. International Internet traffic is often routed through third-party countries before getting to its destination. Traffic between Moscow and New York might be routed through London and therefore show up as part of European cross-border data flows. Traffic between the Canadian cities of Vancouver and Toronto might be routed through the United States and therefore show up as part of U.S. cross-border data flows. And since less-developed countries may have

better Internet connections with the United States and Europe than with each other, it's possible for intra-African traffic, say, to be routed through New York or London. This factor would tend to overestimate the share of cross-border traffic.

- **When comparing estimates/forecasts from different sources, timing matters.** International Internet capacity, as estimated by TeleGeography, has been growing at almost 50 percent per year. Domestic U.S. Internet traffic, as projected by Cisco, has been growing roughly as fast. As a result, calculating cross-border data flows as a share of Internet traffic can be heavily influenced if one source is using yearly averages while the other source (TeleGeography) is using a particular point in time (April of each year). The direction of bias is uncertain.
- **Compression may distort the statistics**. Widespread and growing use of compression means that "we communicate around three times more information through the same installed infrastructure as we did in 1986" (Hilbert 2011, p. 7). It's possible that cross-border data flows may be compressed more intensively than purely domestic data flows.

MEASURING THE ECONOMIC BENEFITS OF CROSS-BORDER DATA FLOWS

Why are we concerned with correctly measuring cross-border data flows? The classic justification for the benefits of trade is that two or more countries working together can produce more than the same countries operating separately. Moreover, the size of the gain from trade is related to the magnitude of trade, all other things being equal. The more trade, the better.

Under the current trade statistics, the magnitude of trade in data is being systematically underestimated. Thus, the benefits from trade in data are being systematically underestimated as well, which, as we will see in the next section, distorts policy decisions.

Moreover, trade in data has somewhat of the characteristic of a public good, since data can be duplicated relatively costlessly. As a result, the fact that the data is created in one country and used in another country does not deprive the first country of the use. To give a specific example, one type of intangible capital stock is "entertainment, literary, and artistic originals," including films. Licensing the right to show a film in a forcign country currently shows up as an export in the national income accounts. However, such a license generally does not reduce the ability of American consumers to view the film, and it does not reduce the intangible capital stock of "entertainment, literary, and artistic originals."

As a result, trade in data creates positive externalities and an extra boost to global growth. Unlike exports of goods, data can be shipped from one country to another without depriving the first country of the benefits. All other things being equal, growth in cross-border data flows can be a far more powerful impetus to consumer welfare and economic growth than growth in trade in goods and services. This means that data trade generates a positive externality for the global economy. If a U.S. university produces educational videos about computer science and makes them available on the Internet, then students around the world can benefit from those videos.

Now we turn to the question of how data trade figures into calculations of GDP and economic growth. As noted in an earlier paper, data can be "consumed" by individuals; can be used as an intermediate input into production; and can be an investment in intangible capital (Mandel 2012).

For trade in conventional goods and services, there is a well-established methodology for assessing such trade's contribution to economic growth. In the calculation of GDP, the dollar value of exports is a plus, while the dollar value of imports is a minus. For the calculation of gross domestic purchases—which are one measure of living standards—the dollar value of exports of goods and services is a minus, while the dollar value of imports of goods and services is a plus.

The arithmetic does not work quite the same for cross-border data flows, for two reasons. First, because data that are exported are still available domestically, exports don't need to be subtracted from gross domestic purchases. Second, imports of data potentially come in at low or zero prices, as discussed above, despite the fact that there is a positive price to originally producing the data and then transporting it across national borders. As a result, imports of data, valued in dollars, appear not to contribute to growth.

Consider, however, that the alternative to importing the data at a low or zero price is to produce it domestically at its full cost, which would be higher than the import price. Viewed from that perspective, there is a growing body of literature about how to value the contribution to growth of imports that are priced much lower than comparable domestic products. I will show how this approach can be used to value cross-border data flows.[7]

To demonstrate how this would work, I will consider the amusing category of YouTube videos of cats involved in different activities (Illustration 9.1). Quite a few of these videos are produced in Japan and get millions of free views (Lewis-Kraus 2012). They provide pleasure for viewers in America and around the world—in that sense they are analogous to going skiing or reading a book. Thus, they raise consumer welfare in the United States for people who enjoy videos of cats. But how should the gain to the U.S economy from these "free" data flows be measured? The key is to realize that there are two relevant prices here. One is the price to Americans of consuming the Japanese-made cat video, which is zero. The second is the maximum price, P^{cat}, that an American would pay for viewing a Japanese-made cat video, measured either in dollars or in value of time. We assume that there is no way of profitably producing a comparable video with Japanese cats in the United States—in other words, in order for someone in this country to produce comparable videos domestically, the videos would have to be sold at an average price per viewing in excess of P^{cat}.

So before YouTube, it was as if the price of a Japanese cat video to Americans was equal to P^{cat}, and the volume of videos viewed was zero. After the Internet and YouTube, the price P of Japanese cat videos goes to zero, and the volume of videos viewed goes to V.

How much does this change contribute to U.S. gross domestic purchases? For the sake of simplicity, assume that X is the size of gross domestic purchases in dollars, excepting cat videos. Let's also assume that there is no inflation and that X is otherwise not changing. Then the straightforward way of calculating growth would be as $(X + P \times V)/X$, where P is the price of a cat video after the introduction of YouTube. But P is zero, so it looks like there is no gain.

Illustration 9.1 Maru the Cat, as Seen on a YouTube Video from Japan

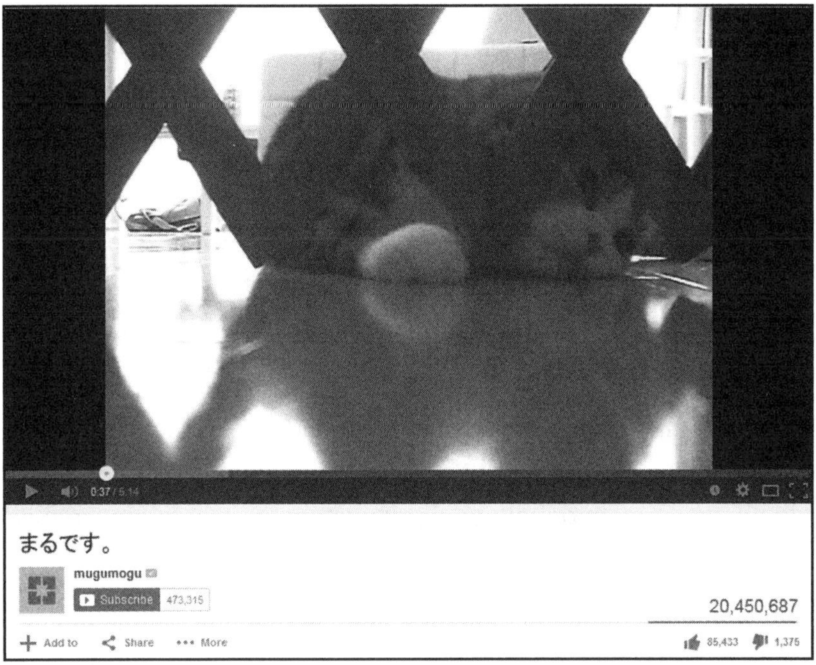

In fact, a better approach is roughly analogous to the procedure used to calculate chain-weighted GDP growth. I take the geometric average of two growth rates—the first assuming that the price of the video is always zero, and the second assuming that the price of the video is always P^{cat}:

$$g = \sqrt{\frac{(X + 0 * V)}{X}} * \sqrt{\frac{(X + P^{Cat} * V)}{X}} = \sqrt{1 + \frac{P^{Cat} * V}{X}} \approx 1 + \frac{P^{Cat} * V}{2X}.$$

In other words, the gain to gross domestic purchases from cross-border data flows of cat videos is roughly equal to the revenue that would be generated by pricing the videos at the average of the actual price (zero) and the price that Americans would be willing to pay, P^{cat}.

2. I thank Alan Mauldin of TeleGeography for providing these estimates.
3. These figures are based on the bidirectional averages of the average for the month of April and the peak during April of each year.
4. See also http://ciscovni.com/forecast-widget/index.html.
5. Non-Internet IP traffic in the United States is mainly consumer video.
6. 1 exabyte = 1,024 petabytes; 1 petabyte = 1,024 terabytes; 1 terabyte = 8 terabits.
7. This growing body of literature on how to assess growth when import prices are less than domestic prices includes Diewert and Nakamura (2010) and Feenstra et al. (2009).

References

Blake, Linda, and Jim Lande. 1998. *Trends in the U.S. International Telecommunications Industry*. Washington, DC: Federal Communications Commission, Common Carrier Bureau, Industry Analysis Division. http://transition.fcc.gov/Bureaus/Common_Carrier/Reports/FCC-State_Link/Intl/itltrd98.pdf (accessed March 18, 2014).

Bureau of Economic Analysis (BEA). 2011. "Chapter 8: Net Exports of Goods and Services." In *NIPA Handbook: Concepts and Methods of the U.S. National Income and Product Accounts*, Douglas R. Fox, ed. Washington, DC: U.S. Department of Commerce, Bureau of Economic Analysis, pp. 8-1–8-31. http://www.bea.gov/national/pdf/nipachapters1-9.pdf (accessed March 17, 2014).

———. 2014. *Gross-Domestic-Product-(GDP)-by-Industry Data*. Washington, DC: U.S. Department of Commerce, Bureau of Economic Analysis. http://www.bea.gov/industry/gdpbyind_data.htm (accessed March 17, 2014).

Castro, Daniel. 2013a. *The False Promise of Data Nationalism*. Washington, DC: Information Technology and Innovation Foundation. http://www2.itif.org/2013-false-promise-data-nationalism.pdf (accessed March 18, 2014).

———. 2013b. *How Much Will PRISM Cost the U.S. Cloud Computing Industry?* Washington, DC: Information Technology and Innovation Foundation. http://www2.itif.org/2013-cloud-computing-costs.pdf (accessed March 18, 2014).

Cisco Systems. 2013. "The Zettabyte Era—Trends and Analysis." White paper. San Jose, CA: Cisco Systems. http://www.cisco.com/c/en/us/solutions/collateral/service-provider/visual-networking-index-vni/VNI_Hyperconnectivity_WP.pdf (accessed March 17, 2013).

Collin, Pierre, and Nicolas Colin. 2013. *Mission d'Expertise sur la Fiscalité de l'Économie Numérique*. Paris: Ministere de l'Economie; Ministere du Redressement Productif. http://www.redressement-productif.gouv.fr/files/rapport-fiscalite-du-numerique_2013.pdf (accessed March 19, 2014).

Under the circumstances, the impact of cross-border data flows on economic growth will be understated as well, and it will be more difficult for policymakers to set the right priorities for trade and tax policy.

There have been several recent proposals for increasing the tax rate paid by international Internet companies, or for imposing additional regulations on them. In one instance of this, a recent paper from the French government suggested a sort of tax on data (Collin and Colin 2013). Such proposals—which would be likely to discourage cross-border data flows—are more likely to be seriously considered in the absence of evidence showing the large positive economic impacts from such cross-border data flows.

Impact of Data Localization

Another example comes from the aftermath of the revelations about NSA monitoring, which created a backlash against U.S. Internet companies and intensified discussions about building "walls" that would keep certain types of personal data from leaving countries such as Brazil.

Several reports have identified the possible negative economic consequences of such actions (Castro 2013a,b; Staten 2013). However, what's missing is the ability to actually track the negative consequences from data protectionism, since we do not currently track cross-border data flows. By comparison, if a country erects trade barriers against a particular tangible product, the impact of such a policy would immediately show up in the trade statistics. It's difficult to measure the harm from barriers to data trade if we cannot measure the data flows to begin with. Weller and Woodcock (2013) note that adverse effects may be incidental:

> It is also the case that regulations that are not explicitly intended to apply to Internet traffic exchange may have that effect. For example, restrictions on the ability to export certain data, such as customer profiles, intended to protect security and privacy, may also limit the development of Internet topology and the growth of Internet assets in some regions. Similarly, tax policies in each country toward broadband and Internet businesses are likely to affect the choice of the locations for investment in Internet assets. (p. 24)

CONCLUSION: THE NEED FOR BETTER DATA ON CROSS-BORDER DATA FLOWS

Businesses in any industry are usually ambivalent about the collection of government statistics on that industry. On the one hand, objective industry-wide statistics can be extremely useful for business decision-making and planning. On the other hand, the collection process can be intrusive, and accurate statistics can potentially attract new competitors or unwanted attention from regulators.

The calculation gets even tougher for rapidly innovating tech industries. Tech companies are unlikely to call for additional investment in statistics that may be quickly rendered obsolete by technological change.

However, the balance changes in a situation where businesses need government support in order to avoid bigger problems. In particular, better information about cross-border data flows will help make the case that data protectionism and taxes on data can be economically destructive.

The bottom line is that the statistical agencies should supplement the current trade statistics with additional metrics on cross-border data flows. This should be part of a large push to better measure data consumption and investment domestically.

Notes

My thanks to the Sloan Foundation for funding this research. I thank Diana Carew of the Progressive Policy Institute, Alan Mauldin of TeleGeography, Steve Bauer and Bill Lehr of the Massachusetts Institute of Technology, and Michael Kende of Analysis Mason for very useful assistance. All mistakes and errors are my own.

1. Many large providers own their own undersea cables, have a share of a cable, or have long-term rights to use part of the bandwidth. Submarine cable is used to carry cross-border data flows across oceans but also often between countries on the same continent, because it's often easier and safer to maintain cables that run along the coast underwater than across difficult terrain. Cables are typically laid with multiple strands of optic fiber, some of which are "lit"—i.e., they have the necessary equipment to be used—and some of which are "dark," or not yet ready for use. Capacity can be increased by laying new cables, by lighting dark fiber, or by improving the capacity of already-lit fiber.

2. I thank Alan Mauldin of TeleGeography for providing these estimates.
3. These figures are based on the bidirectional averages of the average for the month of April and the peak during April of each year.
4. See also http://ciscovni.com/forecast-widget/index.html.
5. Non-Internet IP traffic in the United States is mainly consumer video.
6. 1 exabyte = 1,024 petabytes; 1 petabyte = 1,024 terabytes; 1 terabyte = 8 terabits.
7. This growing body of literature on how to assess growth when import prices are less than domestic prices includes Diewert and Nakamura (2010) and Feenstra et al. (2009).

References

Blake, Linda, and Jim Lande. 1998. *Trends in the U.S. International Telecommunications Industry*. Washington, DC: Federal Communications Commission, Common Carrier Bureau, Industry Analysis Division. http://transition.fcc.gov/Bureaus/Common_Carrier/Reports/FCC-State_Link/Intl/itltrd98.pdf (accessed March 18, 2014).

Bureau of Economic Analysis (BEA). 2011. "Chapter 8: Net Exports of Goods and Services." In *NIPA Handbook: Concepts and Methods of the U.S. National Income and Product Accounts*, Douglas R. Fox, ed. Washington, DC: U.S. Department of Commerce, Bureau of Economic Analysis, pp. 8-1–8-31. http://www.bea.gov/national/pdf/nipachapters1-9.pdf (accessed March 17, 2014).

———. 2014. *Gross-Domestic-Product-(GDP)-by-Industry Data*. Washington, DC: U.S. Department of Commerce, Bureau of Economic Analysis. http://www.bea.gov/industry/gdpbyind_data.htm (accessed March 17, 2014).

Castro, Daniel. 2013a. *The False Promise of Data Nationalism*. Washington, DC: Information Technology and Innovation Foundation. http://www2.itif.org/2013-false-promise-data-nationalism.pdf (accessed March 18, 2014).

———. 2013b. *How Much Will PRISM Cost the U.S. Cloud Computing Industry?* Washington, DC: Information Technology and Innovation Foundation. http://www2.itif.org/2013-cloud-computing-costs.pdf (accessed March 18, 2014).

Cisco Systems. 2013. "The Zettabyte Era—Trends and Analysis." White paper. San Jose, CA: Cisco Systems. http://www.cisco.com/c/en/us/solutions/collateral/service-provider/visual-networking-index-vni/VNI_Hyperconnectivity_WP.pdf (accessed March 17, 2013).

Collin, Pierre, and Nicolas Colin. 2013. *Mission d'Expertise sur la Fiscalité de l'Économie Numérique*. Paris: Ministere de l'Economie; Ministere du Redressement Productif. http://www.redressement-productif.gouv.fr/files/rapport-fiscalite-du-numerique_2013.pdf (accessed March 19, 2014).

Diewert, W. Erwin, and Alice O. Nakamura. 2010. "Bias Due to Input Source Substitutions: Can It Be Measured?" Paper presented at the conference "Measurement Issues Arising from the Growth of Globalization," held in Washington, DC, November 6–7.

Feenstra, Robert C., Alan Heston, Marcel P. Timmer, and Haiyan Deng. 2009. "Estimating Real Production and Expenditures across Nations: A Proposal for Improving the Penn World Tables." *Review of Economics and Statistics* 91(1): 201–212.

Hilbert, Martin. 2011. "Mapping the Dimensions and Characteristics of the World's Technological Communication Capacity during the Period of Digitization (1986–2007/2010)." Paper presented at the Ninth World Telecommunication/ICT Indicators Meeting, held in Mauritius, December 7–9.

Hilbert, Martin, and Priscila López. 2011. "The World's Technological Capacity to Store, Communicate, and Compute Information." *Science* 332 (6025): 60–65.

International Telecommunications Union (ITU). 2012. *Measuring the Information Society 2012*. Geneva: International Telecommunications Union. http://www.itu.int/ITU-D/ict/publications/idi/material/2012/MIS2012_without_Annex_4.pdf (accessed March 17, 2014).

KPMG. 2010. *Accounting under IFRS: Telecoms*. London: KPMG in the UK. http://www.kpmg.com/CN/en/IssuesAndInsights/ArticlesPublications/Documents/Accounting-under-IFRS-Telecoms-O-1001.pdf (accessed March 17, 2014).

Lewis-Kraus, Gideon. 2012. "In Search of the Living, Purring, Singing Heart of the Online Cat-Industrial Complex." *wired.com*, August 31. http://www.wired.com/underwire/2012/08/ff_cats/all/ (accessed March 17, 2014).

Mandel, Michael. 2012. "Beyond Goods and Services: The (Unmeasured) Rise of the Data-Driven Economy." Policy memo. Washington, DC: Progressive Policy Institute.

Meltzer, Joshua. 2013. *The Internet, Cross-Border Data Flows, and International Trade*. Issues in Technology Innovation Series, No. 22. Washington, DC: Brookings Institution. http://www.brookings.edu/~/media/research/files/papers/2013/02/25%20international%20data%20flows%20meltzer/internet%20data%20and%20trade%20meltzer.pdf (accessed March 18, 2014).

Staten, James. 2013. "The Cost Of PRISM Will Be Larger Than ITIF Projects." *James Staten's Blog*, August 14. Cambridge, MA: Forrester Research. http://blogs.forrester.com/james_staten/13-08-14-the_cost_of_prism_will_be_larger_than_itif_projects (accessed March 18, 2014).

TeleGeography. 2012. "Global Internet Reaches 77 Tbps Despite Slowdown." News release, September 6. San Diego, CA: TeleGeography. http://www

.telegeography.com/press/press-releases/2012/09/06/global-internet-capacity-reaches-77-tbps-despite-slowdown/index.htm (accessed July 30, 2014).

———. 2013. "IP Transit Port Upgrades Yield Steeper Price Declines for Buyers." News release, October 8. San Diego, CA: TeleGeography. http://www.telegeography.com/press/press-releases/2013/10/08/ip-transit-port-upgrades-yield-steeper-price-declines-for-buyers/index.html (accessed March 17, 2014).

———. 2014. *Global Bandwidth Research Service*. San Diego, CA: TeleGeography. http://www.telegeography.com/research-services/global-bandwidth-research-service/index.html (accessed March 17, 2014).

United Nations. 2011. *Manual on Statistics of International Trade in Services 2010*. Statistical Papers, Series M, No. 86. New York: United Nations, Department of Economic and Social Affairs, Statistics Division. https://unstats.un.org/unsd/tradeserv/TFSITS/msits2010/docs/MSITS%20 2010%20M86%20%28E%29%20web.pdf (accessed March 17, 2014).

U.S. International Trade Commission. 2013. *Digital Trade in the U.S. and Global Economies, Part 1*. Washington, DC: U.S. International Trade Commission. http://www.usitc.gov/publications/332/pub4415.pdf (accessed March 17, 2014).

Weller, Dennis, and Bill Woodcock. 2013. *Internet Traffic Exchange: Market Developments and Policy Challenges*. OECD Digital Economy Paper No. 207. Paris: Organisation for Economic Co-operation and Development. http://www.oecd-ilibrary.org/science-and-technology/internet-traffic-exchange_5k918gpt130q-en (accessed March 17, 2014).

World Trade Organization (WTO). 2013. *Statistics Database*. Geneva: World Trade Organization. http://stat.wto.org (accessed December 2013).

Authors

Nadim Ahmad is the head of the Trade and Competitiveness Statistics Division in the Statistics Directorate of the Organisation for Economic Co-operation and Development.

Kimberly Bayard is a senior economist with the Board of Governors of the Federal Reserve System.

David Byrne is a senior economist with the Board of Governors of the Federal Reserve System.

Gaaitzen J. de Vries is an assistant professor in the Faculty of Economics and Business at the University of Groningen.

Maureen Doherty retired last year as an economist with the Bureau of Labor Statistics.

Susan N. Houseman is a senior economist with the W. E. Upjohn Institute for Employment Research.

Fariha Kamal is an economist with the Center for Economic Studies at the U.S. Census Bureau.

Jennifer Koncz-Bruner was formerly an economist in the Balance of Payments Division of the International Economic Accounts at the U.S. Bureau of Economic Analysis.

Bart Los is an associate professor in the Faculty of Economics and Business at the University of Groningen.

Hong Ma is an associate professor in the Department of Economics at Tsinghua University.

Michael Mandel is chief economic strategist at the Progressive Policy Institute.

Brent R. Moulton is associate director for National Economic Accounts at the U.S. Bureau of Economic Analysis.

Jiansuo Pei is an associate professor in the School of International Trade and Economics at the University of International Business and Economics.

Dylan G. Rassier is an economist in the Office of the Associate Director for National Economic Accounts at the U.S. Bureau of Economic Analysis.

Jennifer Ribarsky is head of Annual National Accounts, Purchasing Power Parities, and Prices at the Organisation for Economic Co-operation and Development.

Dominic Smith is a graduate student in the Department of Economics at the University of Minnesota.

Marcel P. Timmer is a professor of economic growth and development in the Faculty of Economics and Business at the University of Groningen.

Shunli Yao is director of the Institute for Applied International Trade.

Index

Note: The italic letters *b*, *f*, *n*, or *t* following a page number indicate a box, figure, note, or table on that page. An *f* also designates illustrations. Double letters mean more than one such item on a single page.

About the Institute

The W.E. Upjohn Institute for Employment Research is a nonprofit research organization devoted to finding and promoting solutions to employment-related problems at the national, state, and local levels. It is an activity of the W.E. Upjohn Unemployment Trustee Corporation, which was established in 1932 to administer a fund set aside by Dr. W.E. Upjohn, founder of The Upjohn Company, to seek ways to counteract the loss of employment income during economic downturns.

The Institute is funded largely by income from the W.E. Upjohn Unemployment Trust, supplemented by outside grants, contracts, and sales of publications. Activities of the Institute comprise the following elements: 1) a research program conducted by a resident staff of professional social scientists; 2) a competitive grant program, which expands and complements the internal research program by providing financial support to researchers outside the Institute; 3) a publications program, which provides the major vehicle for disseminating the research of staff and grantees, as well as other selected works in the field; and 4) an Employment Management Services division, which manages most of the publicly funded employment and training programs in the local area.

The broad objectives of the Institute's research, grant, and publication programs are to 1) promote scholarship and experimentation on issues of public and private employment and unemployment policy, and 2) make knowledge and scholarship relevant and useful to policymakers in their pursuit of solutions to employment and unemployment problems.

Current areas of concentration for these programs include causes, consequences, and measures to alleviate unemployment; social insurance and income maintenance programs; compensation; workforce quality; work arrangements; family labor issues; labor-management relations; and regional economic development and local labor markets.